D1064510

FIRST BORN

FIRST BORN

The Death of Arnold Zeleznik,
Age Nine: Murder, Madness
and What Came After

JOHN KATZENBACH

Atheneum   New York

Copyright © 1984 by John Katzenbach
All rights reserved
Published simultaneously in Canada by McClelland and Stewart Ltd.
Composed by Westchester Book Composition Inc., Yorktown Heights, New York

364.1523
K19

For Carter, Elizabeth and Robert Zeleznik

Contents

There are some crimes so irrational, so unpredictable, so explosive . . . that they can no more be prevented or guarded against than earthquakes or tidal waves. . . .

> —*The Challenge of Crime in a Free Society,* the report by the President's Commission on Law Enforcement and the Administration of Justice, 1967

People *need* to be able to make sense out of their environment; otherwise life would be intolerable. To "live with fear" as victims call it—to be suspicious of every sound and person—converts the most elementary and routine aspects of life into an exercise in terror.

Thus the emotional impact of being attacked by a stranger transcends the incident itself; it reaches a primordial layer of fear. . . .

> —Charles E. Silberman, *Criminal Violence, Criminal Justice*

Author's Note

The events described in this book are real. No names have been changed. The reconstructions of events and conversations are taken either from police reports, court records, grand jury memorandums, sworn depositions, hearing transcripts, tape recordings made at the time by participants or the recollections of the principals. For narrative purposes, I reconstructed interviews in several brief passages on the basis of the synopsized reports submitted to various judges by psychiatrists.

This book would not have been possible without the cooperation of many people. Michael Korvick, formerly of the Dade State Attorney's Office, deserves special thanks. Without the help of Jack Denaro, Roy Black, Michael Tarkoff, Michael Von Zamft and Barry Weinstein, all former members of the Dade Public Defender's Office, the book would not have been a feasible project. Miami Homicide Detective Edward Carberry was exceptionally helpful during one lengthy interview, in which he described Vernal Walford's postarrest behavior.

Gregory Torres of the Special Senate Investigating Committee in Boston also deserves much credit and thanks for providing necessary documents. Norman Gorin of CBS-TV's "60 Minutes" show was also helpful.

One never gets to interview everyone, not even everyone that one wants.

There are some others who deserve mention. William Reiss of Paul R. Reynolds, Inc., believed in this project from the very beginning, and I am grateful to him for his sensitivity and support. Neil Nyren of Atheneum was all that one could ask for in an editor. The editors at the *Miami Herald* helped make the time available for this project. Few newspapers would be as flexible. Emma Kada, too, was instrumental in gaining me the hours necessary to stare into the blipping green screen of the IBM Personal Computer on which I wrote this work. My beloved wife and child made far more sacrifices than I to bring this work to completion.

And lastly, I want to thank Carter, Betty and Bobby Zeleznik. It is ultimately their story. They have taught me much. They are, frankly, the bravest people I know. It is to them that this book is dedicated.

John Katzenbach is a featured writer for the *Miami Herald*'s *Tropic* magazine, and the author of the much-acclaimed novel, *In the Heat of the Summer*. Previously, he was the criminal court reporter for the *Miami Herald* and, before that, the *Miami News*, and his work has appeared in many other newspapers, including the *Boston Globe, Washington Post, Chicago Daily News* and *Newsday*. Born in Princeton, New Jersey, he is the son of former Attorney General of the United States Nicholas deB. Katzenbach, and lives in Coral Gables, Florida, with his wife, journalist Madeleine Blais, and their young son, Nicholas.

"The Worst Thing . . ."

> It was the worst thing I've seen in my seven years in the police department. . . .
>
> —The homicide detective

1. What Happened

Their memories remain distinct: an ice-cold clarity.

Thick, wet snow swirled down in Philadelphia the day they left for the holidays. Carter remembered that afterward; it explained in part why the boys were so excited when they felt the first hot rushes of Miami's tropical winter. With that children's singleness of purpose they insisted on a swim moments after the family had checked into the hotel. Arnold, at nine a year older than his brother, Bobby, was ready first, as usual. He clamored for Carter and Betty to hurry, as if each second of the day's warmth were precious. The parents collected towels, and en masse the family went out to the large hotel pool. Betty remembers sitting by the side, her feet dangling in the water, watching as the boys splashed enthusiastically, their bodies sleek and gleaming in the early-afternoon sunlight.

After the swim the boys wanted to explore. Arnold and Bobby seemed suffused with energy after being cooped up on the train overnight. Again, Arnold was ready first. Carter turned to Betty and told her that he would go ahead with Arnold and that she could bring Bobby along in a minute or two and catch up with them in the hotel lobby.

Father and son walked down the hotel corridor together. Twenty-five feet. Fifty feet. It was shaped in a L with the bank of elevators at the intersection. Carter slipped his hand into his pocket and realized he still carried the room key. He frowned at his forgetfulness, thinking: Betty will be unable to lock the door. A man of precision, he felt an instant's frustration. He looked down at Arnold. Their eyes locked for a moment. Carter would remember that later:

1

the little boy's face turned up, his bright eyes, open, inquisitive, filled with excitement, framed by his dark hair. "Just wait here," Carter said. "I won't be more than a minute."

He remembers seeing Arnold waiting. Alone.

Ten seconds.

Carter stepped back into their room. Number 216.

Twenty seconds.

He handed Betty the room key.

Thirty seconds.

She noticed a stain on his trousers.

Sixty seconds.

He got a damp washcloth from the bathroom.

Seventy seconds.

She began to scrub at the spot.

Ninety seconds.

And then they heard the scream.

It was a single, drawn-out, high-pitched sound of panic and helplessness that shattered the easy day's rhythm and lodged permanently in their memories: Help, oh, help me please, help.

Without hesitation the three of them, Carter, Betty and Bobby, burst into the hotel corridor. Arnold had disappeared.

On December 20, 1974, at approximately 4:45 P.M. Arnold Frank Zeleznik, aged nine years, was murdered in room 206 of the Crossways Airport Inn on Lejeune Road in Miami, Florida. He was the elder son of Carter Zeleznik, Ph.D., a psychologist, educator and assistant director of the Office of Medical Education at the medical school attached to Thomas Jefferson University in Philadelphia, and of Carter's wife, Elizabeth. The family was traveling to a planned two-week holiday in Central America. They were scheduled to meet up with another couple and fly from Miami to Costa Rica, to stay on the estancia belonging to other friends. The train ride to Miami was the completion of the first leg. The selection of the Crossways was made with convenience in mind; it was a large, modern hotel, adjacent to Miami International Airport.

One thing they could not understand afterward was the mere chance, the accident of timing and fate and bad luck, that had put Arnold, alone, in that hallway at that precise moment. Carter and Betty had always been careful and protective, but not stifling, with their children. Arnold and Bobby had been reared to recognize oddity and danger and not to be frightened, to be capable of dealing with it. Arnold, especially, had shown a sense of independence tempered by an unusual maturity, even as a baby. He was a curious child, who welcomed experiences and changes, but was not the type to push himself into trouble or get into a scrape. He was, they thought, a child of unmeasured grace.

The family rushed headlong down the corridor to the spot where Carter had left Arnold. At first Carter thought Arnold had been kidnapped; he bounded down the hotel's stairway toward the parking lot, the idea that he had to spot the getaway car reverberating in his mind. Betty, fighting against the sudden onslaught of panic that was taking root in her heart and spreading, gripped Bobby's hand tightly. Heads began to poke from the other rooms. "Have you seen my little boy?" she cried. "I heard him scream." No one replied. They stared at her uncomprehendingly. Later it would disturb her. She would not be able to reason why. At the elevator she stopped a wiry, heavily muscled, light-skinned black man and asked him the same question. He glanced at her, at Bobby, then ignored the question and raced down the stairway.

He was the killer.

The manager of the Crossways, Ray Barbarino, had also heard Arnold's scream. He saw the light-skinned black man cross the lobby and exit through the front door, moving quickly. Barbarino knew he was the occupant of room 206. His attention shifted quickly to Carter, Betty and Bobby as they rushed into the lobby, pleading for help with their search. Barbarino had already checked down the elevator and laundry shafts; when he heard the scream, he'd suspected the child had slipped and tumbled down one or the other. But there had been no sign of the child. Barbarino reached for the passkey, and one of the other employees, no one was sure exactly who, said, "Try room two-oh-six." It was the first place they would search.

Barbarino turned the passkey in the door handle of 206 and stepped inside. To his left was the bathroom. His eyes swept in. In one quick, unforgettable, horrified glance he took in the whole of the murder scene. I must not let them see this, he thought, and he turned, spreading his arms wide as if to barricade the entranceway, his voice suddenly lost, dysfunctional.

They rushed past him in their panic. Unstoppable.

Arnold was in the bathroom, his body illuminated by the unforgiving harshness of the overhead fluorescent lamp. Blood covered his body. It streaked the walls, the toilet and the floor.

With a half moan, half shriek, Betty threw herself down on Arnold, her arms swiftly wrapping around, encircling her child. "I'm sorry," she whispered. "Oh, Arnold, I'm so sorry."

Carter stared for an instant, pounded the wall, then plummeted precipitously into shock. His body temperature plunged; his own heartbeat came perilously close to stopping completely. He was unconscious before he hit the floor.

Bobby's eyes fixed on his mother and brother, a Pietà of horror. He stood motionless, eyes wide, absorbing it all wordlessly.

Barbarino, choking, hurried to call the police and the rescue squad.

2. The Arrest

City of Miami Motorcycle Patrolman Harold Bishop was sitting on his Harley-Davidson when he heard the police dispatcher's first BOLO (be on the lookout) announcement of the crime and possible suspect. The terse, staccato description came crackling over the police radio a few minutes after 5:00 P.M. Subject's name: V. Walford. Negro male, light-skinned. Approximately six feet, between 160 and 170 pounds. Close-cut hair. Wearing dark jacket and light pants. Wanted in connection with homicide. Possibly armed, dangerous.

Bishop thought of the Crossways and its proximity to the airport. He thought straightaway: That's where he'll be heading. With a veteran policeman's instincts, he weaved the big cycle through the afternoon rush-hour traffic and gunned the bike up the entrance ramp to the airport. His eyes scanned the area.

As Bishop cruised through the taxi storage zone, adjacent to the terminal building, he spotted the suspect walking toward a cab. Bishop saw the man wave down a yellow cab and slip into the seat next to the driver. As the cab started to pull away from the area, Bishop made a quick U-turn and caught up with the taxi at a stop sign. He motioned to the driver to pull to the side.

Bishop watched as the suspect emerged from the cab.

He saw dark brown bloodstains on the pants.

His hand went to his service revolver, and he demanded to know the suspect's name.

"Vernal Walford," the suspect replied.

It was less than twenty minutes since Arnold had screamed for help. Bishop handcuffed the suspect and called the dispatcher for a backup patrol car to help transport the subject to the city police headquarters. Bishop read the suspect his rights from a *Miranda* card. He searched him for weapons, but found none. The suspect remained docile, uncomplaining, but his eyes darted back and forth, watching the policeman piercingly.

In the suspect's pocket was this note:

"The God of Israel, say so. The God Israel say this
temple must not be used for any voilence nor any
police office child offer has sacrifices."

It was handwritten in a distinctive, twisted print.

3. The Scene

At the Crossways the gathering of violent death had begun. The first officers
to the hotel had immediately called for homicide detectives, rescue squad
personnel, the Medical Examiner's Office and a representative from the Dade
State Attorney's Office. In addition, forensic technicians had been summoned
and were en route within minutes: fingerprint men; crime scene search specialists; the evidence gatherers. Police auxiliary members, mostly officers in
training, had also been requested to help search for a murder weapon. Dozens
of people, moving swiftly toward the Crossways, caught up in the pattern of
murder. A killing may perhaps be sudden, abrupt and dramatic, but the
immediate aftermath is one of caution, a measured investigative pace. Homicide work is not ordinarily for people in a hurry.

City of Miami Homicide Detectives Edward Carberry and Walter Martinez
were at the site of another death when they received the dispatcher's summons
to proceed immediately to the Crossways. They left the other body with rescue
personnel; it was that of an elderly man, an apparent suicide. They were only
a few blocks away and arrived at the hotel minutes after 5:00 P.M. Uniformed
officers and rescue squad members were already at the location, sealing off
the scene to preserve evidence. The BOLO with the description of Walford
was already on the airwaves. The dispatcher had not informed Carberry or
Martinez about what kind of homicide they had to deal with; Carberry spotted
a rescue squad member he was friendly with, waved him over and asked,
"So, what have we got?"

The rescue squad man shook his head. His face was grim, the first indication that an exceptional horror awaited the detectives. "A kid," the man
said. "A little boy. Just a kid." He escorted the detectives into the nightmare
in room 206.

Ronald Keith Wright, the deputy chief medical examiner for Dade County,
was en route to his home in the southern portion of the county that Friday
afternoon when the murder took place. He had barely entered his home when

his office called, directing him to retrace his steps and head for the Crossways. A pipe-smoking intellectual man, Wright guessed that it was something unusual for the office to call him rather than assign it to one of the assistants.

He got back into his car and caught the Palmetto Expressway back into the city from the suburbs. The traffic was much lighter heading in that direction, and he made good time.

At age thirty, Leonard Glick was new to the major crimes section of the Dade State Attorney's Office. On December 20 he was assigned to the homicide detail; in the rotating system of that office, a prosecutor was delegated daily to attend any homicide scenes where the detectives felt they might need legal expertise. It was also considered a way to give the prosecutors on-site training; a prosecutor familiar with the particular depravity of murder scenes will be that much more effective at conveying the horror of the crime to a jury. It is one thing to look at pictures; another, to look at wasted flesh and blood.

Glick was at the Dade Public Safety Department, the county sheriff's department, when he received the notification that there was a scene at which he was needed. He walked outside into the still-warm early evening and waited for a city of Miami patrol car to pick him up. He was slightly nervous. It was only the second homicide scene he'd ever been to. He did not know what to think; he'd been told it was a child's murder. Momentarily he thought of his two daughters. The police cruiser slammed up, lights and sirens going. He jumped into the back seat and wondered why they were traveling code 3, accelerator jammed down, to the scene of a dead body. He hung on as the driver flung the car through the preholiday traffic.

The Zelezniks were only barely aware of what was happening to them as policemen and orange jump-suited rescue squad members gently led them from room 206. They were moved to another suite on another floor; later they would not remember which. Their clothing was taken from 216 and brought to the new room. Betty's clothes were streaked with Arnold's blood, but she was oblivious to the macabre sight she presented. For a few seconds they were left in the lobby, before being accompanied to the new room. At first the three of them huddled on a couch together. A *Miami Herald* photographer snapped off a shot of them that would run on the wires and in papers across the nation in the morning. They were in advanced shock, staring sightlessly out dulled eyes at the activity surrounding them. Functioning more out of the darkness of hysteria than any reasoning of the mind, Betty walked up to a lobby telephone and began dialing numbers. The hotel operator came on the line and requested Betty's room number. "I don't know," she said. "I can't tell. It's being changed. I can't remember. It's an emergency, you see, my child is dead. He's been killed. My child has been killed." The operator persisted, demanding a room number before she put through the call, and Betty continued to plead into the telephone that she couldn't remember, that her child had been murdered and that it was an emergency. Suddenly a woman, a stranger, took the phone from her hand and gave the operator her own room number. Then she placed a card with her name and telephone exchange in Betty's hand and told her that if she needed to talk with anyone, to call on her. Betty would later wonder what happened to the card. She would never forget that telephone operator either. But now, with an open line, she couldn't recall whom she was insistent on telephoning. She knew only it was someone at home, a neighbor, a friend, part of her family, someone back home in Fort Washington. She never completed the call. Turning in helplessness, she placed the receiver back on the hook. Then she allowed herself to be led to the new room, where she and Carter and Bobby all lay together on a bed, their arms encircling each other.

Glick was unprepared for the sight that awaited him.

He was aware the victim was a child, but he did not know the nature of the murder or the actual location. By the time he arrived at the Crossways the lobby was filled with cops, technicians and the curious. The Miami press corps was beginning to arrive, though the evening news stations were perilously close to their 6:00 P.M. deadlines and the *Herald*'s first edition was already streaming from the presses. He saw Martinez and Carberry in the lobby and approached them. Martinez told him that the two officers who'd transported him to the Crossways had mistakenly been told he was the child's father; that explained the rush through traffic and their quiet, non-communicativeness. Neither of them had wanted to be the one to tell the father what had happened at the Crossways.

Glick said he wanted to see the scene, and Carberry said, "It's bad." Glick followed the two detectives to the second floor, pausing at the elevator to note a smear of what appeared to be drying blood on the wall next to the elevators. As he walked down the hallway, Glick was struck by the quiet, by the drawn faces of the policemen and the crime scene analysts already dusting for fingerprints and cataloguing the potential evidence. There was little conversation and none of the jocular black humor and gallows jokes— the slight defense against the recurring routine of brutality—that almost invariably accompanied the processing of a murder scene. My God, Glick thought, how grim everyone is.

Then he stepped into room 206.

It was a scene of transcendent horror in a very small place. The prosecutor couldn't believe that such a small child could bleed so much. It seemed as if the maroon streaks of drying blood were spattered everywhere. They discolored the child's green shirt and shorts. Glick swiftly averted his eyes, swallowing hard. He left the bathroom and glanced around the hotel room.

At the head of the bed, propped open and resting on the pillows, was a large red-jacketed Jerusalem Bible. It was open to pages 1426–1427. The Book of Daniel. The cover of the Bible was folded over to page 1184. Pages 1185–1186 were missing, torn from the spine. This section was Isaiah 28:3 through 29:17.

Glick's eyes traveled to the bedroom dresser. An uneaten takeout chicken dinner rested, untouched, on the surface.

As he watched, Glick saw one of the crime scene analysts gently take a blue cardboard box and wrapping paper from one corner of the room. He noticed, too, that the room's occupant had left without taking his clothing. A simple brown duffel bag lay forgotten on the floor of the closet.

Around him the processing was under way. Ron Wright had arrived and was in the bathroom inspecting Arnold's body. He had not touched anything yet. The prosecutor kept his hands in his pockets; he had been taught to do that. No sense in adding to the crime scene fingerprints that would just have to be eliminated later. He remembered hearing the clicking of a camera shutter; everything was being photographed. He decided to leave with Carberry and Martinez. He walked past the bathroom where Wright was lifting a piece of gauze from Arnold's neck. It had been placed there by one of the first rescue squad members. Glick hurried outside.

Wright was nicknamed Doctor Death by police and prosecutors. He was a familiar face at the scene of almost any homicide. His immediate superior, Dr. Joseph Davis, was considered among the preeminent pathologists in the nation, if not the world. After decades of torn, tattered, shattered and disrupted bodies, Davis had drifted into the theoretical aspects of pathology, leaving much of the day-to-day work to Wright and the assistants. Wright was generally the first called. He had a wry sense of humor and a voluminous knowledge of medicine and the law (he also had his *juris doctor* degree). He was an expert at transforming the cold facts of death into human terms from the witness stand. He understood the game of law and courtrooms better than many of the participants.

And he knew instantly, as he walked into the scene, what he had to deal with. A madman, he thought. Only a madman. That means an insanity defense. That means a trial in which the killer's mental status becomes more important than what actually happened here. He saw all this as an equation, and he saw his first duty as preserving, within his memory and with a camera, the horror in that bathroom.

He shot dozens of photographs, unhappy with each. He could easily picture the sequence in the courtroom. He would be on the stand, the prosecutor would haul out the stack of photographs and the defense attorney would object. At side bar, out of the jury's hearing, the judge and lawyers would wrangle over the photos. Too explicit. Inflame the passions of the jurors. Render them incapable of measuring a verdict based on the law rather than on emotion. He saw the defense lawyer easily winning that fight and the photos being discarded. So, he thought then, I'm going to find a way to get these photos into evidence. He concentrated on the problem analytically. Finally he perched himself above the body, and peered down through the fisheye lens he'd attached to the camera. That'll get in, he thought, and it will do the job. They'll see what really happened here.

Glick, Carberry and Martinez walked down the hallway and outside onto a small balcony. Glick sucked in the cooling evening air, as if trying to clear his lungs of the still residue of death; then he joined the detectives in searching the hallway for the murder weapon or any other evidence. The knife, he thought, must be somewhere close by. He noticed another smudge of dried blood near the elevator and pointed it out to one of the passing technicians. Then he went downstairs and outside to where some of the uniformed officers and auxiliaries were hunting through the nearby underbrush and landscaping for the murder weapon. They had no luck.

A short time later he gave up the search and joined the two detectives. They decided it was time to talk with the Zelezniks, and the trio went to the suite where the family was waiting. Glick was startled when he saw Bobby, curled in his mother's arms; except for the hair color, he seemed so much like his brother, down to the same outfit of green shorts and shirt. He shook his head, trying to clear the eerie sensation.

Carter had a dampened white cloth covering his eyes, like a bandage covering a wound. Glick and the detectives introduced themselves. They did not say much, but Carberry told the family that a suspect had been arrested. Glick told Carter that the killer would be held to the most rigid standard of the law. It was all he could say, he thought.

Carter got up from the bed. His visage changed then, from a stretched canvas of damage to anger. "You guys better not screw up," he said. His voice rose, straining the limits of his control. "You better not mess this thing up. I don't want this guy to get away with it. I don't want you guys to screw it up." Then he dissolved again, his sorrow just as swiftly replacing the outrage. The detectives nodded, said little and left the family alone. Formal statements, they knew, could wait until later.

When they left the room, the family had returned to the bed, their arms entwined in grief.

4. At the Homicide Office

Bishop had escorted Walford to the city of Miami police headquarters, which housed the homicide office. It was a grimy building that shouted sorrow from the fading paint on its walls; within two years the department would move into an ultramodern fortress on the fringe of the downtown Overtown district. Bishop seized a sturdy wooden chair and handcuffed Walford's wrists to each side; he had spotted what he believed to be blood underneath the suspect's fingernails, and he didn't want the potential evidence destroyed before a sample was taken. The two men eyed each other: Bishop, immense, barrel-chested, and Walford, muscled, wiry, his eyes continuing to flit about. "You know what I want to talk about?" Bishop asked.

"Yes," Walford replied.

"Will you talk about it?"

"No."

The two men stared at each other. After a few moments Bishop again pulled the *Miranda* card from his pocket and once again read through the litany of rights guaranteed Walford. "You understand your rights?" he asked.

"Yes."

"How did you get from the hotel to the airport? Did you run? Did you ride?"

"I walked."

"Were you carrying anything?" Bishop was thinking about a knife.

"I don't remember," Walford said.

And then Walford began to shake.

His head started to twitch from front to rear, back and forth, faster and faster. The rest of his body, still cuffed in a sitting position to the thick wooden chair, remained rigid, as if separate. "What're you doing?" Bishop demanded, but the shaking continued. "Get ahold of yourself!" Bishop shouted, but without effect. Bishop summoned up his largest voice: "Dammit! I said get ahold of yourself!"

Walford's eyes slowly turned toward the officer, and the quaking began to diminish, recede. Bishop went back to asking questions. "You got a family?"

"Oh, yes," Walford replied. His voice abruptly shifted then, becoming swift, rambling, erupting from his mouth in a high-pitched, singsong Caribbean accent. "Oh, yes, I have a wife home in Kingston, yes, and we have ten children; ten children we had but not now, no, no. No more ten children because five of them died! Died! Yes, dead! And I was at the airport to go home, but no one would give me the money, the money to go home. But God! I told them about the Word! Of God! But they would not pay! I told them of the Word, but they would not pay! God! God!"

Bishop interrupted. "How did your children die?"

"Oh," Walford said, suddenly coy, "I do not know."

"Did you kill the little boy at the Crossways? Did you take a knife and cut his throat?"

Walford smiled.

Walford laughed.

He shook his head slowly, deliberately, back and forth. "I know my rights!" he said. He drew out, elongated the word *know*: *knooooow*. "I see my rights, right there!" He nodded vigorously at the rights card. "You cannot speak to me if I do not want it! And I do not want it! I do not have to talk with you! God! I care only to talk with my"—he paused, "my attorney." His voice was raised in singsong victory. "My at-tor-ney!" Walford said, drawing out and accenting each syllable.

"You," he said, piercing Bishop with his glance, "you cannot speak."

Bishop swallowed back his frustration and anger. He showed no emotion. It was difficult. He waited quietly, eyes locked on Walford, until the detectives arrived, accompanied by laboratory technicians.

When Carberry and Martinez first saw Walford, he was still handcuffed, alternately grimacing and grinning. They spoke briefly with Bishop, who filled them in on Walford's behavior, his demands for an attorney and what he had said to the motorcycle cop. Carberry thought at first that it was just an act, a charade: another killer deciding to put on a show for the detectives. The detective was a young man in his late twenties with two small children at home. He could not rip the picture of Arnold in the bathroom from his mind's eye; he felt the child's helplessness for an instant as he watched the lab technicians remove Walford's bloodstained clothing for processing as evidence. What chance did he have? the detective thought as he saw the rippling muscles that scored across Walford's arms and shoulders. Walford's body was impressive; the muscles were tightly bunched and ridged, an athlete's figure.

Walford was given the loose-fitting jeans and work shirt from the county jail. Larry Stamper, a technician, took photographs throughout the process.

Click! Walford stood, head thrown back, haughty, his hands in cuffs held before him, but with a look that knew no constraints. Click! Walford's eyes were wide with anger, muscles tightening, protruding, tense as an animal's before springing. Click! His teeth were bared, snarling, furious.

Carberry watched Walford. He fought off the basic policeman's urge, that most common desire to act as society's avenger. Let him just try to make a break, he thought. In his mind's eye, he saw the Zeleznik family again, collapsed together in pain and sorrow, and he thought in a small way one shot would even the score. Then, as quickly as the desire came, it fled. He set his teeth together and thought instead: We're not going to let this animal get away with it. There aren't going to be any screw-ups. No legal mess. I'm not going to see this animal walk out of a courtroom because he gets some clever attorney. I'm going to nail him and see him on Death Row. Carberry walked slowly up to Walford. He smiled. "Mr. Walford," he said between clenched teeth, "I'm Detective Carberry. I'd like to ask you some questions."

Carberry and Martinez took Walford into an interview room. They pulled out a standard city of Miami rights form; it repeated the *Miranda* warnings, spelling them out in greater detail. Walford and the detectives read each element together, pausing only to ascertain that Walford knew what each right entailed. At the end Walford looked at the two detectives and nodded his head.

"I understand," he announced.

"What happened in the hotel?" Carberry asked.

Walford grinned widely. His hands were cuffed in front of him. He lifted his hands, pointing one finger, then thumped it down against the rights form on the table before him. He tapped the section that starts: "You have the right to an attorney..."

And then he laughed. "I know my rights, oh, yes, oh, yes, my rights, my rights, my rights. You cannot!" His laughter was joyless, filled with anger. As he laughed, his head started to shake again, over and over, back and forth, twitching electrically, as if charged by some unseen current.

A short time later, in the main squad room, Walford was removed from the cuffs for fingerprinting. He listened as the detectives, Bishop and the technicians conferred. When the photographer turned the camera lens toward him, he bared his teeth in a snarl. "Knock it off!" Bishop yelled. Walford, grinning again, complied. A few seconds later, still listening to the policemen, he jumped up, enraged.

"God! God! God! God, not man! God of Israel say so! God say so! God of Israel!"

And then he lifted his arms, holding them directly out from his sides, continuing to call out to God, held rigidly in place on his own imaginary cross.

Walford was taken from the homicide office and placed in a holding cell while detectives completed the paper work that accompanied the arrest and questioning. There were several other men in the cell with Walford. When Bishop walked past the cell a few minutes after Walford had been placed inside, one of the men waved to him. "Hey," the criminal said, "I want to talk." Bishop approached him.

"What is it?" he asked.

The arrestee paused, looking back over his shoulder. "Hey," he said, "I don't want no trouble, but the dude you put in here, the weird one, says he's gonna kill himself some policemen tonight. Thought you'd want to know."

Bishop stared past the man toward Walford, who stood stiffly in the corner, as if at military attention, chin tight to chest, arms held rigidly down his sides, heels together. The motorcycle cop went and told Carberry and Martinez about the information. The three of them went back to see Walford.

"Mr. Walford," Carberry asked bluntly, "did you say you wanted to kill a policeman?" Bishop hovered close by, muscles tensed.

Walford spread his mouth wide, baring his teeth again. He laughed. "No, Constable, I did not say that."

He was then placed in an isolation cell. The policemen could hear him talking to himself in his singsong accent about God.

5. Night

Carter, Betty and Bobby spent the night at the Crossways.

Carter had managed to call a friend of his, a doctor at Jefferson Medical College, where Carter worked, and the friend had readily agreed to fly down and help arrange to transfer Arnold's body back to Philadelphia. Betty had spoken with her twin sister in Michigan, and she was flying east to meet the family when they returned home to their house in the Fort Washington suburb. The conversations had been brief, otherworldly explanations of what had happened; the shock of the event had rendered both parents exhausted. They didn't really know what they were saying or what they were doing; a type of automatic pilot took over. They did not eat that night, although the hotel management urged them to try to put something in their stomachs. They stayed together, the three of them, in their room at all times. They were afraid to let each other out of their sight, even for a second. It was a physical need, too; they held hands, wordlessly, touch being the only reassuring tool they had to continue through the night.

Few thoughts penetrated the thickness of their grief.

They tried to measure just how long Arnold had been out of their sight. Seconds. They tried to think of him alive, but the image was ripped from their imaginations, replaced by the indelible portrait of his body, awash in blood, legs twisted grotesquely. It terrified them, a mental whimper.

Bobby, they thought. He mustn't be left alone. The younger brother stayed huddled on the bed. He needed to be touched and held. He was.

For much of the night a young man, a police trainee who'd been at the crime scene earlier, stayed with them. He was in uniform, quiet, outside the door or sitting in the corner. Later they weren't certain of his name, but his presence was palpable and reassuring. Years later they would talk with gratitude about the young man and what he did for them that night: He made them feel safe in a world suddenly filled with terror.

They did not speak about what had happened through the night. They did not sleep much, perhaps stealing a few minutes at random from the darkness. Later Betty remembered the silence in the room, the sensation of Bobby and Carter beside her, their breathing mingling with the nighttime street sounds, the noise of reality distant, shut beyond the walls and windows, but still barely distinct, as if a reminder. She watched through the length of the night as the shadows deepened, then began to lighten with the onset of morning. She wondered, though, if they would ever really emerge from the darkness.

6. Morning

In the morning a police cruiser picked the family up at the Crossways and drove them slowly to the Dade County Jail. The homicide detectives had arranged for Walford to be shown in a line-up: the suspect and five black jail guards and policemen, all dressed alike. The cruiser traveled through the city streets slowly, unhurried. The long night had left the family pale and shaky. Carberry watched the three enter the building, wondering how they could hold up under the strain. He had worked late into the night, writing the reports of the murder, then had sat up with his wife until nearly 3:00 A.M., drinking, replaying the scenes from the day that were scoring his mind. He escorted the family into a waiting room.

Prosecutor Glick arrived soon after. He, too, had spent a restless night, fighting sleep and time and again walking gently into the bedrooms of his two small daughters, to listen to their rhythmic breathing and reassure himself that they slept peacefully.

Roy Black and Jack Denaro were also present.

The two men were members of the Dade Public Defender's Office. Both young men, they had already carved considerable reputations for themselves as criminal defense attorneys. Each would eventually go on to the top of their profession in private practice. Very different personalities—Black, devil-may-care and witty; Denaro, cerebral and a onetime seminary student—the two shared office space in the PD's suite on the eighth floor of the Metro Justice Building in downtown Miami.

Each man had independently started working on the case as soon as he'd heard of it late Friday afternoon. The word had coursed through the Justice Building about an unusual murder, a child, and an unusual defendant. In the early morning, Saturday, they had persuaded a county court judge to appoint them to Walford's defense, working under the correct but legally premature assumption that he would be unable to obtain his own counsel. Both men were determined to see that Walford's rights were observed. Both men were determined to reach Walford before he made any incriminating statements to the detectives.

For each man it was as if the inherent horror of the crime had demanded that much swifter a response, as if by the horrendous nature and quality of the murder, it were that much more important to see that the killer was protected.

Their first meeting with Walford was instructive.

It was before the family arrived at the jail, and Walford was being kept in a small room just off the line-up studio. The two public defenders greeted Carberry, whom they knew well from other homicide cases, and requested to meet with Walford.

"We want to see our client. Alone. Right now," Black said.

Carberry shrugged. "He's been acting kinda strange. I think you guys might want to have some protection in there with you—"

Black cut him off with a quick negative. They didn't want any detectives eavesdropping on their conversations. Carberry said, "Have it your way," and motioned for the jail personnel to let the two attorneys into the room. Black stepped through the door first, hand extended in greeting. Denaro was a step behind him.

"Hello, Mr. Walford," Black said cheerily. "My name is Roy Black, and this is Jack Denaro. We're here to represent you."

As Black's hand wavered, unrecognized, in the air, he saw Walford's expression change, Jekyll to Hyde. It twisted into a grimace, and his teeth were suddenly bared like a menacing dog's. He sprang to his feet, his hands, though cuffed, shooting up, pointing through the ceiling. He shouted, "God, not man, shall represent me! God, not man!"

With each repeated "God, not man!" Walford's face contorted further, and he advanced on the two surprised attorneys. They stepped back as they saw Walford gather himself before springing forward. Denaro leaped through the door, trying to pull it shut behind him. Black, coattails flying, seized the door and hauled it open, jumped through the doorway and slammed the door shut behind him in the same motion. For an instant all they could hear was Walford's cry, "God, not man! God, not man!," repeated over and over again, fading through the closed and bolted door.

"Jesus Christ," Denaro said, "that guy is nuts."

But it did not alter their desire to defend him. Indeed, it only increased their interest.

The Zelezniks knew nothing of Walford or of his increasingly bizarre behavior. They moved everywhere linked together, their hands and arms touching, as if they could somehow pool their internal resources sufficiently to carry them through the day. They were escorted into the line-up room; a typical darkened closet type of area with a one-way glass mirror looking in on a stage in an adjacent room. The rear wall was marked with heights. They were introduced once again to the detectives, to Glick and to Roy Black. Then the family was separated; Betty was left in the viewing room while Bobby and Carter waited outside.

It was explained to her that each man in the line-up would step forward on command and turn, turn, turn, making a 360-degree circle in front of her. She was told to wait until the line-up was completed before she made any selection. A court stenographer sat unobtrusively in the corner, his dictation machine making small clicking sounds as he copied down the conversation.

"They are going to stand right in front of this mirror, okay?" Detective Martinez said. "They cannot see you. Right?"

"Yes," Betty replied. "Will these be the only men?" The detectives could see anxiety growing in her face, hear it in her voice.

"These will be the only men you will be viewing. Okay?"

"Yeah," Betty said. She had been placed with her back to the mirror while the line-up was put in place.

"All right," Martinez said. "Turn around."

Betty turned slowly and stared through the glass. She paled instantly, and her voice began to quaver. "Oh, God, help me," she said.

"Now wait until you see every one of them, all right?" The detective was trying to keep her under control.

"Yes," she replied. But her voice continued to shake, and she continued to speak as each man stepped forward, pirouetting in front of her so close she thought she could reach out and touch them right through the glass. "They weren't dressed like that," she said in confusion. "Oh, God help me. Oh, God help me, God help me," she pleaded.

Number one stepped up. "God help me to make my choice." Her voice was desperate.

Number two came forward. "God help me. God help me make my choice."

Number three followed suit. "God help me, God help me, God in heaven help me." She began to moan softly with tension.

Number four faced the mirror. "God help me, God help me, God in heaven help me."

Number five stepped to the front. His movements were crisp, military. Each motion he made was stretched as tight as a drill sergeant's command. His face seemed locked, eyes front, emotionless. "God help me," Betty continued pleading. "Why wouldn't I know? Why wouldn't I know?" Number five stepped back to the wall and snapped to a parade rest.

Number six came to the window. "Oh, God help me," Betty said again, but defeat rode her voice.

She turned away from the window, and her eyes, red from tears and strain, fixed on the two detectives. "He looked so light yesterday," she said. "Oh, what if I'm not sure, should I give a guess?"

"Try to," Martinez said.

"He looked so light yesterday."

"Will you try to remember what you saw yesterday?" the detective probed, trying to force her mind to focus on the few seconds killer and mother had met outside the elevator.

"He seemed to be taller. I thought he was light, like around the edges," she said. Her voice was filling with frustration and despair, cracking fast. She desperately wanted to point out the killer. It seemed so important.

"Do you recognize any of these men?" the detective asked.

"I'm not sure. I am not sure. It might... is it all right if I give a might? It might be number six. I don't know for sure. I was afraid this would happen. I thought of him as being lighter." Her voice trailed off in despair.

"Okay, Mrs. Zeleznik." The detectives, aware of the defense attorney's presence, decided to take her out.

"Is it possible to look at them again?" she asked, but the policemen shook their heads. Betty was led from the room. The line-up had taken seven minutes.

When Bobby was brought in, Carter walked beside him. Roy Black said quickly, "If his father wants to stay in here, I have no objection, if he does not say anything." Glick and the detectives nodded in agreement.

"Now, Bobby," Carter said, "just let me hold your hand." Glick was again struck by the eerie resemblance between the two brothers. Bobby seemed almost a carbon copy of the murdered child, he thought.

Martinez placed Bobby with his back to the line-up studio. He bent over, putting his hand on the boy's shoulder, adopting a friendly tone. "If you recognize anyone, I don't want you to tell me about it until after you see all of them, okay?" Bobby nodded his head. "Don't say anything until the end, Bobby," Glick said. Again the child nodded.

"Now he can't see you, so you can move up here, okay?" The detective brought Bobby right up to the glass. Bobby clutched Carter's hand tightly, and Carter stood beside him. Bobby watched in silence as the six men stepped up before him, one after the other, performing the ballet of identification.

Bobby said nothing until the line-up was finished.

"Bobby," Martinez asked gently, "do you recognize any of those men?"

"I think it might be number five. I think it might be him. I can't remember," the child said.

"Okay." The policeman pushed gently, his face registering no approval or disapproval. "Are you sure?"

"I am not sure," Bobby said, but his tone was decisive and strong. "But I think it might be him."

"Okay, Bobby," the detective said. "That's good enough."

Martinez, of course, knew that number five was Vernal Walford. And he knew that despite the child's professed doubts, Bobby had still made a positive identification.

At the Dade County Medical Examiner's Office morgue that Saturday morning Dr. Wright led Dr. Daniel Ashler into the refrigerated room where bodies were stored before autopsies and to await the funeral home workmen. Ashler was Carter's friend and co-worker. He looked down as Wright pulled back the sheet covering Arnold's face, a motion seen in so many movies that it was almost a cliché. He nodded as his eyes traveled over the waxy, stiffly frozen features before him. "Yes," he said, "that's Arnold." He thought for a moment as his body filled with ineffable sorrow: Poor Arnold. And then his thoughts turned to the living: Poor Carter. Poor Betty. Poor Bobby. How will they survive this?

Dr. Wright lowered the sheet, and the two physicians discussed the transfer of Arnold's body back to Philadelphia.

The autopsy was performed in the early afternoon. It was mostly a formality; Wright and everyone else who'd been in the room where Arnold's body had been discovered knew that he'd been killed by slashing stab wounds to the neck, viciously administered. Wright was accompanied by technician Sam McMullin. They wanted to see if they could find any signs of defense wounds. There was a deep cut on Arnold's right hand, a bruise on his lip and a bruise on his left arm. No other signs of struggle. An acid phosphate test was run to determine whether Arnold had been sexually assaulted. It would be negative.

When the line-up was completed, Glick and the two detectives joined a group of jail guards in escorting Walford back to an isolation cell in the county jail. At first Walford said nothing, marching along in quick-step. Glick watched Walford's face as best he could. He saw the eyes dart about, suddenly locking in on an object, penetrating it, absorbing it, then just as swiftly staring off into space. Glick was almost overcome with the emanations of malevolence that flowed from those eyes. He half shuddered with relief when he watched Walford locked into a cell.

Months later Glick, his wife and two children would be visiting friends staying at a Miami Beach hotel. When they left their friends' suite of rooms, the two little girls went running ahead, laughing and dashing down the long carpeted corridor. For a second the two girls disappeared from his sight, and he felt his heartbeat quicken. He called out fearfully for the girls to stop, his own feet suddenly picking up the pace and rushing after them. And one night, years later, he would be in his living room, watching television with the girls. One of them slipped from her seat to the floor, legs akimbo, beneath her torso, her head flung back. For just an instant he stared at her; then suddenly, uncontrollably, he yelled, "Don't sit like that! Sit up straight!" The little girl peered at him curiously, and his wife said, "What's bothering you?" It was not until later that night, in his bed in the darkness, that he realized his daughter had slipped into the same position in which years earlier he had seen Arnold Zeleznik.

Carberry worked on the homicide reports. He listed the evidence seized:

The Bible
The note
The package and paper
The bloodstained matchbook
The bloodstained clothing
Some nineteen sets of fingerprints lifted at the scene
Blood samples taken from Arnold and from beneath
Walford's fingernails
An address book

* * *

Eight days after Arnold's murder he would dictate a thirteen-page single-spaced supplementary report of the crime. It would include the information obtained on the Monday after the murder from a woman who worked at a Sirgany International gift shop in the concourse area of Miami International Airport. She'd seen Walford's photograph in the *Miami Herald*, called the police and told them that Walford had purchased a knife from her the morning of the killing. It had been a six-inch bladed hunting type of knife. She signed a copy of the *Herald* next to Walford's photo: "This is the man I sold the knife."

At the beginning of Carberry's report, he wrote: "This case cleared by the arrest of Vernal Walford, NM, 31, of 33 Penn Street, Jonestown, Jamaica. . . ."

Five years after the crime Carberry would sit at his dining room table, reviewing his file of notes and evidence, the words he'd written years before. When he looked down at the stack of glossy photographs taken at the crime scene, his eyes filled with tears.

Years afterward, too, Ron Wright would say, "I remember the case, but only vaguely." Then he would lean back in his chair at his desk, ponder the memory and, without notes, recollect with precision all the details of the case. "It stayed with me, I guess," was his explanation.

A police cruiser returned Carter, Betty and Bobby to the Crossways when the line-up was finished. There was nothing further they could do or say to affect the case; there was nothing for them in Miami. Dr. Ashler had arranged for Arnold's body to be shipped on a Delta flight that evening, and they were handed their tickets, too. There were no more statements to be taken, no more identifications to be made. They had been told they would be kept abreast of the developments in the case as it wound its way through the court process of arraignment, indictment, hearings and trial.

Betty later remembered how everyone on the flight was very kind. They were met by a Delta representative who took them to a separate waiting room where they could sit alone. He personally ushered them onto the flight. The stewardesses seemed to hover over them with food and drinks. The family tried to eat the dinners that were set down in front of them, but they could not. Betty tried to remember when she had last eaten; but her throat was too tight and dry, and the food tasted only of sorrow.

The dull, ever-present roar of the jet's engines served as a backdrop to the thoughts that coursed through their emotion-dulled minds. Images from the murder, the line-up, the policemen, the attorneys, all crowded their thinking. Questions seemed to shout through the images from the recesses of their grief: Why had this happened to them? How could it have come to pass? Who was this murderer, this man who had snatched Arnold from the hallway and their lives simultaneously? Over and over: Why? Why? How? How?

And Betty wondered, too, what would happen to all of them now. What was there for their future? Where would they find justice? Where would they find peace?

And would they be able to keep going at all?

When the onslaught of questions slowly began to recede from their minds, they could feel only a coldness, as if there were no warmth inside the airplane or in the world. And Betty prayed then that the airplane would crash and they all would be killed in the same flashing moment, so that they would not have to go on and face the incomparable pain of each new second.

CHAPTER 2

Arnold

1. Carter

Carter Zeleznik is a large man, gray-bearded, his thinning hair pushed abruptly back from his forehead, giving him a Rasputin-like, mad-monk quality. He is round-shouldered, his athlete's past long forgotten. He wears suits that seem put together by happenstance and hang loosely from his large limbs. When he walks, it is with purpose, a gangly, flapping quick march, as if to say that destinations are important, travel a barely tolerable delay.

His glance is penetrating, intensive, a severity that seems to complement his academic's nature. He has a precise manner, as if he has fully investigated and studied the consequences of each new step he takes. His voice is filled with the locutions and language of the psychologist and the educator. Sometimes he slips into the droning of a man who seems to have spent too much time at the head of a classroom, but when Carter moves into a subject closer to his heart, his voice picks up an excitement, a great emotional momentum, an absorption. His tone carries a constancy of determination; he is a man engaged—independent-thinking, intellectually self-reliant—who dissects his way through any problem. If one method does not work, another must be found. Examine the elements of the problem. Delineate the parameters. Inspect the interaction of each factor. And then, when a course becomes clear, follow it steadfastly through to its conclusion.

He is not, however, stiff or remote.

He is quick with a joke and has a huge puppy-dog spontaneity about him; his great long arms will suddenly fly out and sweep Bobby into the air and dangle him on his shoulder. His handshake is a grasp and pump, enveloping.

He wears his emotions and his beliefs outwardly. He is a man who does not believe in concealing any feeling or thought. When he laughs, it is in short bursts of uncontrolled happiness. He rides the surface, an odd blend of mathematical precision and untethered flexibility. And when thrust into the extraordinary vortex of December 20, 1974, he was forced to rely on every resource gained through his unusual life.

Carter Zeleznik was born on either April 24 or April 25, 1925, in Detroit, Michigan. He always celebrated his birthday on the former date, but when he first applied for a passport some twenty-odd years after his birth, he discovered his birth certificate carried the latter date and misspelled his name. He corrected the name mistake but left the date. He would later tease his boys that he really deserved two birthday parties, and they would roar in mock protest.

Carter grew up in the affluent suburb of Grosse Pointe, the son of a well-to-do lawyer. The memory of the Depression childhood fills his early recollections. In one day he saw his father slip from wealth and comfort into a life in which he was another struggler trying to survive the hard times. This is not to say that the family went to the bread lines. His father still had his profession and his ability, and if the Depression meant troubled times, it translated into less on the table rather than into nothing.

One memory stands out: Carter was a child of eight or nine when he accompanied his father to collect on a note owed by a local businessman. The sum was $4,000, a large amount in those times, enough to tide a family through months, if not years. Carter watched as his father went to the store owner to call in the note. The store owner's family was there, too, watching, their grip tenuous on their business, their possessions, their lives. He watched his father talk with the store owner as the two of them walked through the business, a little ways distant. He did not hear what was said, but after a few moments he saw his father stop and tear the note up. Then he came over, took Carter's hand, and the two of them left the family with their business intact.

He thought it was the act of a large man.

Carter graduated from Grosse Pointe High School in the late 1930s and went on to the University of Michigan at Ann Arbor. The war broke out while he was a student. He did not volunteer but waited for his draft notice to come up.

In the interim, he ran on the track team as a sprinter and studied anthropology. He thought he would become an archaeologist as well as an anthropologist: a student of societies and the ways of man.

When he was drafted, the war in Europe had entered its final stages. He was assigned to a replacement brigade, trained at Fort Dix as a rifleman and shipped to the European theater of operations shortly after the Battle of the Bulge had reached its bloody conclusion in the winter of 1944. Advance columns from Patton's Third Army were already pushing toward the Ruhr River. He spent his time in the rear echelon, failing to see actual combat, but his eyes grew accustomed to the impressions created by combat and the afterbirth of battle. He became a part of the army of occupation.

One wartime vision would come to haunt his memory. Shortly before his reassignment stateside he took a leave and traveled to Switzerland. The difference between that nation, spared the damage of war, and the remainder of Europe was striking. There was something also in the manner of the Swiss, their sense of order, protectiveness and stubborn independence. He looked at the rows of carefully tended mountain gardens, the carved wood and gingerbread homes and saw peace. It stayed in his mind's eye through the years, a fantasy of a quaint, protected world divorced from violence, crime and unrest. He harbored the dream of returning to live there.

After the war Carter entered an academic nomadism that carried him to the University of Michigan, McGill University in Montreal, Yale University in New Haven and other places. He continued to study anthropology and archaeology, but discovered more of his time was being spent in psychology-oriented pursuits.

He spent years in Ethiopia, teaching disciplines ranging from mathematics to social studies at an English-language academy. He traveled in Africa, unsettled in career and future, and would recall later the withering heat of the Gulf of Oman as he stared out from the deck of a small steamer en route to Aden and counted the fins of the sharks as they patiently followed in the boat's wake.

There was time, too, spent on an archaeological dig in Asia Minor, in Iran. It would later become a favorite story; the expedition to which he was attached was at least partially funded by the Central Intelligence Agency, a fact of which most of the members of the group were unaware. Especially Carter. The agency tried to debrief the members afterward. Carter's debriefing was impressively short. He hadn't known he was supposed to be looking for the types of things that interest intelligence gatherers and consequently didn't have much to contribute. He was, he later said, laughing, a most inept and unaccomplished spy.

Carter's years passed swiftly, following academic pursuits, searching for grants, traveling. Following the recommendation of a close friend, he applied for a job in the Office of Medical Education at the Jefferson Medical College. In essence, the department monitored the continuing education of doctors produced by the college. It was a job more closely aligned with his interest in psychology; Carter would one day grin and boast laughingly that he'd never been forced to take a job for which he'd actually been trained. He decided to switch disciplines, leave anthropology behind and pursue his doctorate in educational psychology. That academic revamping was well under way when he decided to go out to Michigan at Easter 1961, to visit his family.

Boarding the plane to return to Philadelphia following the holiday, he saw himself as a man growing well into his middle age, surrounded by books, papers and studies, an academic hermit, alone save for the ideas springing from his imagination.

2. Betty

Elizabeth Mosca was born in March 1928 in Philadelphia. She and her twin sister, Rita, were the youngest in a large family. There were five older brothers and sisters.

Her father had arrived in the United States more than a decade earlier as a teen-ager, without money, the language or a profession, but with the immigrant's dream and the desire, wit and enthusiasm to make them work. He emigrated alone from the small city of Abruzzi, north of Rome; his two older brothers were already in Philadelphia, working as stonemasons, part of an influx of immigrants who worked in the building trades during those years. It was to that profession that Betty's father gravitated: but he was really a merchant at heart, and owning his own business was at the core of his dream.

Betty's mother, in contrast, was the daughter of an established, prosperous North Philadelphia family, stern, middle-class and owners of a grocery store.

Her mother and father met when he was making deliveries to the store. Their courtship was the stuff of Norman Rockwell America. Her father would come to visit and spend most of his time trying to convince Betty's mother's parents of his worth, while Betty's mother, properly chaperoned, listened quietly, attentively, a forgotten part of the ritual. The young couple would go for rides in the family car on weekend afternoons, Betty's father in front, Betty's mother in back, a chaperon by each.

When they had the opportunity to fall in love was a mystery, Betty would recall, laughing. Nonetheless, they did. In the old-fashioned way Betty's father asked for permission to marry Betty's mother in 1915, obtained it from his father-in-law-to-be, and the couple was married that same year. They started a family and took over the grocery business.

The grocery store was on the ground floor, narrow aisles of food stacked tightly into a small place. Betty and her family lived in an apartment on the upper floors. The store was on Glenwood Avenue in Philadelphia, which was then a polyglot neighborhood, mixed black, Italian, Irish, German, an area of low-income families in brick row houses. The grocery was an integral part of the neighborhood, a place of familiarity and friendship. Her parents knew most of their clients by name. As a child Betty would help out in the aisles, fetching items for shoppers. All the children helped; it did not seem much like work to them.

Betty grew into a trim, small woman, with an open face and quick smile, handsome with an elegant sturdiness about her and her hair cropped short, away from her face. She is direct and forthright but at the same time manages a kind of deference, a self-effacing sense of humor. Her laugh is vibrant and contagious. She is a woman of enthusiasm, infectiously so, friendly, outgoing, polite, accommodating, always the first to ask if her guest is comfortable and happy.

When she spoke of her own history, she frequently interrupted it with laughter. The memories were rich, palpably enjoyable. Even when she spoke of hardships and frustrations, it was without regret; she saw all the elements of her story as part of the whole, the make-up of her life. She would not have traded any part of her growing up.

She thought of her household as protected, dominated by the strength of her mother and father. The traditional elements were there: The mother ran the household; the father ran the business, although her mother also controlled the books. She saw her parents as partners, engaged in the dual courses of business and rearing a family. They were a close family, Catholic, church-going, hard-working. There was much love in the household.

She had an orderly, happy childhood, filled with some privilege and some good luck. Her older brothers and sisters married and started their own families, while she and her twin stayed on in the house. She went to the Little Flower Catholic High School and, after graduation, began to attend the Wharton School of Business at the University of Pennsylvania. She attended mostly night classes and worked in the store during the day, though she didn't really consider it work. She was uncertain, too, about business school, not really knowing what she wanted to be.

With Bobby sitting on the couch next to her, she told an anecdote, introducing it with an elbow nudge to his ribs and the words "Bobby loves this story." Once, when she was a small child in grade school, she was in line with her fellow classmates. For some reason the teacher started to ask the children what they wanted to be when they grew up. Betty remembered a sense of apprehension as the teacher approached her. "When it came to be my turn, I started to cry. I couldn't tell them. I didn't know. I said I wanted to be a little girl. And they said you can't be a little girl all the time. And I said, 'Well, I guess I'll just be a mommy then.'" Her voice filled with laughter as she remembered the little girl's dream always to be a little girl.

She thought of herself as sheltered in many ways from anger, tragedy and hardship. Her parents kept the "bad things" away from her. In the Mosca household troubles were not openly discussed, nor were bad times and struggle.

She came to see her mother as "all-giving"—the type of woman who would give up a possession to another if she merely thought the other really desired it. She would hand it over without a second thought. She also saw her mother as the silent strength of the family. If her father was called the boss, it was really only a convenient charade. Her mother controlled the operations of the family. Her father ultimately relied on his wife.

She acquired from her mother a kind of inner strength, an ability to absorb, to go on, to take charge with subtlety. But her own childhood was a time of happiness. She would not need to employ those qualities for years.

"I've never had anything really bad happen to me," she said. "Until Arnold. Well—" she hesitated—"when my mother died."

The death of Betty's mother at the end of Betty's teen-age years was the first real emotional hardship she faced. It was a quick death, a heart attack, over without any lingering pain. The memory causes Betty to pause, take a deep breath and continue slowly. Because she has known only a few terrible times, she feels them all the more vividly. She is a woman who is unafraid of her emotions, but at the same time she wants them in perspective.

"And that was hard to take when my mother died. She was sixty-two, so she wasn't very old. And it was unexpected. And it was rough. But I could tell myself, and I could rely on the fact, that she lived a good life. And she did most everything she wanted to do. And at the time she died, I thought: Well, she's really better off. She would have gone downhill, you see. They had just retired and she wasn't active for the first time in so many years, and she didn't like that. She had been active so many years, so alive, and retirement didn't sit well with her. But it was hard to take, still."

If there was a tragedy in that most difficult, most ordinary of events, it was the effect the death of Betty's mother had on her father. He suffered greatly in his wife's absence: too many years together; too many days, hours and instants shared. His daytimes and nighttimes blended, filled with an irrepressible loneliness. His depression was compounded by his diabetes, which rendered him a semi-invalid, bed ridden much of the time and dependent on insulin shots. The family could afford a nurse, who spent the days with the elderly man, but it was Betty, by then the only unmarried member of the family, who watched after him at night and shared the house with him.

She realized then that he would be alone without her, and she came to the conclusion that it was up to her to take care of him. Though she continued with some of her classes, more and more of her time was occupied in easing the old man's transition through the degenerative stages of the illness toward inevitable death. Eventually the schooling simply evaporated under the demands of nursing her father. It was a role she did not complain about, something instead that she took to heart, that she felt she owed, a debt for the happiness of her own childhood. If she regretted the loss of her own future to the old man's, she did not let it show.

3. Carter and Betty

Betty had been reluctant to take the time away from her invalid father; but her twin had insisted, and she finally agreed to fly out to Detroit at Easter time 1961. It had been some time since she had seen Rita; like all twins, they had been extremely close, growing up. After her marriage Betty's sister had moved to the Midwest, and the separation was painful for both of them. She flew out, spent a few enjoyable days and then boarded a United Airlines return flight to Philadelphia.

Carter was on the same flight. He was in the row ahead of Betty, but there were some empty seats, so he was able to converse with her and the people next to her throughout the flight. Most of the talk was with her seatmates, but Betty knew he was really watching her. He met her at the bottom of the airline ramp after the landing in Philadelphia. He accompanied her to the baggage claim area, where he asked her if he might give her a call sometime. Not encouraging, Betty replied cryptically, "I'm in the phone book."

Carter, unabashed, called the next day.

They were married in December 1962.

It became a family joke, especially after the boys had been born. Carter would announce that he and Betty were "united on United."

4. The Boys

Arnold was born on April 7, 1965; his brother, Robert, about a year and a half later. For Carter and Betty, Arnold's birth was the manifestation of the most extraordinary good luck, the type of fate that changes lives. There they both had been, devoted to their own particular pursuits and solitudes, when suddenly they had met and their lives, seemingly locked in one direction, had abruptly, wonderfully changed.

Arnold was the symbol of that change, their sudden joy.

In looks he favored his mother. He was dark-haired, with her openness. In temperament he seemed a blend of the two parents. He had Carter's inquisitiveness and curiosity and Betty's politeness and sense of decorum.

From the start Bobby idolized his older brother. The boys grew quickly, inseparable, but very differently. Bobby's appearance was more like his father's. He was blond and big-boned, while Arnold was more compact. While Arnold was energetically outgoing, glib, a whirlwind of activity constantly hungry for new knowledge, experience and learning, Bobby was more reflective and intense. He could focus his attention on a subject for a far longer time than other children, absorb more and understand more. They both had quick intellects, were at the heads of their classes. Each, in his own way, fashioned a great pride for their parents, who thought themselves beyond blessing.

After Carter and Betty had married, they planned to move to the New Jersey shore area, where Carter had been offered a teaching position in a school for gifted children. They had made the commitment to bring Betty's father with them. But he died, too much sorrow with the passing of his own wife coinciding with his diabetes. Carter and Betty swiftly shifted gears.

Carter reacquired his full-time position in the Office of Medical Education at Jefferson Medical College and continued work on his doctorate. They found a home in the Center City area of Philadelphia, where Betty established a household and set to the task of mothering the two babies.

In one of Carter's academic incarnations he had come under the benign influence of philosopher Warren McCulloch. He had taught Carter about the medieval Chinese Sung dynasty. During that period the Chinese had developed a method of child rearing that Carter and Betty adapted to their life in Center City. Essentially it held that up until the age of four the child was basically to be treated with total freedom. Few strict efforts at discipline were to be used. The idea was to create a sense of self-confidence in the children. They were not allowed to cry and were free to do almost anything, within obvious reason. Then, at the age of four, when the child had learned self-reliance and self-confidence, one could set whatever rigid rules one wanted.

That was the approach Carter and Betty followed, albeit within the limits that each child created. Both children flourished under the system; learning was both an adventure and a game. Arnold and Bobby grew both emotionally and intellectually.

5. Memories

Betty remembers:

When Arnold was a child of four or five, he decided that he was capable of going to the store for a bottle of milk all by himself. The two of them talked about it, in that unique way mother and child have. He was all seriousness.

"Mama, I can go to the store by myself. I am big enough now."

"Arnold, are you sure? You haven't done that before; we've always gone together. And you will have to cross the street by yourself. I won't be there to hold your hand."

"No, Mama, I can do it. I know how to look both ways and wait for the green light to become red. I can do it."

"Well, all right, Arnold. If your father approves, you can go to the store tomorrow by yourself." That night the two parents talked over the trip. It was a journey of only a block and a half or two blocks. The people in the store knew Arnold. There was only the problem of crossing the street, and he wanted to do it badly; when Carter had arrived home from work, it had been Arnold's first words as he raced to his father's arms, an instant before his younger brother. When he'd been put to bed that night, he'd had a Christmastime excitement about him. Betty had seen the boy's face light with pride when Carter had agreed to the plan.

In the morning Arnold announced, "Mama, I'm ready now." Some of the excitement was out of his voice, replaced with a solemnity more appropriate to the child's vision of the seriousness of the event.

Betty asked, "Are you sure, Arnold? You don't have to go. You can go in a month or so if you'd like to wait." The child paused, considering.

"No. No, thank you, Mama. I'm ready now." So Betty handed over the few coins for a bottle of milk and walked Arnold to the door. He went down a few steps, turned and waved. Then, with a determined, decisive pace, he set out for the store. Betty, suffused with a mother's blend of joy and fear, gave Arnold a few seconds' lead to get down the street; then, as she had discussed with Carter, she followed him, keeping Arnold in her sight but staying hidden from him. It was not difficult. He was striding along with confidence, clutching the money in his hand, his eyes locked straight ahead on the street corner with its imposing stoplight, his biggest hurdle, and the sanctuary of the store beyond. Betty watched him hesitate on the edge of the curb, watching the streetlight, and her heart tightened. Arnold saw the light change, peered first one way, then the other, gauging the traffic. There was none. He stepped across the street swiftly and decisively and headed into the store.

Betty followed, carefully looking in through the window at Arnold, who deliberately paced to the milk counter, seized a bottle and sashayed up to the check-out counter. He paid and exited. Betty dashed down the street so that Arnold wouldn't see her, and danced back inside the house moments before he came striding down the sidewalk. She affected a look of nonconcern as he came through the door. She watched him set the change down on the table and place the milk in the refrigerator. Then he turned to her. "I did it, Mom, see, I did it." And with a jump and a leap, he soared into her arms, where he couldn't see the tears of happiness that rimmed her eyes.

Carter remembers:

Arnold had a gentleness that blended with politeness. He was not an aggressive child, never had a fight, but at the same time he had an insistent curiosity. Once a family friend, a psychologist, came to visit. For fun, he took Arnold aside and showed him a jigsaw puzzle of the United States. He then described what is called the four-color problem. The problem concerns the number of borders that each state in the Union can have that touch a different-colored state. It is a famous mathematical paradox. The friend thought it would stump the child in a few minutes, but Arnold paid close attention to all the explanations, tried diffent combinations and sought different solutions. Over and over again he provided the family friend with correct answers to the mathematical questions.

Finally, he handed the puzzle back to the psychologist. With a grin the friend looked up at Carter. "I'll be damned," he said. He added, "I've never seen a child that young accomplish a feat like that."

Arnold was four.

Once another friend was visiting and at the dinner table told a bad joke. Not an ugly joke, just an unfunny joke. There was a second's awkward quiet; then Arnold filled in the silence with a polite, friendly laugh. Later Carter and Betty almost choked with their own laughter, thinking about the sense of decorum and manners that Arnold had displayed. He had said afterward he didn't want the guest to think his joke unfunny.

It was not long after that that Arnold began to take the train by himself.

The Zelezniks were beginning to feel constricted by life in the Center City area. There really wasn't room for the boys to play and to run; both were exceptionally energetic, and the compact city streets and traffic limited their horizons. Additionally, the Zelezniks were concerned about the growing crime rate in downtown Philadelphia. They began to consider moving to the suburbs, and as part of that scheme, Arnold was enrolled in the New Horizons Montessori School in Fort Washington, just outside the Philadelphia city limits. Every day Carter would walk Arnold the half dozen blocks to the commuter train station and see him onto the line. A teacher at the school volunteered to meet Arnold at the Fort Washington stop. Carter rode the train with Arnold a few times, to make certain he knew the proper place to get off; then Arnold started to ride alone.

Carter had contacted the city officials in charge of the line to see if he could arrange some special escort but had been rebuffed. Undaunted, he spoke with some of the line's conductors and asked if they wouldn't help keep an eye on Arnold. The men were delighted. It wasn't long before Arnold knew all the conductors; they would let him walk the train corridor with them, allowing him to call out the stations as the train approached. His high little boy's voice would soar with the names of the stops—Philadelphia, Germantown, Fort Washington—in his best imitation of the conductors. Waving, he would depart. He loved the train.

One afternoon, after Carter had walked over to the station to meet Arnold after his day's schooling, the child got off the train, laughing. Several of the conductors hung from the passageways, watching and grinning. Arnold ran down the platform toward his father, waving his prize in his hand: The men had given him his own dark blue conductor's cap. After that he wore the cap every day.

Betty remembers:

It was hot, summer, and the family had driven down to the New Jersey shore to go swimming. At the first beach the family went to there was a sign that said: No Ballplaying. No Floats. The boys could see that other children were playing in the surf with floats. Arnold pointed and said, "But they are using floats out there." He spied the lifeguard and went up to the man and asked whether or not floats were allowed. The lifeguard offered to rent Arnold a float despite the sign. The boy returned to his parents, shaking his head.

"I don't understand. The sign says no floats," Arnold said, "but the lifeguard rents them out. Who's right?"

Betty said, "Well, Arnold, you can't use the float because the sign says not to, even if the others are using them. They are wrong, and the lifeguard is wrong." The family then got into their car and drove over to Ocean City, which allowed floats on the beach and in the surf. Arnold had been troubled by the discrepancy, though, and Betty had taken him aside and explained that sometimes it was hard to follow rules but that they should obey the law even if it meant going against their own wishes.

Carter remembers:

In 1972 Carter took Arnold, who was just seven, downtown to one of the big political rallies in a large hotel. Arnold had been excited and curious, clutching his father's hand as they walked through the crowds carrying placards and waving banners. Father and son found themselves shunted off to the side, adjacent to a rear stairway, when they were suddenly caught up in the press of the entourage of advisers and Secret Service personnel surrounding Vice President Hubert Humphrey. The flow of people thrust Carter and Arnold up to the wall, but not before they were spotted by the vice president. Humphrey stopped, walked over to Arnold and bent down to shake his hand. Arnold seized the politician's hand eagerly, then looked up directly into his eyes.

"How are you, son?" said Humphrey.

"Mr. Humphrey," Arnold said, his little boy's voice clear, "if you become president, will you end the war in Vietnam?"

It was a child's question, simple, direct and unadorned by all the tragedy and trauma that accompanied the query. Humphrey paused, looking deep into Arnold's eyes. After that second's hesitation, without rancor, but in a voice of elderly affection, he answered, "Yes, I will, son. Just for you." They shook hands again, eagerly, and with a little wave, the vice president swept on.

Carter and Betty finally decided that life in the Center City area was too hazardous; it was a devastating irony, later, when they would think that they had moved to Fort Washington in order to escape the dangers of violent crime.

They rented a huge, rambling house on Fort Washington Avenue. It filled quickly with the boys' toys, games, baseball mitts, balls, rackets, rocks, books, strewn clothes, friends, loud voices and happiness. Carter commuted to Jefferson Medical College daily; Arnold and Bobby, to the New Horizons Montessori School. Betty tried to keep some sense of organization in their lives. It was difficult.

Arnold loved baseball and followed the Phillies religiously. He played shortstop on his Little League team. He said he wanted to grow up into a ballplayer. It was all he would talk about some days.

It was mostly a gentle time, almost idyllic. The boys grew. Bobby was quieter than Arnold but followed his older brother's footsteps; Arnold was non stop action, as if he were compelled to engage each moment of his young life for all it was worth.

The Costa Rican trip came up suddenly. The Zelezniks were invited down only a few weeks before they would have to depart. Carter and Betty talked it over briefly; it would be an opportunity for the boys to see a whole new culture. The year before the family had traveled to Europe, where Carter had led them through Switzerland. During that trip, they had picked out a little plot of land on one hillside, and as the boys had run in the mountain fields, Carter and Betty had sat on the grass fantasizing about the imaginary house they would construct. The porch here, overlooking the lake. The garden by the side, where it would capture the sun. A small studio for Betty, who loved to paint, with a northern exposure. A study for Carter, lined with his books.

Costa Rica, however, would be different. Winter was fast approaching, Christmas a few weeks away. The boys were excited; they wanted to go. Betty felt slightly unprepared; the offer, the arrangements and the decision all came a bit too quickly. She felt rushed but with a sense of resignation agreed, letting the boys' enthusiasm catch her up and carry her along.

They decided not to fly to Miami, but to take the train. It was partly a concession to Arnold's love of trains. He was delighted, racing about the Thirtieth Street Station in Philadelphia, barely containable. Thick snow was falling, and all the Amtrak schedules were out of whack. The Florida train, the Silver Meteor, was delayed, but Carter realized they could take another train to Washington, D.C., and have several hours sightseeing before the Florida train caught up with them. It was the kind of spontaneous decision Carter loved, something to get them all on the move, something exciting for the boys that would let them know that the holiday had really begun.

In Washington, Carter asked a porter what sights they could see that were close to Union Station before their connecting train arrived. He pointed them toward the Capitol building and toward the U.S. Supreme Court. Snow was still falling, but much less hard than in Philadelphia. The family trudged over to the Supreme Court, only a few blocks away.

Outside the building there is a great stone stairway, which stretches up, white and imposing. Betty stared up at it from the street, feeling dwarfed by the huge white marble columns rising up against the overcast sky and the towering WPA architecture. She watched as Carter climbed the stairs toward the entrance, holding Bobby's hand. Arnold, as always, had raced ahead.

For a second he was framed in the entranceway, beneath the words carved in the façade of the huge building: "Equal Justice Under Law."

For a moment Betty felt an odd dizziness, an apprehension, and she shaded her eyes, steadying herself as she looked up at Carter, Bobby and Arnold. Then, shaking off the sensation, she followed the three up the stairs and into the building, worrying more about catching their train so as not to miss their connections in Miami.

CHAPTER 3
Fifty-five Degrees

1. The Return Home

It was weeks before they turned the thermostat up.

When the Zelezniks had left their house in Fort Washington in early-morning darkness on the nineteenth to catch the train, it had been snowing and the temperature had dropped into the thirties. Despite their need to hurry and the impatience of the two boys to get on with the vacation, Carter had still taken the time to walk through the rambling old house and turn all the thermostats down to fifty-five degrees. No sense, Carter had told the family, in heating a house when no one was there. And when the three survivors of the trip to Miami returned home so precipitously in the evening darkness of the twenty-first, there seemed no need to bring warmth into the house; they had no desire to return the thermostat to a comfortable level. Instead, Carter, Betty and Bobby sat huddled together on the living room couch in the chilled, dark house, staring into the ashes of an unlit fire in the fireplace. They didn't bother to put a match to the wood. Betty explained later that they hadn't really noticed the temperature; the cold inside them was so much deeper than the frost in the air that they were scarcely affected.

On board the huge Lockheed 1011, Bobby said, "Arnold had always wanted to fly on a jet. Now he'll never get the chance." He said little else but stared out the window while the lights of Philadelphia grew brighter as the plane approached the landing. When the Zelezniks arrived at Philadelphia International Airport they were met by two of their closest friends, a psychiatrist and a lawyer, and by Betty's twin sister, Rita. Delta arranged for them to be escorted from the airplane; they had not taken their winter coats on the trip to Costa Rica, and it was close to freezing when the plane touched down, so the Delta representative told them to keep the blankets they had received on the plane.

Carter, Betty and Bobby emerged from the plane, wearing the blankets like robes; they seemed mortally stricken, ashen-faced, bewildered by the depths of the event, like refugees from some unspeakable horror, which was precisely what they were. They were walked through the cold air into the terminal, past a bank of television camera lights and a crowd of newspaper reporters and photographers.

They remembered the lights, as if the brightness had illuminated their tragedy.

Betty, Bobby and Carter could not remember, later, if they said anything to any of the reporters.

Bobby, though, clutching his mother and father's hands, said, "We must be brave. Arnold would want us to be brave." His parents thought he was right, of course, but his words, so accurate an assessment of exactly what Arnold would have wanted, struck more cold into their hearts. Betty wondered again where they would find the strength to continue; each passing instant seemed harder than before. There was no talk in the car as they settled into silence for the drive back to the house in Fort Washington.

Betty's twin sister had come in from Detroit to stay with the family. A few days after the return from Miami, Rita snapped a photograph of Carter, Betty and Bobby out in the big yard next to the old house. The three of them are turned, facing the camera. Bobby is seated on a small bicycle between his parents. Carter is on the right, stooping over, holding the handlebars. Betty stands on the left, just behind Bobby. The three of them are dressed in identical orange sweat shirts with the logo of the New Horizons Montessori School imprinted on the front. Each, high on the left arm, wears a black armband. The camera's shutter captured their faces, creased and strained with the effort to smile, the effort to mask the immutable sorrow inside; at play in the yard without joy.

There were two services for Arnold. The first was public, and many people crowded into the Urban Funeral Parlor on the Bethlehem Pike. It was two days before Christmas. Arnold's teachers from grade school, eyes rimmed red with tears, were there, and Arnold's classmates, looking slightly uncomfortable in their suits and neatly pressed dresses, their faces marked with the confusion of a child's perception of death, their hands gripped tightly in their own parents' hands. The neighbors came. Carter's co-workers from Jefferson Medical College. Betty's family.

Arnold lay in the small coffin, dressed in his Philadelphia Phillies uniform. The second service, on the twenty-eighth, eight days after the murder, was for Carter, Betty and Bobby alone. In the morning the three of them drove to St. Alphonso's Church in Ambler, where Father Thomas Kelly performed a requiem mass of the angels. Carter, Betty and Bobby sat, heads bowed, in the front pew. They remained silent as selections from Beethoven's Fifth Symphony flooded over them. Then, the music swelling inside them, the resurgent strains of Beethoven's Sixth, the *Pastorale*, filled the solemn church air.

"Blessed are the little children," Father Kelly said, "for they shall enter the kingdom of heaven."

One of the hardest, most awful feelings was that they had left Arnold behind. They suddenly felt so incomplete.

There were both public and private qualities to their grief. They made little effort to conceal the disaster that had overtaken their lives.

At first, as is part of the ritual of death, they were inundated with friends, family, well-wishers and neighbors. People filled the Fort Washington house, bringing food, drink and solace, if it could be dispensed. Betty said later that it seemed the doorbell was constantly ringing, the door opening to another cheese cake or salad or baked roast, as if by eating they would somehow alleviate their sorrow. Betty had mixed feelings about the guests who filled the house. There was a part of her that recognized the honesty and the heartfelt need of their friends to help them, but it was balanced against an inner anger that resented the intrusion. Sometimes she wanted to scream at the people who stopped by: Let us alone! Don't try to comfort us! Stop trying to make us feel better when we don't want to!

She resented feeling obliged to the guests. More often than not, the people who would visit would cry so bitterly and so uncontrollably over Arnold's loss that it fell to Betty to comfort them. She would gather her own tears and say, "It's all right, don't worry," over and over again, but in her thoughts she just wanted the people to leave.

She recognized, though, that there was a selfish impatience in that feeling, and she bit back her tongue and accepted the gifts and condolences and embraces and tears with grace and thanks. As she half listened to the words of comfort that her friends tried to muster for her, she thought: No one can really understand. She did not speak these words out loud but held them back with the same gut effort that she used to try to hold her tears.

Still, it was hard for her to fight the overwhelming feeling in the pit of her heart that all she wanted was for all the noise and people to stop, so she could be left alone with her husband and her remaining child inside the darkened, cold house, where she could simply sit and become absorbed by the grief that gripped her.

There were hundreds of moments lost in this pain.

Betty felt she couldn't *do* anything. The only tasks she could perform were those that were essential. A load of wash, for example. When Carter got up in the morning, if there wasn't a clean shirt to wear, he would simply put on a dirty one without caring. Betty found it difficult to do even the laundry or the dishes or any of the routine chores that she was accustomed to doing.

She thought the family was just existing. When it was morning, they would put some food in their mouths. Hours would pass. Then it would be lunchtime. Then it would be afternoon. Then it would be evening and time to eat again. Then it would be time for bed, and they would try to sleep; but the night darkness closed their memories in on them, and they would lie awake.

Small things score her memory.

There was one woman, the wife of a highly regarded Philadelphia psychiatrist and a family friend, who came by. The husband had been active in helping with the arrangements at the funeral home, trying to organize the tasks of death, trying to be supportive and caring. What Betty remembered afterward, though, was meeting the woman face-to-face, back at the house and away from the other well-wishers. The woman and her husband had one child of their own, a little boy close in age to Arnold. The woman had started to speak and became suddenly awkward, grasping at words. She motioned across the room at her husband, the psychiatrist, the man who dealt daily with the vagaries of human tragedy and depression, and said, "If it had been our boy, his son, it would have killed him. Right there. He would have died on the spot. I know it. He couldn't take it."

Betty couldn't reply. For the thousandth time that day she fought the tears in her throat that billowed up like sails filled with wind.

But her eyes fell on Bobby, sitting quietly aside.

Betty had often considered Bobby to be Arnold's echo; he emulated his older brother so much it seemed sometimes that when Arnold requested something, Bobby would follow within ten seconds with the same demand. He always wanted to do what Arnold did, be what Arnold was. Now, with Arnold gone, where did that leave him?

She had her strongest thought then, the idea that would carry her through the hardest days: that if it hadn't been for Bobby, the knowledge that Bobby still had his life, his future, everything in front of him, then yes, it would have killed them, too, just as surely as if the murderer had plunged his knife into their necks. She thought: He is our life now; we owe it to him, we must keep going for him. Even if it means pretending sometimes, we must keep going for him.

In the crevices of his imagination Carter, too, had the same idea. When the hurt became too severe, like a pain grasping the muscles of his heart with a mail-clad grip, he would look at Bobby and swallow great gulps of air, swallowing at the same time the bilious desire to give up living and replacing it with an angry, unfettered determination to keep on going.

A few days after the funeral Betty received a letter from Arnold's grade school teacher, Terry Young. In its way it was typical of the notes and letters that were delivered to the house; at their core they all had the same uncompromising grief that the loss of a child spurs. Betty would remember this letter, however:

Arnold Zeleznik: Arnold Zeleznik was a student in my class from September, 1971 until June, 1974. He came to my class after several years in the Children's House of Green Montessori School in Center City, Philadelphia. He was in my class for the first three years of elementary school, then went on to the upper level of the elementary program.

Throughout the three years, Arnold was consistently an eager learner. He had an interest in all learning which was infectious and was often communicated to other, less-interested children. He loved math, history, especially American history, biology and geography. He was an avid reader.

He learned quickly and often and would go rapidly through various pieces of learning, or else leap over certain sections as he reached the end point. This was very true in math. He often took the initiative. On one occasion, he saw a museum mentioned in the back of a biography he was reading, and he wrote away for information on how our class might take a field trip to it.

Socially, he got along well with all the children. He had friends throughout all the years. When younger, he was more of a follower socially, but by his third year, he was definitely a leader. He and his best friend, Andy R., set a tone in the class of cooperation, enthusiasm, involvement in learning and in all the class activities. This positive tone was dominant enough that the other boys picked it up and were more cooperative and less disruptive than they had been the year before.

Arnold's energy and enthusiasm carried over in the area of sports. He enjoyed all games, but his favorites seemed to be baseball and hockey. His sense of fairness was also very much in evidence here. He would try to help the other team players play better.

I would like to make one final personal note about Arnold. Our older daughter, Danielle, was four years old when Arnold started at New Horizons. I remember very clearly how he was kind to her on the playground at recess time. This was not an occasion when I was around, so it was not a case of teacher-pleasing.

Also, for the last year and one-half that he was in school, my other daughter, Rachel, was also in the school, in the Children's House. At times, being very little, she would come searching for her mommy. I then needed someone to take her back downstairs. Very often, I preferred to have Arnold take her. He seemed to be her special big friend. . . .

When Betty read the letter, she choked with tears, each truth more painful than the previous one. Even after the letter had been added to the boxes and drawers that became cluttered with memories of Arnold, she did not forget the words contained within it.

Carter returned to work on January 2. Betty and Bobby took him to the train station to see him off for Center City and the medical college. He stared through the smudged window at the two of them, standing on the platform, waving as the train pulled from the station. His memory was filled with the vision of Arnold, when he was younger, riding the same route, walking through the cars, conductor's hand in his, conductor's hat proudly on his head, calling out the station names in his high, clear, excited child's voice.

If he did or said anything during that day, he does not recall it. He did, however, type out a letter to himself. It was four pages long. It began with a description of arriving in Miami and raced through the events of the afternoon of the twentieth. It ended:

. . . He was in death as in life a beautiful boy.

Since that time and in some way for the rest of our lives, we have been grieving our loss, Arnold's loss, the world's loss.

Today, January 2nd, 1975, I finally returned to work. As I left for the train Bobby said to his mother, who like myself is not as strong as he is: When Arnold left us, he left us his courage. Now all we have to do is use it. . . .

Most of that day, though, he sat at his desk, spinning in the chair, not restless but stymied by the feelings that filled him. A man who had always been engaged in the pursuit of some knowledge, probing some task that needed to be performed, he was suddenly, precipitously trapped in an unfamiliar lethargy. He looked at the papers and studies and piled-up work in front of him and saw only the memories of his murdered child.

He thought, later, a kind of madness came over him then.

In early January Carter had to attend an out-of-state conference. Betty and Bobby joined Carter in the car for the drive; no one was being left alone at home. They went; Carter participated. Their memories are blank, however, as to what was said or done. Betty couldn't recall later what the conference was about, though she and Bobby wandered through the rooms, trailing after Carter. Carter would sit in the hearing rooms, not listening to the speakers and the panels, his eyes falling on the other conferees, thinking: They do not know my pain; they do not know how empty I feel.

They had no idea what was happening with Vernal Walford. They had had no contact from the Dade State Attorney's Office or the Miami police. They simply assumed that they would be told when to come to Miami and be kept abreast of all important developments. After all, that is what they had been assured.

At the same time they first became aware that Walford had been released from Northampton State Hospital prior to the murder. Friends living in the New England area sent them newspaper clippings from the *Boston Globe* and the *Springfield Union*. Both papers had followed up the killing with reports about Walford's release from Northampton; each paper discovered that Walford had been committed by a psychiatrist on a ten-day writ for observation. Once inside the state hospital, however, Walford had been allowed to change that involuntary order to a voluntary commitment, which by law was only seventy-two hours. He had been allowed to sign himself out of the hospital after fewer than forty-eight hours.

Both papers reported, too, that during his stay at the hospital, Walford—then under the alias Robert Miller Grant—had hallucinated freely, made weird gestures, muttered bizarre, religious commandments, talked angrily about white men and said that, as Jean Caldwell wrote in the *Globe*, "... he disliked people in this order: men were not bad, women were less than men and children did not count at all."

Both newspapers also swiftly discovered that during his abortive stay at the hospital Walford had attacked two of the attendants, leaping on the back of one man and trying to strangle him. Swift help by other attendants and other patients had managed to pry Walford free before he killed the man.

When asked why he had assaulted the attendant, Walford had told hospital personnel that voices had told him to kill the man. He had then been strait-jacketed, shot up with Thorazine and put in a padded cell.

The following day he had been released.

He had signed himself out in order to get home for Thanksgiving dinner, the papers reported. William Goggins, the hospital superintendent, defended the action and was quoted in each paper as saying the release had been "appropriate" on the basis of information the hospital had had at the time.

The newspaper reports infuriated Carter.

Still caught up in grief, he began to rage. How could they just let him go? he wondered.

There were small things that Betty could not bring herself to change. When it came time to set the dinner table at night, she automatically seized four knives, forks and spoons from the silver drawer. Arnold's absence was a palpable void; she could not force herself to set only three place settings, so for months the family ate at the table with a place set for Arnold.

The nights were the hardest times. The darkness seemed to fill their imaginations, the memory of the crime and Arnold's torn body gaining substance and dimension in the dark and shadows. Bobby could no longer sleep in the room he'd shared with his brother, so he would crawl into the bed between his parents and fall fitfully asleep, his breath coming in short, rasping sounds. Carter barely slept at all but lay awake until morning light, staring wide-eyed up at the ceiling, listening to the darkness noises. It was equally difficult for Betty; she was unable to get any rest from her memories and her grief until the night she slipped from the bed, leaving Carter and Bobby behind, and went alone into the boys' bedroom. She looked around at the toys, games and clothing strewn about haphazardly in the room. Each pile, each angle seemed to speak loudly of Arnold. She looked at his bed in the corner, freshly made. Then she pulled down the sheets and blankets and climbed inside, for the first time feeling warmer, a small step closer and, if not at peace, at least temporarily comforted. And she slept.

Betty hated to go out of the house. Even the simplest errands angered her and seemed inappropriate and irritating. Bobby trailed beside her as Betty went restlessly from room to room. He did not seem to find these odd travels unusual. He said little but could not stand to be alone.

There was one day, perhaps six weeks after the murder, when Betty was forced to go out shopping. She remembers how frustrated she felt; she needed some simple household items and had to go to one of the nearby shopping malls. She couldn't bring herself to burden a neighbor with the mundane task, and though she hated to go out—it was like leaving the house unprotected—she knew she had to. Bobby was at school, supervised, being watched, and Carter was at work in downtown Philadelphia, and there was nothing for her to do save get dressed, get into the car and drive over to the shopping area. She entered the store briskly, hurrying, wanting to get back to the house. She swiftly found the items she needed and carried them over to the check-out counter. A middle-aged woman was working the register; she took the items from Betty and began totaling them. Betty handed over her credit card to pay for the purchases. The woman glanced down at the card for an instant, then looked hard at the name embossed there. The saleswoman's eyes opened wide then, and she gave a little gasp of recognition. She looked up, and her eyes locked on Betty's. The two women stared across the counter at each other for a moment.

The saleswoman finally broke the silence, saying, "You're the lady with the child who was . . ." But she was unable to complete her sentence, and the two of them, strangers, in the middle of the day, under the bright lights of the shopping mall, broke uncontrollably into tears.

2. Some Decisions

It was necessary to reorder their lives.

Carter and Betty reached the same conclusion independently; each, within grief, within hurt, feeling physically and mentally beaten by Arnold's murder, recognized that the family was in danger of simply stopping. Carter especially realized that the vision of Arnold's murdered body in room 206 had very nearly killed him. He realized, too, that the shock of the murder was still with them daily, affecting every move, every idea. The family had to get up, go on, go forward. Neither he nor Betty knew exactly what those words meant, how the physical, emotional and psychological advancement would manifest itself, but he was convinced they had to do something.

Simultaneously Betty looked closely at Bobby, as he followed her throughout the house, dogging her every step. She saw the damage and the danger. It was a formless fear, not a thing she was ever able to put her finger on precisely, but she knew within her heart that they would remain frozen, forever crippled by that horrible moment when they had burst through the doorway into room 206, unless they did something. Anything.

There was no intensely dramatic moment that marked this first decision. Betty and Carter talked, in the way of any close couple that has faced a tragedy, and decided that they had to begin a process of restoring their lives. Otherwise, they thought, they would lose Bobby to a world of depression. Betty said afterward that she was afraid that Walford might have murdered them all with that single slashing blow of his knife.

So, in the midst of their sadness and loss, Carter and Betty made a vow to return to, if not normality, at least a routine. To become a family again.

How to do it was the question.

CHAPTER 4

"No Man Speaks for Me!"

Date: 12/23/74
Time: 8 A.M.
Quiet in cell . . . staring. Gives no response to questions.

Time: 9:15 A.M.
Remains quiet.

Time: 10 A.M.
Visited by investigator from p.d.'s office. Little or no verbal response.

Time: 10:25 A.M.
Visited by Dr. Rothenberg and representatives from p.d.'s office. Inmate yelling loudly, screaming.

Time: 10:35 A.M.
Visited by Dr. Mutter. Yelling. Screaming. Very hostile. Began talking in a deliberate distinct speech pattern in a loud voice.

Time: 10:50 A.M.
Quiet again. Mr. Black requested that patient not be medicated until seen by Dr. Corwin this afternoon. Will refer to Dr. Casademont for medication order.

Time: 2 P.M.
Inmate stated, "that he's to obey only the Lord," and that he will "kill" for the Lord.

Time: 3 P.M.
Patient given thorazine 300 mg. in orange juice which he flushed in toilet. Secured eight officers to restrain patient and thorazine 100 mg. was administered intramuscular. Patient fought vigorously and bit a correctional officer on the leg. (Dr. Sanders suggested that we draw lab studies when feasible to determine possibility of hepatitis.) Patient does not demonstrate loud or aggressive behavior except when he is approached by staff. . . .

—Dade County Jail medical unit log sheets

1. The Obvious Defense

After his arrest, the abortive questioning, the scraping of blood samples from beneath his fingernails and his booking on murder charges late on the twentieth and into the morning of the twenty-first, Vernal Newland Walford was placed in a stripped security cell within the medical unit attached to the Dade County Jail, called Ward D. The ward was associated with Jackson Memorial Hospital, the large public hospital in downtown Miami. On the morning of the twenty-first, prior to the line-up in which Bobby Zeleznik accurately identified him, Walford was also given a preliminary bond hearing, as required by Florida law. He was ordered held without bond on first-degree murder charges by County Court Judge Ruth Sutton. The public defender was also ordered to represent him. Walford did nothing at the hearing, except stare icily ahead. Black and Denaro were there, already conceiving the defense.

From the instant that they had heard of the crime the previous evening, they had known that insanity would be their only possible argument. They had known it simply from the fact of the crime. How could one describe the act that had occurred in room 206 other than to call it madness?

Merely a crazed act and bizarre behavior, however, would not translate into what Denaro called "a true verdict, a verdict that spoke the truth, exactly what the word means." It would have to be a construction of many devices and elements, all rigged together with the intelligence and obsession of the two fine lawyers.

By the Monday after the murder they had sent the following letter to the jail, to the police and to the state attorney's office:

TO ALL LAW ENFORCEMENT OFFICERS
in re: Vernal Walford

BE ADVISED that Mr. Vernal Walford, aka Bob Grant Miller, arrested December 20, 1974, and presently incarcerated in Safety Cell #1, Jail Clinic, Dade County Jail was appointed the Public Defender by Judge Sutton on the 21st of December, 1974. Be advised further that Mr. Vernal Walford has been diagnosed as psychotic within the last three days and that since the time of his arrest has openly exhibited his mental disease until Jail Authorities this day administered to him the anti-psychotic drug thorazine.

KNOW THAT BY THIS LETTER we, the undersigned attorneys, instruct you not to talk to Mr. Walford outside the presence of one of the undersigned attorneys.

s/ Roy E. Black
Assistant Public Defender

s/ Jacob M. Denaro
Assistant Public Defender

Of course, the letter's legal authority to prevent any further interrogation was questionable. In particular, the attorneys knew that several days before Arnold Zeleznik's murder, another little boy had been kidnapped from outside his house in Coral Gables, a Miami suburb. Though there was no evidence linking Walford to the disappearance, Black and Denaro were worried that detectives might try to hang the case on their client, just to clear it from their books. The letter was designed to be sufficiently intimidating to make any officer think twice before trying to take a statement from Walford. The lawyers were anxious, too, that Walford not confess whatever twisted reasoning lay behind the killing to anyone except them and the line-up of psychiatrists that was gathering to examine him. That was a secret they wanted to control. Denaro, especially, believed that the logic behind the murder, no matter how insane, was the key to the defense.

They needed to know why.

They needed to know how.

And they needed to know whom and what they were dealing with.

There was a great leap from Jack Denaro's breathless exclamation upon first meeting Walford, "That guy is nuts!," to understanding his madness. The two lawyers began a frenzied collection of their own, accumulating facts, impressions and information as rapidly as possible. Walford's competency hearing was set for January 31. Their defense had to be twofold and prepared by that hearing. Out of what they would learn from Walford, about Walford and the psychiatric reports, they would construct an insanity argument: that he did not understand right from wrong at the time of the murder. At the same time they needed to be able to show that he now was too far out of control to be put on trial for Arnold's murder.

2. Black and Denaro

Sometimes when courthouse people in the Dade County Metro Justice Building spoke of Roy Black and Jack Denaro, it came out as one word, as if they were one person: "BlackanDenaro."

The two men were an unusual blend of similarities and contradictions. Their backgrounds were strikingly different, but the sum of their experience created an amalgamation that worked remarkably effectively in a courtroom. "Together," Roy Black said later, "we created a kind of synergistic energy." Each had joined the Dade Public Defender's Office in 1971, hired out of the University of Miami Law School by Phillip Hubbard before he'd gone on to become a highly respected appellate court judge. In the late sixties and early seventies the Dade Public Defender's Office was a haven for the iconoclasts and independents who were graduated from law school during those turbulent years. It gained national attention in 1968, when it sued the Miami Beach police for arresting demonstrators illegally at the Republican National Convention.

The office was operated in opposition to the famed Dade State Attorney's Office headed by Richard Gerstein, a prosecutor of wide renown. It is sometimes said, around courtrooms, that there are two types of people: those who like putting people in jail and those who like getting them out. The Public Defender's Office, naturally enough, attracted the latter. Black and Denaro were the top of its class. They started in what is known as the pits, handling misdemeanors, and quickly advanced into the felony divisions. It was a quick step to defending accused killers.

When Arnold Zeleznik was killed in Miami, it was before the city gained the homicidal reputation it currently regrets. His murder was 1 of fewer than a 100 that would be processed during 1974. By the end of the decade, when Miami would convulse with riots and refugees, the murder total would soar to close to 700 county-wide. Arnold's death, however, occurred at a different time, with a different mood. It was so out of the ordinary that it captured public attention easily. So, too, it captured Black and Denaro's attention, and because of the exceptional quality of the murder, the two men were able to justify devoting all their time to it. Ironically, had the murder taken place five or six years later, the overburdened members of the Public Defender's Office would doubtless have had considerably fewer resources to devote to it. The outcome might very likely have been different. Indeed, assigning the top two lawyers exclusively to the case would have been unheard of.

But in 1974, that is what happened.

From the instant the news of the crime filtered through the Justice Building on the afternoon of the twentieth, the murder and the defense of the killer dominated the imaginations of Roy Black and Jack Denaro. It compelled them far more than any other case they had had. Both men used the same word: a fascination.

Defending Walford absorbed them.

In their professional lives the two men would come to represent arsonists, contract killers, multiple rapists, wife beaters, husband stabbers, drug-dealing kingpins, panicked junkie killers, child molesters, cop killers, motorcycle gang sadist-murderers, corrupt cops and the occasional white-collar criminal. Walford, however, was something different, something each man independently had difficulty putting into words. To be a criminal defense attorney is to accept a single principle above all others: the right of the accused to a vigorous defense. This principle requires the defense lawyer to hold the state prosecutors, the judge, the jury and the law to the strictest standard. It is to live in a world of gray shadow, where language, actions and events all can be manipulated, where nothing is painted black and white. It is a constant hunt for the rough edges, the meager crack, in which a doubt can be created, sown and nurtured. It is a world in which one's morality and one's sense of right and wrong are superseded by the requirements of the Constitution. It is a world in which the moral sense of guilt and innocence is subjugated to the legal sense: Can these qualities be proved? It is a heady, exciting, powerful world, a theatrical contest of will and facts and brains. It is ultimately the most dangerous game; the heads on the wall are real.

To the two young attorneys Walford was the absolute test of the principles of the defense lawyer. Who could be more outcast from society than a mad, black, foreign child murderer? What act, they thought, could be more evil?

And so who deserved the greatest defense? The unflagging defense? The defense without cost? The combined energies and intellects of the two finest lawyers in the office?

Walford.

In 1974 Roy Black was twenty-nine. He had been born in New York City, the son of an executive with Jaguar Motors, a onetime Grand Prix race driving Englishman married to an American. The family had first lived in the city, then moved to the suburbs, to Stamford, Connecticut. When Roy was an adolescent, his father decided he'd had enough of the executive life and moved the family to "the tallest mountain outside of Kingston, Jamaica." They'd lived there and in Nassau. Roy had gone to prep school in New York City and then in 1963 to the University of Miami on a swimming scholarship. In 1967 he'd traded that for an academic scholarship and attended the university's law school. After graduation he'd received the highest grade in the state on the Florida bar exam and been invited to give a speech before the state supreme court. It had been the time of the infamous Chicago Seven trial. Black had chosen to speak about the rights of the accused.

He was a tall, athletically-built man, who wore thick glasses, his straight sandy hair hanging down across his forehead. Outgoing, jocular, he loved recounting the legal prank, the moment of cross-examination during which the witness is caught in a lie. He was filled with rapid-fire stories of wild cases, the events that happened behind the more studied moments in the courtroom. Once, after having defended a black man accused of the first-degree murder of a white policeman, Black had emerged from the courtroom to a bank of television cameras. The jury had returned a second-degree murder verdict; Black had argued that the killing, which had taken place in a wooded area, unseen by other policemen or witnesses, had been an act of self-defense. Instead of the death penalty, his client faced a life term without any mandatory time; in reality, perhaps seven years behind bars. It was an exceptional legal victory, but the first question from the barrage of television reporters had been "Do you plan an appeal?" He had swallowed hard and replied, "Of course, there are elements that we'll investigate." Then, as the cameras swung to the defeated prosecutor, Black had roared with laughter. "Hell, appeal? We won!" On the evening news shows his laugh could just be made out in the background. He liked that even more.

One of the jokes, probably apocryphal, that the judges in the Justice Building liked to recount was how one of their membership had finally ordered Jack Denaro to buy a different suit. He had, it seemed, one brown suit. Wore it to every court appearance. It was a ruling from the bench, the story went, so Denaro had gone out and bought one blue suit—then alternated the pair.

Denaro, possessed of a wiry build and wiry black hair, an intense, unusual man with an ironclad stare but a quick wit, had come from a large Italian family and grown up in upstate New York, near Rochester. Three years older than Roy Black, Denaro had first attended the seminary at St. Bernard's College in that city, thinking he would join the Catholic priesthood.

Some innate sense, however, had told him it was the wrong vocation. He had chosen, instead, to go to law school at Union University in Schenectady, and graduated in 1967. He'd come to the University of Miami's law school to do legal graduate work, and he'd received his master's and doctoral degrees in international law in 1968 and 1970. His dissertation topic had been the legal implications of cross-boundary crimes, the jurisdictional questions raised by an airline hijacking, for instance.

He had not intended to become a trial lawyer or a criminal defense attorney. He had been recruited, however, by the persuasive Phillip Hubbard, who had argued to him that it was more important to act the law than to become a legal academician. Denaro, unsure, had stumbled into a different religion. The onetime altar boy, who'd spent years studying Scripture, philosophy and the great thoughts of mankind, was suddenly enmeshed in a world of killers, rapists, savages and wildmen.

He loved it.

He saw it as an art form, a performance on a stage coupled with a blank canvas on which to paint his vision of facts and events. He developed a monk-like obsession for preparation, for outlearning and outknowing his prosecutorial adversaries. He was sleepless on a case and a master of device. Once, in a highly-publicized murder trial against a top prosecutor, he deliberately misstated a key measurement that had been testified to by a crucial witness. Denaro's entire version of the facts depended on that measurement—the way it had been testified to. Without thinking, the prosecutor leaped to his feet with a vigorous objection. Denaro hadn't hesitated but had continued his closing argument, the key measurement underscored in the jury's minds not by him, but by his adversary. A transcendent maneuver, the prosecutor ruefully acknowledged later, his case lost.

Denaro was once asked in an interview why he'd chosen criminal defense work. He quoted Camus and the myth of Sisyphus. "It is in the nature of man to strive," he said.

3. A Collection of Events

The week following the murder Denaro went to the Crossways. He scrawled notes on a legal pad as he walked through the Formica and fluorescent lights of the thickly-carpeted hotel:

. . . Ray Barbarino, resident manager.

Said W. belligerent at breakfast. Said W. talked with other diners, including a man and children who sat down nearby. He ordered four eggs and hotcakes. The waiter explained the order would have to be a la carte.

Walford then got into an angry discussion with the waiter over the size of the bill. The waiter at one point touched Walford on the shoulder. W. stepped back, saying he didn't like to be touched.

Barbarino said that several of the housekeepers saw Walford spend much of the day sitting in a green chair outside the second floor elevator doors.

Another employee saw Walford with the Bible in his hand about 15 minutes before the murder. The Bible cover was red. Said "he was funny looking."

At 3 P.M. was when Walford went to the kitchen and talked with the chef as the latter prepared the chicken dinner that was found . . . in the room.

Chef said Walford said he was waiting for a phone call.

Chef said W. seemed like a real nice person.

Walford (from clerk) checked in at 8:45 on 12/19. Called from the airport for a room. Carried one bag, jacket on, overcoat. First was put in room 204, but because that was undone, was moved to 206. Paid cash through Sunday 12/22.

Zelezniks in at 2:30 P.M. on 20th. Took swim.

Barbarino said he heard the scream, thought first there had been some kind of accident. Ran directly to elevator shaft, checked that, then went to the laundry chute. Came back to the front and the clerk says he saw Walford leaving rushed. Went to room 206 and saw the body. . . .

Only a few steps behind the police, Black discovered that Walford had purchased the murder weapon at the Sirgany International gift shop in the concourse area of Miami International Airport earlier in the day on the twentieth. He spoke to the store clerk who had spotted Walford's photo in the *Miami Herald* and had identified it for the police.

She told Black how Walford had come into the store. It was a typical airport gift shop with wide-open doors, filled with knickknacks, stuffed animals, magazines, games and T-shirts, a potpourri fashioned to appeal to any and all interests. The knives were in a glass case next to the register. Walford, the clerk said, had spent the day out in the concourse area, carrying his Bible, accosting travelers, preaching and demanding they repent. His voice, sometimes raised in exhortation of the Lord, sometimes in lament for people's sins, had carried into the shop.

Walford had spotted the knife as soon as he'd entered the gift shop. He'd wanted it emphatically, she said. When she handed it over to him to show him he'd said he would buy it. When she had asked for the knife back to wrap it back in its box, he'd refused to give it up. To obtain the proper price, she had had to read the tag from another similar blade. She'd taken his money and handed him the box. He'd crushed the box around the knife savagely, she said, a single angry motion.

Then he'd disappeared. Bible in one hand. Knife in the other.

Arnold Frank Zeleznik, taken three months before his death.
COURTESY CARTER ZELEZNIK.

Vernal Walford, shortly after his arrest. COURTESY DADE STATE ATTORNEY'S OFFICE.

Betty, Carter and Bobby Zeleznik, minutes after the discovery of Arnold's murder.
PHOTO BY JOE RIMKUS, JR., *MIAMI HERALD*.

The Zelezniks today. PHOTO BY G. LOIE GROSSMAN.

4. Competency

Under Florida law, a hearing would have to be held and Walford judged competent to stand trial before any trial date on murder charges could be set. Black and Denaro instantly agreed that this first hearing would, in effect, control Walford's entire experience with the criminal justice system. In Florida the standard for competency was significantly different from the famous M'Naghten standard of right and wrong which governed a criminal trial in which insanity had been raised as a defense. Briefly put, to be competent to stand trial in Florida in 1974, a defendant simply had to understand the nature of the charges lodged against him and be able to assist in his defense.

It was a fuzzy standard.

While a psychiatrist might reach any clinical conclusion, based on the exaggerations of Walford's madness, the two attorneys had to confront certain facts: Did Walford understand the charges against him? He'd fled from the scene to avoid capture; he had hidden the murder weapon to avoid detection; he had refused to answer detectives' questions about the murder. It could easily be argued that Walford had a clear understanding of what he'd done and the illegality of his act. Could Walford assist in his defense? A more difficult question. In effect he'd already done so, by demanding an attorney and exercising his constitutional rights when confronted by police following his arrest—an exercise the vast majority of even the most street-wise of suspects failed to engage in. But could he provide the detailed answers to questions from Black and Denaro that a first-degree murder defense demanded? At times, yes; at other moments, no. Was that sufficient to order a trial?

Black and Denaro thought it a close question.

Despite the extraordinary quality of Walford's disease, a fact apparent from the beginning, it was possible that the curious conjunction that schizophrenia, Walford's innate arrogance and intelligence, and the rules of criminal procedure made, would cause a judge to order a trial.

They knew, given the murder and the publicity, that they could expect no discretionary rulings by any Dade County judge. No close question was going to go their way. The evidence of incompetency had to be overwhelming.

There was little doubt in their minds that Walford was legally insane and the act he'd committed pardonable under the M'Naghten standard of insanity. There was equally little doubt in their minds that the murder of what Denaro called "a beautiful, guiltless little boy" would outrage a jury. Given a choice between a guaranteed twenty-five years behind bars (or a death sentence—the penalties for first-degree murder) or turning Walford over to a state division of mental health plagued by bureaucratic foul-ups, inmate escapes and neglect, with no legal control over how long he would be behind bars, which option would jurors select? Would they listen to a bunch of doctors discussing the highly technical elements of legal insanity, or would they follow their own instincts and think of preserving the community instead?

Each lawyer knew the answer to those questions.

Consequently, they believed it was of paramount importance to avoid any trial. Walford had to be declared incompetent. Black and Denaro sat in their cubbyhole office high in the Metro Justice Building, plotting the scheme of the defense late into the evening of each day. They did not know then, at the beginning, how Walford himself would come to control what would happen.

The two lawyers realized that the five psychiatrists already scheduled to examine Walford would reach independent conclusions about his mental status. Two doctors had already been appointed by a judge to perform evaluations. The attorneys wanted the widest possible examination, however. Consequently, Black and Denaro started sending other doctors over to see Walford, so that they would have a diagnosis in advance of the official reports and far in advance of the State Attorney's Office. One of the first of the many doctors who would eventually see Walford was psychologist Robert Sylvester. His report was for Black and Denaro alone.

Psychological Evaluation of Vernal Walford.

Vernal Walford was examined in the Dade County Jail. Walford was awakened in his cell in the dispensary area... by the guard who accompanied me. [Since his arrest] he had been violent, assaultive and extremely difficult to control. Hence I was asked to examine him through the bars of his cell.

He was nude and remained sitting on a pad of rubber-like soft material, which served as a mattress. All loose items, such as toilet articles and clothing, had been removed from the cell as it was feared that Walford might attempt suicide.

He was pleasant enough, in a restrained, suspicious way, and answered my questions in a patois that appeared to be a mixture of Jamaican English-American and French. I was able to understand only in part his long, rambling statements. If I asked him to repeat a word or phrase, he would become instantly angry, gritting his teeth and repeating the word in a slow, overemphasized manner that made it all the more difficult to understand. He is obviously functioning with only the slimmest of marginal emotional control....

He finally said he would not talk to me anymore until I had gotten him some clothing; whereupon he laid down and seemed to fall asleep at once. I checked him a couple of times during the next hour, but he had not moved....

Walford is obviously suffering from an acutely severe psychotic state which is clearly paranoid schizophrenic in nature. Throughout my examination of him, he would suddenly thrust out his arm, pointing the forefinger and little finger at me in the symbolic "Devil's Horns" gesture to ward off evil spirits....

From his long discourses, I was able to elicit the following specific bits of information. Walford said that "God has given me a mission to punish man for his sins, especially the white man." The words "white man" were accompanied by the finger gesture. The word "sacrifice" appeared many times in the discourse, but without reference to the alleged offense....

He said he had never been in Miami before and described how difficult it had been to get a passport and leave Jamaica. Only the intervention of Jesus Christ, working through God, enabled him to come to the United States. This was, he said angrily, how the white man [the finger gesture] tried to do evil to him and prevent him "from carrying out God's will." It was interesting to note that Walford spoke well, grammatically, and with an unusually good vocabulary. His voice cadence rose and fell as he spoke reverently of God and of Christ, then rose in hate and anger at the oppression of the white man and his sins....

There is not the slightest doubt in my mind that Walford is acutely psychotic and experiencing a psychotic episode of extraordinary intensity....

He acts only and is motivated solely by a "message from God." Thus he expiates his own guilt and mistakes by proclaiming that everything he does is the result of God's direction to him. From...the picture I was able to observe, he could have been psychotic for some years, certainly for as long as even five or ten years. As such, his condition is chronic....

Sylvester's report also included his speculation that the murder could have been some type of "human sacrifice" prompted by Walford's biblical obsession coupled with the stress of the Christmas season, the unfamiliarity of Miami and the dominance of the weird Caribbean religious cultures from which he had sprung. There was no exact evidence of this, the psychologist cautioned, but it was a possibility. He ended his report with the urgent request that Walford be hospitalized in maximum security without delay.

The idea that Arnold's murder was a "human sacrifice" was one which grasped the press mightily. Since the first reports of the killing the "ritualistic" aspects of the homicide had been stressed. It seemed the easiest explanation for the murder method: Arnold had been held, throat cut, blood draining to the floor. To label the crime thus also took it far away from the mainstream of any other type of murder; it was the type of quick sensationalism that attracted even the staidest of newspapers. Black and Denaro did nothing to discourage that kind of speculation in the papers. The more crazed the act appeared, the more momentum their arguments gained.

"He's a vicious animal..." Roy Black told one inquisitive *Miami News* reporter. He emphasized the word *animal*.

At the same time the lawyers were working hard to discover exactly who Walford was. His Jamaican extraction was obvious, but where had he come from? What was he doing in Miami? What had brought him to room 206? Where was he going? The list of questions seemed interminable. Neither man knew which answer to what question would be crucial, but it was imperative to answer as many as possible.

As with the police, the press informed them that Walford had been incarcerated at Northampton State Hospital in Massachusetts. They started to piece together what happened in the days prior to the murder. They spoke with Lucille Fernandez, a name obtained from the police. She was Walford's girl friend in the Hartford, Connecticut-Springfield, Massachusetts area.

It was early evening and closing on darkness. With a tape recorder attached to the telephone receiver, Black and Denaro made the call from the cubicle they shared on the eighth floor of the Metro Justice Building. Denaro did the talking, with Black coaching in the background.

"Hello. What is your name, ma'am?"

"Lucille."

"Lucille Fernandez, correct?"

"Right."

"Okay, my name is Jack Denaro. Our office represents Vernal Walford."

"Uh huh."

"You are Mr. Walford's girl friend?"

"Yeah."

"Okay now, how long have you known Mr. Walford?"

"I went through this three times already."

"It's extremely important."

"Well, I just came in, I walked in the door, and I was trying to get my daughter some dinner right this minute. You couldn't get this from the police department?"

"No, we won't be able to get it from the police department for some time to come. I wouldn't trouble you unless it was of the highest urgency."

"Yeah. I know. I want to help."

"When did you first meet Mr. Walford?"

"In July, in Hartford at a party with friends."

"What was he like?"

"Like a normal man."

"How long did you go with him?"

"Until he left. He said he had to go home. He's married. He received some money from Detroit. From Shirley Robertson. We weren't friends. Two hundred dollars. He said she used to be an old girl friend of his."

"What else?"

"Well, he was baptized Sunday before last."

"Now wait a second. What day are you talking about?"

"Last Sunday, and the Sunday before that."

"In other words, the Sunday before the little boy died."

"Yeah. The Alden Baptist Church. Springfield, Mass. Four blocks away. When he first came here, we used to go to church. And my daughter."

"What did he say his religious background was?"

"He didn't say. He said he likes to go to church. He didn't smoke. He stopped drinking. So when he got hit over the head, he stopped everything, you know. He just wanted to go to church and get more deeply involved in the Bible. I guess they found it with him. He got deeper and deeper, and uh, well, I better go back, because he got hit."

"When did he get hit?"

"It was before Thanksgiving. The man on the job hit him. He was working at Milton Bradley here in Springfield. He never told me his name. He said he went to work. When I came in from work, he was sitting at the table. So he says, when I walked in, my daughter and I, guess what? He said, this guy just walks up to me and hits me cross the head with a doll."

"With a what?"

"A doll. A thirty-two-inch doll."

"What is that, a tool?"

"A baby doll. He works at a toy factory."

"Oh."

"Well, this is when it all started. He says it was a piece of the glass. He wears glasses, and he says a piece of the glass went behind his eye, and it cut it back there, the eyeball."

"Did he go to the hospital?"

"Well, not right away because he started acting funny that night and he went downtown with me. I said you want to go to the hospital, but he says No! I'm gonna forgive the guy, ya know. And he begins to talk strange. I said, yeah, it's nice to forget, right? Okay, so we go downtown. He and I and my daughter and when we get into the store, I don't know what happened, but he started to go from person to person, Repent! Repent! Repent all your sins! So I says, what's wrong with you? And he was saying it so loud. He says, I got to go, got to go. He says, if you don't hurry up I'm gonna leave you. I said what's wrong with you? because he never acted this way before. You know, he's a quiet guy and intelligent. But he says, hurry up, hurry up. My daughter was following him, and I grabbed her because the way he was running out of the store, she could follow him and get in front of a car. When we got outside, he started screaming. Screaming loud so some people laughed at him. I said Bob—I didn't know his real name, just Bob Grant—people are looking at you and they are going to have you arrested and put you in a mental institute. So he said, I don't care. I'm supposed to tell. I'm supposed to spread the word. God is coming. God wants his people to repent. So I said, well you do this when God call upon you to be a minister. And you go to ministry school, then you have a church and you tell the people these things. He said, No! No! I must go out tonight and tell everybody. I got so nervous I drove home. And he was still talking, you know, you've got to repent of your sins. So I said, calm yourself down, do you want to go to the hospital? He said no, take me home fast. So I came back to my house and he jumps into his clothes and he put on all red, well, not red, but cranberry, he had a cranberry suit. He says, I'm gonna dress up in this red and from now on my name is Red. He put on red socks, everything red. And he rushed out of the house. He says I gotta go and spread the word. I say maybe you should go to the hospital. Maybe that hit disturbed you. He said no, I gotta go, gotta go, to New York and Hartford and spread the word. And he says if anybody asks for him to say that Red went to spread the word. And he was like, laughing, you know. So he ran out. The next day he comes back, so I say, did you spread the word and he says Oh yes. And I saw the sun on the bus and I was telling people to look at the sun. I said, sun at night? He says, yes, I saw this big light and the bus driver said he was going to put me off if I didn't keep quiet. So I kept quiet. So I said, oh yeah . . ."

"From the time he moved in with you until the time he got hit on the head, he didn't act unusual, did he?"

"Until he got hit on the head."

"He acted like a normal man?"

"Yeah."

"He never acted disturbed or unusual or irrational before that time?"

"No."

"What did he tell you about his background?"

"Since he got hit on the head, he says my name is Vernal Newland Walford. He says, I must tell the truth. He says I must tell I am married. I couldn't pronounce it. He told me he was born on January the sixth, 1943, in Jamaica. He said he lived in Canada."

"What else did he tell you he never told you before?"

"About his God."

"This is very, very important. What specifically did he say?"

"My God. I must go and tell the world that Jesus is coming. I says, who? He said, Jesus is coming, if you don't believe me, but he's coming. He says, you must repent of your sins, repent, and I must go out and tell the world, tell everybody that they must repent of their sins."

"Did he say anything about a sacrifice?"

"No."

"Did he ever mention a sacrifice?"

"No. Never."

"What else did he say?"

"It was hard to talk with him. He just ran out of the house. He had packed his clothes because he went to Jamaica and then came back."

"I'm confused."

"He went to Jamaica. He was gone about a week. He said he had to take care of business and see his children. Before Thanksgiving. Before he got hit. The day after he comes back he gets hit in the head."

"How did he act when he came back from Jamaica?"

"The way he acted before. Normal."

"He went running out on a Thursday, came back on a Saturday. What did he say?"

"He sat around. He didn't get violent. He went to the book."

"What book?"

"The Bible."

"What color was the Bible?"

"Red. It says Jerusalem on the front. I asked him to read the Twenty-third Psalm. It didn't read like our Bible. It sounded like garbage to me. It just didn't say The Lord is my shepherd, you know. It reads it, but it doesn't explain it the way our Bible does. So he starts explaining it. He was calm you know. All day he wanted me to sit down and listen to him. He was always talking about his God."

"When did he go to the institution?"

"Monday. He went to work, and they sent him to the Springfield Hospital emergency. They called me up and says, We've got Bob Grant in here, and I said, well, what's wrong? And they said at the doctor's office he was making up sounds. I said what sound? and they said the sound was like ha, ha, ha, ha, ha. Like his voice was going up and down. So they took him to emergency. And emergency took him to the institute. But he got out later that week. . . ."

And so Denaro thought: A man gets hit in the head with a doll, and it catapults him into a madness that results in a little boy's death. If the pieces were falling together, in terms of a legal reply to the murder indictment, each piece only added another question to the puzzle. It began to gnaw away at him.

5. *The Paradox*

Meanwhile, Walford remained naked in his cell.

His actual behavior ranged from that of the wildly energetic, loud, abusive, assaultive, raging madman to a near-catatonic stillness, in which he stared blankly, absently out at nothing. The jail ward records reflected that awkward discrepancy. One minute, madness; the next, nothingness. Mingled occasionally were periods of lucidity, during which he would respond to questions, make simple requests, such as for a blanket, and remain quiet and pensive.

Those moments created a problem for Black and Denaro. The design of their defense was to create in Walford the maddest man imaginable. Much of the time Walford performed in precisely that fashion, but the moments of lucidity contradicted the portrait. If they were coupled with Walford's actions immediately after the murder, it was possible he could be seen in a different light altogether. Sometimes Walford's actions were not the acts of a madman. Sometimes he behaved as would someone who knew he had committed a terrible act, had to evade detection and so, when captured, had retreated into madness and bizarre behavior. It seemed to protect him.

He was, in a way, a paradox.

Insane, yes. Stupid, no.

Knowledgeable. Intelligent. Educated.

But acutely, chronically psychotic.

Then they thought of the videotape.

The idea occurred to the two attorneys during one of their evening skull sessions. They needed to find a method of capturing Walford at the height of his madness, at the moments when his control dissipated and the electric impulses in his brain took over. If in reality Walford experienced moments of lucidity, it was necessary, when the two lawyers brought their arguments that he was incompetent to stand trial into the courtroom, that he be viewed as without any semblance of sanity. In 1974 there was little legal precedent in support of using a videotape in a criminal court proceeding. Denaro believes now that Walford's tape was the first case in the nation to utilize the new procedure.

It wasn't as simple as pointing a camera at him, however.

Of primary importance, Black and Denaro agreed, was the elimination of all controlling antipsychotic drugs from his system. It would do their argument little good to have a videotape of a drugged-out Walford sleeping naked on the hard cement floor of a Dade County Jail cell. Consequently, they needed a court order to remove him from any antipsychotic medicines. They knew that the jail personnel, already impressed with Walford's strength-through-madness, would scream at eliminating drugs. The cell could barely contain him; they needed the additional chemical strait jacket. Obtaining a court order wouldn't be hard; every capable attorney in the Justice Building knew enough friendly judges to acquire signatures on whatever warrants they had in mind. Denaro secured the necessary signature by approaching a judge in the midst of the annual Metro Justice Building Christmas party. They would also need Walford's jailers to cooperate, however.

The two men went to see Dr. Carlos Casademont at the jail. Dr. Casademont, a psychiatrist, was in charge of Ward D. It was he who had made the initial diagnosis of paranoid schizophrenia that had led to Walford's being placed on high dosages of Thorazine. Black and Denaro made it appear as if their visit was just one of happenstance—dropping by, so to speak, to talk about their weird client.

As the three men were shaking their heads in amazement over some of the vagaries of Walford's behavior—at various times he had been spotted neighing like a horse, barking like a dog, eating his own feces, doing countless push-ups on the floor while reciting the Twenty-third Psalm—Denaro casually opened the subject.

"You know," he said, "it would be remarkable if we could find some means of recording Walford's behavior."

Dr. Casademont nodded his head. "I have been thinking the same thing," he replied. "I've never seen anyone who exemplifies paranoid schizophrenia like Walford. He is a classic case. More than a classic case. Perhaps even unique."

"You mean," Black chimed in, "we should preserve the behavior as an educational tool?"

"Right," Denaro replied. "So that students, like medical students or law students, could see the extent of madness."

"That would be valuable. My students would truly benefit," Dr. Casademont said. "But how?"

The hook was planted.

"Oh, I'm not sure," Denaro said. "Photos maybe?"

"That wouldn't really capture his movement," Black said quickly. "Students wouldn't really see his behavior."

"That's right," the doctor said, warming to the subject. "It would have to be something more elaborate."

"Like a motion picture," Black said, nodding.

"I've got it," Denaro said. "A videotape. One of those new portable units."

"That would do it," Black agreed quickly. Casademont nodded. "But," Black said, "we'd have to bring it in when he's at his worst. How do we arrange that?"

"He'd have to be off the antipsychotic medicines," Casademont said.

"That's right," Denaro added. "But wouldn't that be dangerous?"

"Not if we did it for only a short time," Black answered. Again the doctor nodded in agreement.

"Tell you what," Denaro said. "We'll try to obtain a court order and see if we can find a videotape technician." A signed order was already in his pocket. A videotape cameraman had already been contacted and was on twenty-four-hour stand-by.

"For the students," Denaro said.

"For the students," said the doctor.

That evening Walford stopped getting antipsychotic drugs.

He howled as his rage grew unchecked.

The actual filming took place within a few days. Black and Denaro, accompanied by Dr. Arthur Stillman, a psychiatrist, went to the cell with the cameraman. The first time they went, Walford was still in drugged sleep. They went back the next day and were rewarded with the type of behavior they wanted. Occasionally, Roy Black would try to ask, "Mr. Walford, Mr. Walford..."

But Walford raced on, oblivious.

6. A Defect of Reason

The final picture on the tape was not sharp, the black and gray tones mingling, sometimes seeming to waver, at other times indistinct for lack of proper lighting. There was only one person visible on the screen, one character in this particular television show. The camera had first focused on his eyes, burning, electric, staring balefully into the lens. At the start he was seated, but with a sinewy, feline grace, he languorously seemed to re-form in a standing position.

His hair was closely cropped, military-style. His extraordinary physique was revealed on the tape; his muscles seemed to be on the verge of bursting through his skin. His arms were thick and bulging; his chest was broad, expanding as he gathered in great deep drafts of air. His stomach was defined, rippled the way a sudden gust of wind worries a still pond. The veins on his neck stood out; someone watching the man on the videotape would almost be able to feel the blood being pumped under great pressure throughout his body and into his brain.

He was naked.

With a movement so sudden that the camera seemed to recoil, Walford reached for the bars to his cell and shook them violently. His teeth were bared back, animallike, and his mouth opened wide with a howl of less than human anger. With another abrupt motion, Walford began a bizarre dance, his energy run wild. He threw himself to the hard cement floor and began to snap off push-ups, fingertips extended, his body rigid and unbendable, as if carved from metal. Up and down he moved, like a piston in an engine gone crazy. His singsong voice replaced the howl, and words became clear: "The Lord is my shepherd, I shall not want...."

The Twenty-third Psalm rolled out, over and over. His tongue seemed to savor the message, and he elongated the words, drawing them out, delighting in them, rendering them part of his howl: "The Loooooooorrrrrrddddd is m-m-m-m-my shep-HERD! I shallllll not waaaaaaannnnntttt!"

His voice undulated in intensity, mimicking the up-down movement of his stiff body.

Then, as quickly as that exercise had started, it ended. Walford jumped, froglike, to the side of the toilet bowl. He bent over, squatting like some jungle primate, and scooped out handfuls of water. He splashed his face and body, making washing motions. He drank, and his scream started up again. "Waaaatttter!" he shouted.

A voice from out of camera range broke into the tape. An angry occupant of another cell shouted, "Somebody shut that crazy fucker up, man!" Walford turned toward the voice and grinned wildly. He threw his head back in a great mirthless laugh. He leaped to the bars again, snapping his teeth angrily and shaking the bars. The entire cell seemed to shake with the loosed energy inside.

"God! Not man!" he screamed. He pronounced the word *Gahhhd*. He repeated the phrase several times, changing the inflections in his voice. Then he stepped back from the bars, looking out at the camera, and his visage changed once again. He adopted an almost insouciant look on his face, and he shook his finger at the camera half-menacingly. Then he changed again, as quickly as flipping a book's page. He raged. He howled. He stretched his voice to its limit, racing about the cell in frantic, endless expenditure of energy.

The camera continued to film Walford quietly. The finished tape was about forty-five minutes long. It ended, as it had begun, without introduction or explanation.

It was Vernal Walford at his worst.

It was precisely the impression the defense wanted.

Years later frustrated prosecutors would claim that Black had stood outside the cell, waving his arms, taunting Walford into the rage captured on the tape. There is no evidence of that. When the drugs were stopped, it was inevitable that Walford's madness would build explosively.

7. A Procession of Psychiatrists

In the weeks before the competency hearing Walford was visited by a number of forensic psychiatrists. There was a drill involved; the doctors all worked frequently with the courts and had attained a level of professional prominence through pretrial evaluations. They administered certain cognitive tests, designed to demonstrate an accused's sense of place, time and understanding. Then they talked, usually about the crime, trying to detect whatever glimmer of madness or sanity existed. All the doctors sent to see Walford were experienced, respected men; all would have swiftly recognized any efforts to deceive them. Their reports to the court would carry great weight.

It is one of the failures of the modern American system of justice that psychiatry often has to bring its subjective views and opinions into an arena designed for fact. Psychiatrists and psychologists who perform forensic evaluations rarely feel that the specificity required in a courtroom is appropriate to their specialty. They routinely object to the pinning down, the requirement for absolute judgments that are demanded by lawyers.

But that does not prevent them from entering courtrooms.

Many see their job as an inherent evil; they feel that there is no way the two professions can actually be reconciled. At the same time, however, they are required to troop in with their opinions. It is not unusual in a criminal trial to have one group of doctors lined up with a defense team and another with the prosecution and have them battle it out. One side's eloquence may perhaps be the factor that sways the judge or the jury. A recent example of this, of course, is the trial of John Hinckley, the attempted murderer of President Reagan.

*   *   *

In Dade County the doctors followed the same routine. They received a phone call from the judge's office—or the prosecutor or defense attorney—and they went over to the jail. Ordinarily the interviews lasted from fifty minutes to several hours. The doctors asked simple questions: What day is it, what month, who's the president of the United States, what are you charged with? Then they might move into the more complex: Why did you do it?

Walford, of course, presented unique problems.

On January 6, Roy Black, Jack Denaro and Dr. Sanford Jacobson went to see Walford. As usual, he was naked in the cell. The doctor paused and looked at Walford, who stood in the center of the cell staring at the three visitors. "Mr. Walford?" he asked.

"Definitely," Walford responded.

"My name is Dr. Jacobson."

"I know. I have seen you. Others like you." His answer was clipped, his voice filled with the tolerance one shows a child.

"Do you know these gentlemen?" Jacobson motioned toward Black and Denaro.

"Yes. I have seen them. They are my attorneys."

"They are from the Public Defender's Office. Do you understand what they do?"

"No. Explain it to me."

"Well, you have to have an attorney—"

Walford interrupted angrily. "Oh, I have to have an attorney to speak for me! Why should I have an attorney when I can do it for myself? You're crazy!"

"Have you ever been to court before?"

"Ohhhhh, I know the rules and regulations!"

"Have you been to court before?"

"Definitely! I don't have to see them. They are all the same."

"Well, in the United States it is different than Jamaica."

"Oh," he said, as if dismissing the subject as beneath him, "I am sure they have some crooked procedures."

"Can you tell me something about yourself?"

"Why should I?"

"Well"—Jacobson hesitated—"you don't have to—"

Again Walford interrupted swiftly. "That's it. That's it. I don't have to, so why should I?" His voice filled with a laugh, the words flowing nonstop in singsong Caribbean accented English. "I speak to you, you speak to me. So, take it and go."

"The judge wants me to talk to you—"

"Speak!"

"Where were you born?"

"I will speak very slow, very distinctly and correctly. My date of birth is the seventh day of January, nineteen hundred and forty-three."

"You will be thirty-one what day?"

"Today is what day?"

"That's what I want you to tell me, if you know."

Anger jumped into Walford's voice. "Today is what day! I wouldn't ask if I knew!"

"Today is Monday, January sixth. So that means your birthday will be tomorrow?"

"That's it!" He laughed a great sudden laugh, as if he'd enjoyed a huge joke. "If you know the key, why come to me for the lock?" Then he hesitated for a moment. "I believe in God, not man," he said.

"When did you come to Miami?" the doctor asked.

"That," Walford said with precision, "is a different story. I will explain. Listen to me carefully. I was brought in last year. February. I was in Jamaica, sitting on my buttass, praising God. But the Americans in a ship came to Ocho Rios. They asked us if we had any grass. We told them yes. Myself and my two brothers. Don't interrupt! I will tell you! I was in the penitentiary. For renting a car for another man. And having an accident. The judge said, 'I will give you six months to sit in the penitentiary and learn about God.' It was all a plot! A P-L-O-T!"

Jacobson shook his head as Walford launched into a complicated story about a marijuana deal with white men in the days after he'd been arrested for failure to return a rental car. The marijuana deal had apparently required him to come to the United States. However, Jacobson wanted to know about God. "Did you learn about God in the penitentiary?"

"Definitely. I said, 'Father, I swear to thee,' and I heard the words go like this: 'You are Vernal Newland Walford?' And I said, 'Definitely, Father.' And He said, 'I am the God of the gods of the gods of heaven and earth. I am the one!' I was shaking. I said, 'I will obey you.' My backside was in the air...." Walford abruptly put his forehead to the floor and launched his feet in the air, standing on his head. "Inside it was cool, but outside it was hot. Something happened to me then. My whole face was great! I believe in God! God! I learned from that moment. I speak to everyone clearly and distinctly and correctly. And things come to me in one blow with understanding. I am smart through God! I was dumb one time, but God made me smart! Made me know the Scripture from beginning to end. Made me know how many tricks there are in the Bible. The white man's Bible. All lies and tricks!"

He spit viciously into the toilet. Jacobson tried to interject a question but was cut off. Walford, unchecked, his excitement growing, began to pace throughout the cell, recounting his twisted version of the Garden of Eden.

"Eve gave Adam the apple. White men wrote that! No! Eve gave Adam a cunt to suck! And she sucked fucking dick! And Adam fuck her in the butthole. Commit Sodom! And then he go commit suicide. He was a black man."

"Who committed suicide?"

"Adam. Because he was ashamed!" Walford grabbed the bars of the cell, shook them, tossing his head back and bellowing in rage.

"Why are you so angry?"

"Because you people are deceiving me! You tell me to eat the apple! That's the fucking lie! You're liars and deceivers!"

In an instant Walford shifted back to the drug deal. He raged on about the white men he'd done business with, but he said God had told him to take a trip with the men and come to the United States, even though he did not trust the men and thought that their payment was phony. "You gave them the grass?" Jacobson asked.

"Listen to me, you fucking fool. He said take the trip. He said you people provoke Him. Tell him lies. The word of God. Father said find the word and trick them!" Walford flung himself through the cell, a animallike growl filling the air.

Jacobson changed the subject. "Why are you in jail?"

"Ahhhh, I got arrested."

"Why did you get arrested?"

"No. You tell me."

"For murder."

His anger left abruptly, and he laughed long and hard. "Ahhhh, they can choose anybody."

"Well, what about it? Is it true?"

"What about it? What about it?" He danced across the cell. "Fuck off. I don't know. If you don't know, I don't know. You came in here to fucking ask. Well, go away. Go away!"

"Weren't you there, where it happened?"

"You don't know." It was a statement. "If you knew, you wouldn't come in here asking."

"I wasn't there," said the doctor.

"I was not there either," replied Walford. He laughed again, then shook the bars of the cell. Then he turned his back abruptly. "I have nothing to impart to you. Go away, I've finished with you."

"You don't want to talk to me?"

"No. No more."

"How about the hospital up North?"

"No. I am fucking trickier than you. If you know, you wouldn't ask. You don't know. They don't know..." He made a great sweeping gesture with his arm, the muscles rigid and tense. "I am in here as a suspect, that's all. They don't know!" He dragged out the word *know*, emphasizing it.

"They say you killed somebody."

Walford snorted contemptuously. He spit into the toilet. "Any man can say that. That is what you hear, not what you know. That's a rumor. A roooo-murrrr. Ha, ha, ha, ha. A tale. Not a fucking fact. So don't ask me!" He began to shadowbox, striking the pose of a prizefighter. Then he savagely struck at the bars, throwing straight jabs with frightening speed. The cell resounded with the slapping noise.

"Tell me about the hospital in Massachusetts."

"I was sent there by another bunch of psychiatrists. I was hit by a doll, and it caused a piece of glass to fly into my eye. I was working. I asked, 'Father, should I work?' and He said, 'Definitely!' At the job they said, 'We need some Popeyes. We need some Donald Ducks. We need some Mickey Mouses.' They said, 'Can you do it?' and I said, 'Definitely!' I had a piece of paper. My brother's wife gave me a piece of paper; it said I was Bob Miller Grant. So I could work. My brother said he would sell his soul for money. I should have killed him on the spot!"

"Is it right to kill?"

Walford snorted again, his eyebrows arching up, his hands on his hips, arms akimbo. "Listen to me. Is it right for you to ask me questions? Don't shrug your shoulders! Did I tell you that I kill?"

"I don't know—"

He leaped in, interrupting. "You are trying to be tricky. Tricks!" He laughed. "Tricky. Tricky Dick. I will pardon Mr. Nixon for what he's done, but all of them are fucking crooks." He laughed again, hesitated for a moment, then added, "I took the papers to Immigration in Massachusetts and said, 'I believe in God, not man! This is phony. Send me back to Jamaica. Send me back to my country. I got here illegally, and I got these papers. I was bought here illegally. But God teaches me there!'"

Walford began to breathe in and out harshly, his voice becoming a growl, animallike grunts rising out of his chest. He rattled the bars savagely, as if trying to break free of the frenetic impulses that coursed through his imagination. The importance of what he'd just said was lost on the doctor and the two attorneys; they did not realize what a crucial statement he'd made. It would be seven years before what Walford had done would become known.

He dropped to the floor of the cell and began doing push-ups, reciting

Scripture. Up he went, fingers rigid to the cement floor, "My kingdom come...."; down he went, his body as straight as a steel bar, "...deliver us from evil...."

"Good Lord!" Jacobson said to no one.

He watched as Walford continued.

"Vernal, Vernal, why are you getting so excited?"

"Because you people know the truth!"

"The truth in the Bible?"

"That's right! I am telling you what is in the Bible!" He jumped to his feet and raced back and forth. Then he began dancing in a slower, more deliberate fashion. His voice grew even more singsong. "Eve gave Adam her pussy to suck!"

"What has that to do with your getting arrested?"

Walford stopped. He cocked his hand comically to his chin. "That's what I just don't know," he said. Then he laughed. "The policeman came to me. He said, 'You look like a man who is a suspect!' He said, 'Get out of the taxi!' He pulled out his pistol and cocked it like that." Walford held up his hand, mimicking a gun. "He said, 'If you run I will kill you.' He looked in his pocket for what they called my rights. I said, 'I don't want to say anything.' He said, 'You want to keep quiet?' I said, 'Definitely!'"

"They arrested you and charged you with murder."

"Don't be a fucking fool. Suspect. Suspect only!"

"Are you mentally able to stand trial?"

"I can stand trial!"

"You won't talk to them." Jacobson gestured toward Black and Denaro, who had remained silent throughout the interview.

"I don't have to. I know court procedures. These fucking lawyers don't know a thing. They weren't there!"

"Does God still talk with you."

Walford sang his response. "He walks with me...He talks with me..."

"Why?"

"Because He loves me! Ha, ha, ha, ha, ha!"

"What does God think about what you've done?"

Walford laughed again. "What have I done?" Then suddenly he grabbed the bars and pulled his face as close to the doctor's as he could. For a second he stared into Jacobson's eyes. "I can tell," he said. "I can tell—" his voice was filled with glee—"that you suck pussy a lot!" He laughed again, then waved his hand at the doctor. "Go and suck some more pussy!"

Jacobson took an instant. Then he said, "The police found blood on your clothes."

"That's irrevelant!" He mispronounced the word, in his hurry to reply. "Irrevelant! Irrevelant! I won't answer!" He turned his back.

"Okay, Mr. Walford," the doctor said. "Thank you."

But Walford, beginning to race about the cell again, simply screamed, "AhhhhhHahhhhh!" as the trio left the cellblock. They could hear the shouts echoing as the bars and locked doors closed one after the other behind them, and they stepped away from madness, back into the world.

Denaro, though, thought hard about the question "What does God think about what you've done?" Walford had seemed so crazily confident in so many of his replies, but to that question he'd wavered. So often he had responded, "Definitely!" with his bizarre self-assurance, but not to that question. Denaro wondered why there was a sudden lack of confidence. He wondered if there wasn't some crack in the armor of Walford's madness. And he resolved to find out.

8. The Reports

Jacobson's report to the court was written the next day. Drs. Arthur Stillman, Charles Mutter, Albert Jaslow and William Corwin followed suit within the next few weeks. The five doctors were the most often used, most respected psychiatrists performing forensic evaluations in Dade County's courts in 1974.

Jacobson's was the most extensive, but each report reflected the vagaries of Walford's behavior when each doctor had arrived outside the bars to his whitewashed security cell. They ranged in length from two to six pages, depending on the doctor's experience when they tried to interview Walford.

I was unable to obtain pertinent history [wrote Dr. Mutter]. . . . He bared his teeth and snarled. He arose and performed a native dance. He appeared disoriented. He was autistic. His affect was grossly inappropriate, guarded, suspicious and hostile. . . . Diagnostic impression is acute paranoid schizophrenia.

He is extremely dangerous and should not be released under any circumstances. . . .

I saw him on two occasions [wrote Dr. Corwin], . . . attempts to question him were met with hostility, shouting and screaming. . . . From time to time he would go into a dance, undulating his hips in a highly sexual manner. At times he would protrude his rear towards the examiners in obscene gestures, or would roll head over heels on the jail floor. At other times he would lie down prone on the mats in the cell and appeared indifferent and unresponsive.

Frequently he would grimace or strike poses and he presented a tendency to strike attitudes and poses which are suggestive of schizophrenic behavior....

... At times he laughed at a private joke [wrote Dr. Stillman] and was very guarded about how much information he would give. Many of his ideas seemed rather bizarre, and his behavior was bizarre, to say the least, filled with religious delusions, autistic thinking, visions of visitations from God.... He seemed preoccupied with ideas of God and sacrifice.

He is of superior intelligence but demonstrated limited insight.... His ability to reason abstractly and discriminatively seemed adequate at some moments and he could follow an argument in logical abstract terms for some distance. At other times he became very concretistic, hung on a word and insisted that he be listened to....

Clinically, we are dealing with a severely disturbed, schizophrenic of the paranoid variety.... Such a state has existed for a lengthy period of time and could not have arisen all at once. The natural history of paranoid schizophrenia is that it is developed over a long period of time, usually in an intelligent person....

Jacobson's report analyzed Walford's responses during their meeting. One conclusion the doctor arrived at was: "At present it is clear that the defendant is severely and acutely psychotic. Within the range of my clinical experience, have I rarely, if ever, seen an individual who offers such a severe and dramatic combination of anger, rage, agitation, bizarre thinking, grandiosity and psychosis...."

No report asked: What chance had Arnold? None tried to envision the nightmarish, twisted grimace on Walford's face when he spied the nine-year-old boy alone in the hallway. There was no shuddering mention of the horror that the boy had confronted. Indeed, his name appeared in none of the reports.

And then there was Dr. Jaslow's report.

As far as Black and Denaro were concerned, the other doctors had reached a consensus: Walford was incapable of standing trial and was insane at the time of the crime. They'd reached those conclusions despite their acknowledging that Walford had his moments of lucidity and that he wanted to go to trial. For each, however, Walford had been in the throes of his madness when

interviewed—to a greater or lesser degree, but still captured in psychosis.
Jaslow's experience had been different:

Although it was my understanding [the doctor wrote] that he had been extremely
agitated and even negativistic to a certain extent with previous examiners, he was
quite responsive and cooperative with me to the extent that he talked quite freely
in certain areas of involvement. . . .

He stood up most of the time during our discussion, but at times excused
himself to sit down on his mattress. . . . During the session there were certain
behavioral mannerisms that reflected his basic disturbance, and each time he had
a need to spit into the toilet he voiced the expression, "Forgive me, Father."

He seemed to be fully aware of the nature and meaning of the proceedings,
and when he had finished his extensive recounting of the details that had surrounded his full history from the time he had been in Jamaica until he arrived
back in Miami, and when he was pressed in the area of the circumstances surrounding the alleged offense, he pointed out that he had every right to remain
silent and would perhaps bring these matters up in court.

All of his statements were given in a stentorian voice with great clarity and
deliberate enunciation of the words and he seemed to relish his control of the
situation. . . .

He described the pillow of clouds that had come over him. . . . Jesus of Naz-
areth . . . seemed to guide him and speak to him throughout the course of his
progression. He described other bizarre experiences, such as his hair turning all
white, including the hair on his face, and there was a complete expansion of his
entire head. . . .

At various times he would describe how God would talk to him and tell him
what to do, and he thought nothing of this. He still refused to talk about the
circumstances surrounding the alleged offense. He then became somewhat rhythm-
ical in his movements and his slapping of his hands eventually led to a form of
dancing and there was inappropriate laughter and loudtalk.

He was capable of assisting in his defense . . . even though he could answer
the charges against him they would certainly be greatly colored by his disturbed
thinking. . . .

Concerning his mental state at the time of the alleged offense, I cannot give
a truly objective opinion since I have no information from the patient himself. . . .

When Denaro and Black saw this report, they thought: Here's the problem.
Even with the others aligned against him, Jaslow's vision of Walford was
more than adequate for a judge to order a trial. They began to scheme, to
invent a method of isolating the doctor and ultimately getting him to retract
his report.

9. Proper Courtroom Procedure

Walford's first appearance before Dade Circuit Court Judge Gene Williams on January 17, 1975, was instructive. When he entered, his eyes darted about courtroom 4-1.

To his right, to his left, behind him and situated in the aisles, burly green-shirted jail guards watched him, waiting for his first explosive movement. Walford's hands and feet were cuffed; the chains would rattle occasionally when he shifted in his seat at the defense table, a counterpoint to the attorneys arguing before the judge in front of him. It was the Friday four weeks after the murder in the Crossways and the courtroom was filled to capacity, the theater type seating occupied by the Miami media, prosecutors, defense attorneys and several score of the curious.

Roy Black and Jack Denaro took turns arguing each motion on Walford's behalf. Sitting opposite them was Assistant State Attorney Leonard Glick. This preliminary hearing, prior to the competency hearing, would be the only hearing Glick would handle exclusively. Although he had been to the murder scene and perhaps had a greater appreciation of exactly what had happened than any other prosecutor, it was felt he was too inexperienced to handle the major case. In the subsequent hearing, consequently, Bernard Yedlin, a more experienced prosecutor, would take the lead.

Glick began the proceedings by reading the first-degree murder indictment. The Dade County grand jury had indicted Walford on his birthday. Janet Reno, who in the following years would become the Dade state attorney, presented Detective Carberry to the twenty-one grand jurors. The indictment followed seconds after his recitation of the facts.

"What is the indictment?" Walford asked in a loud voice. He was ignored.

The two young public defenders' first act was to enter a plea of not guilty to the charge of first-degree murder and to request a trial by jury. Judge Williams wrote the plea down on the docket sheet, occasionally taking notes. The not guilty plea and the jury trial request were standard, formal responses, a legal way of saying, "Play ball," and getting the case of *State of Florida* v. *Vernal Newland Walford*, Eleventh Judicial Circuit number 75-179, begun.

Black and Denaro conferred briefly in the center of the wood-paneled courtroom, then launched into a series of routine motions designed to preserve certain elements that could be raised on an appeal if Walford were convicted. Walford's eyes drifted wildly about the courtroom, occasionally fixing on a person or object and boring in with excessive intensity. Judge Williams watched nervously from the bench.

They asked him to dismiss the first-degree murder indictment against Walford because of the unconstitutionality of the state's death penalty.

Denied.

They moved for any favorable evidence turned up by police or prosecutors during the course of their investigation of the murder to be turned over to the defense.

Granted.

They requested that Walford's criminal record, if any, in the United States or from his homeland of Jamaica be turned over to them.

Granted.

They moved for a list of all potential jurors who might be seated to hear the case.

Denied.

They asked for more time to file more motions.

Denied.

In his chair at the defense table Walford began to shift about, his seat suddenly uncomfortable, his patience suddenly strained. The hearing had almost concluded when he interrupted the proceedings, standing abruptly at the table and shattering the orderly process that was taking place around him. "May I say something to you?" More a demand than a request.

Jail guards tensed, eyes locked on Walford. Judge Williams peered over the edge of the bench, over the edge of his eyeglasses, down at Walford. "No, you are represented by attorneys here." Walford broke into the judge's words, as if catapulted by the judge's explanation.

"I am represented by no man! By God! No man speaks for me! I speak for myself! They are only talking what they know. But they don't know! I know, so I talk. I was the person there! They can't speak for me. I know. My tongue is not tied!" he shouted.

"All right. Keep quiet," Denaro pleaded.

But Walford ignored him. He turned swiftly, gesturing with his head at his two attorneys, eyes rolling. "My tongue is not tied, no way at all!" His voice, still marked by the singsong Jamaican accent, filled the quieted courtroom. "I am not deaf! I am not dumb!"

Walford stepped away from the defense table, chains clanking as he moved. His eyes blazed with righteous indignation, boring in on the judge.

"This hearing is concluded," Judge Williams said quickly. He nodded toward the jail guards, who leaped to Walford and grabbed him, further pinioning his arms to his sides.

"I don't know what you're saying! You listen to me!"

"The defendant is remanded to custody of the Department of Corrections," Williams said, recoiling in his chair.

As the guards' grip tightened on his arms, Walford shouted, "If I don't speak, no man can condemn me! You know I am here! You think my tongue is tied!"

Walford threw his head back, his voice bellowing, tortured with rage, completely out of control. "God! Not man!" he screamed. "God, not man!"

The guards pushed and pulled him toward a door in the rear of the courtroom that led to a hallway and holding cell. The hallway was the direct route to a walkway between the jail and the courtroom building. Walford struggled against his bonds, against the hands that held him, his voice piercing the frozen tableau of attorneys and spectators. "God! God! God, not man!" As the doors to the courtroom closed behind him, his voice continued to carry into the stilled courtroom, echoing through the walls, out into the corridors, filling the fourth floor with his message, "God, not man! God, not man!," repeated over and over, endlessly charged by Walford's raging thoughts.

10. Denaro

To be a defense attorney is to enter a state beyond cynicism. For Black and Denaro, Walford's behavior at his first hearing, two weeks prior to the crucial competency hearing, was ideal.

He'd scared the judge.

He'd scared the prosecutor.

He'd scared all the courtroom personnel.

He'd acted uncontrollable.

He'd acted utterly mad.

In short, he had taken over the hearing, thrown all the reasonableness of the law abruptly out the door and made the hearing as paranoid and as schizophrenic as he was. He had, in effect, created a tone more persuasive to the defense's view of matters than they could possibly have hoped for. It could not have been better if they had sat down with Walford beforehand and carefully scripted his behavior. The very spontaneity of his screams had overwhelmed the stately courtroom atmosphere.

If the scheme of the defense was proceeding according to plan, however, there was a missing element that worried Jack Denaro. He reviewed what they'd learned of Walford, as gleaned from conversations with the doctors, Lucille Fernandez and Walford's brother Carl, who lived in Hartford.

The conversations with Carl Walford had been largely useless. The brother had spoken in rapid-fire Jamaican-accented English almost impossible to comprehend and had been reticent to reply to Denaro's questions. From the others, however, the attorney had learned:

Walford was married. His wife, Noletha, lived in Kingston with five children. Five other children had been born but died. How? the attorney still wondered. Walford had been in the Jamaica Defense Force and reached the rank of corporal. He'd been a champion middleweight boxer—that in part accounted for his extraordinary physique. He'd been involved in the illegal narcotics trade in Ocho Rios Province. Was he connected with the Rastafarians? No evidence of that, Denaro thought. Walford's God seemed to be uniquely his. He'd come to the United States illegally but had the knowledge and the paper work to be able to travel freely out of the country and return. What other illegal behavior did he engage in? Denaro wondered.

He'd been hit in the eye. And become crazy.

Why was he trying to return to Jamaica?

What was he running to? What was he running from?

Denaro, like everyone who came into contact with Walford in Miami, couldn't understand how the mental hospital in Northampton, Massachusetts, had ever released him. It seemed beyond comprehension to the attorney, as he stared at Walford through the bars of the security cell, watching his client box with the voice that penetrated only his own imagination.

What became Denaro's greatest concern and his greatest source of fascination, however, was the paradox: Walford had committed this heinous crime for a reason and now, when asked why, would refuse to reply, play word games or rage angrily.

It did not make sense. If God had instructed him to kill Arnold Zeleznik, why would he not lay claim to that divine connection? Why not shout it to the world?

That was the mystery that consumed Denaro. If everything within the legal world was progressing satisfactorily, the nether world of Walford's mind was still an open question, unresolved.

Denaro thought: I must know why.

He started going over to the jail at odd hours, sometimes in the morning, sometimes in the evening, sometimes in the middle of the night. At first he simply took up a position just beyond the bars, outside the madman's reach, and stared, fixing Walford with a half-glaring, half-questioning look. When Walford would ask him what he was doing, the madman suddenly uncomfortable beneath the unwavering gaze, Denaro would not reply. He sat silently as Walford raved, twisting and furious, before him.

At the core of Walford's rage was the Bible; "excessive religiosity" is an integral part of paranoid schizophrenia. Walford preached and prayed and exercised as he quoted long passages from memory. Denaro thought of the plea: "God, not man." He thought, too, of the night Walford, dressed in red, had raced into the streets of Hartford—and the morning of the murder he had been occupied at the airport, preaching, trying to force the passers-by to repent. So, the onetime seminarian thought, if there is a method of reaching Walford, it must be through the Bible.

Denaro went to Walford's cell a few days before the competency hearing. It was evening, and the harsh fluorescent jail lights forced the confrontation. The two men stared through the bars at each other. Walford's eyes raged; Denaro thought his own did also. He started with the opening to the Book of Psalms: "'Blessed is the man that walketh not in the counsel of the ungodly, nor standeth in the way of sinners, nor sitteth in the seat of the scornful.

"'But his delight is in the law of the Lord. . . .'"

Walford quieted.

"'The ungodly are not so: but are like the chaff which the wind driveth away.'"

Walford shifted uncomfortably.

"You know why I am here?" Denaro asked.

"Deliver us from evil . . ." Walford replied. Tentative.

"I need to know," Denaro said.

"For thine is the power—" Walford said.

"We must know," Denaro emphasized the first word.

"—and the glory."

"You must tell us what you've done."

"For ever and ever . . ."

"You will tell me," Denaro said. He quoted from his memory: "'. . . Abraham built an altar there and laid the wood in order, and bound Isaac his son, and laid him on the altar. . . . And Abraham stretched forth his hand, and took the knife to slay his son. And the angel of the Lord called unto him out of heaven, and said . . . lay not thine hand upon the lad. . . .'"

Walford threw his head back and let loose a long, cascading cry of anguish that resounded down the corridor. The other inmates began to shout for him to shut up. Denaro ignored their cries and said, "You will tell us what we need to know."

Walford shouted, "Get thee behind me!" He made the devil's horns sign with his fingers. He danced across the cell; but there was a wariness in his actions, and he kept his eyes fastened on Denaro. The attorney fixed him with a final hard stare, then turned on his heel abruptly and paced out, without turning back. He heard Walford's shouts behind him and thought: A crack in the armor of madness.

Denaro returned to Walford's cell the following day. He stared at Walford for an instant, just long enough to obtain the naked man's complete attention. Walford was silent, as if waiting. Denaro continued, with another quote from the Book of Psalms: "'Who shall ascend into the hill of the Lord? or who shall stand in his holy place?'" He pointed his finger at Walford. "'He that hath clean hands, and a pure heart; who hath not lifted his soul up unto vanity, nor sworn deceitfully.'"

Walford shook, his entire body trembling.

"Who be you?" he asked.

"You know who I am," Denaro replied.

"You are my attorney!" Walford shouted. He stretched out the word: *at-turrrr-neeeee*.

"Perhaps more," Denaro said.

Walford spit. "Tell me," he asked.

"No," Denaro said, "it is for you to say. We must know about what you've done."

"Do not forsake me," said Walford.

But Denaro, feeling he had the upper hand, turned and walked away.

Just before the day of the competency hearing, Denaro was once again on his way to Walford's cell when he was stopped by one of the jail ward's nurses. "We had to move him to a cell in the back," she said.

"Why?" Denaro asked.

"He and the other inmates were shouting back and forth. It was getting out of control. You know what he said?"

"What?"

"He said to the others, 'Come here! I'll get you! I am Jesus Christ!' and he was snarling, like, and rattling the wire mesh on the bars. It took six guards to move him, and he bit one of them in the back. You know what really set him off was when somebody else used the word *Goddamn* couldn't handle that profanity at all."

Son of God, thought Denaro. It was what he'd expected. Walford's behavior was so grandiose. Why not shoot for the top?

Outside Walford's cell, Denaro said, "'Behold, I will send my messenger....'"

Walford nodded. "'But who may abide the day of his coming?'"

Denaro replied, "God told you what to do?"

"He talks with me."

"He told you to take the knife?"

But Walford, suddenly wary, turned his back.

That's it, the attorney thought. He's just not sure, not sure at all. The voice told him what to do, and now he's worried that he did the wrong thing. He doesn't know. Inwardly Denaro jumped with excitement. There must be some phrase, he thought, that will trigger this. He recalled Walford's reluctance and petulance when asked by Jacobson about what he'd done. "What have I done?" Walford had replied. Gamesmanship. But it masked a greater fear. Suppose Walford was afraid he'd misunderstood the command? That's it, Denaro thought, that's it.

The right question occurred then to the former seminarian. But he held off asking.

11. The Hearing

The competency hearing had a nearly surreal quality to it.

As theater, perhaps Ionesco or Beckett would have enjoyed it. As an exercise in the law, it was unusual, to say the least. It began about 11:00 A.M. on Friday, January 31, 1975. Judge Gene Williams, the chief of the Criminal Division of Dade Circuit Court, was presiding. For the state, Assistant State Attorney Bernard Yedlin; on behalf of Walford, Roy Black and the ubiquitous Jack Denaro.

The hearing began with Dade County Jail nurse Sandra Cominsky being sworn as a witness. She was there to tell the judge that the jail personnel were refusing to take Walford out of his cell and transport him to the courtroom. Though the distance was only a few hundred yards, all inside, the jail authorities felt that Walford was too much a risk. Too many guards already sported bruises and bites from trying to move him from cell to cell.

In addition, Nurse Cominsky explained, after the previous hearing before Judge Williams, Walford had warned the jailers ominously that he wouldn't go handcuffed to court again.

The courtroom was jammed with people. Every seat was occupied. The newspapers, wire services and television stations all had reporters inside the courtroom, waiting for Walford. Additionally, word had "leaked" a few days earlier about the videotape. A front-page story describing what Black and Denaro had done, but with only veiled supposition about what the tape contained, had been stripped across the *Miami News*. Even the steady coterie of elderly men and women who hung around the courthouse, "the buzzards" in Miami, had battled over seats.

Judge Williams seemed tense.

As Nurse Cominsky was completing her refusal to bring Walford to the courtroom, Roy Black entered through the doors leading to the main fourth-floor corridor. He was wheeling a dolly with a large television set, the videotape recorder and black-jacketed rolls of video tape. As he came through the doors, a crowd of television cameramen and newspaper still photographers poised outside the door snapped off pictures. The television lights flooded the courtroom for an instant, as the door was held open for Black.

Williams exploded: "I told him [a courtroom bailiff] to get all the cameramen away from there!" And I want them away from there right now! I want some deputies here right now! I want some deputies. I want those cameramen off this floor! No cameramen, no cameras on this floor!"

The judge turned to a Dade Public Safety Department courtroom deputy. "Go outside there and get them out of there. I thought I had given instructions that no cameramen were to be out there."

"We requested they move. They came back," the deputy replied.

"I don't want any requests. Take them off this floor! If they resist, take their cameras away from them and impound them!"

He turned toward Roy Black. "Mr. Black, was it necessary to do that at this moment that you did it?"

Roy Black allowed that it was.

Bernard Yedlin was considered a topflight trial prosecutor by his opponents. Shortly after the Walford case he went on to become a well-known and respected criminal defense attorney. He had handled competency hearings before—that was nothing new to him—but he was new to the Walford case. Glick, who knew the most about it, had been reassigned. The case the state had was that provided by the police: In terms of Walford's guilt or innocence of the murder, there was no room for doubt; the evidence was open-and-shut.

In the area of competency, however, which windowed on Walford's mind, the state was significantly less prepared.

Black and Denaro had not invoked Florida's reciprocal discovery rule, as was their right. Had they done so, they would have gained access to the entirety of the police effort in the case. But invoking the rule would also have exposed their work: the videotape; the private reports by doctors, the interviews they had performed with Walford's brother and girl friend. They would have been required to hand that information fund over to the state prosecutors, thus uncovering their approach and their theory of defense. The state could then have countered with doctors of its own, perhaps even a videotape of its own, showing Walford fast asleep or calmly eating a meal.

But prosecutors had none of that to show on January 31.

The state's approach to the issue of Walford's competency was exemplified in the first questions Yedlin directed at Nurse Cominsky. "Ma'am, what is it, exactly, the behavior that Mr. Walford exhibited?"

"Mr. Walford bites. Mr. Walford screams. He spits. He is uncooperative in asking him to leave his cell, to walk out of his cell. He had to be taken out by force."

"Let me ask you this: That's voluntary on Mr. Walford's part, the spitting, the biting? Does it appear to be voluntary?"

"Yes, sir."

"I have no further questions," Yedlin said, sitting down.

The hearing continued, without Walford. He remained in his cell as the case got under way, perhaps the lack of his presence a stronger argument than any bizarre behavior he might manifest in the courtroom. The empty chair at the defense table took on an exaggerated symbolic importance, the imagination running wild with the possibilities of what Walford might have done had he been there. Of course, he might have done nothing. That was the rub; no one could tell.

Five psychiatrists were scheduled to testify in the hearing: Drs. Carlos Casademont, Arthur Stillman, Sanford Jacobson, William Corwin and Albert Jaslow. It was the defense's motion that Walford be declared incompetent; consequently, the burden of proving that incompetency was on its shoulders.

Its greatest problem remained Dr. Jaslow and his report. He had said that Walford could stand trial for the murder, with the only caveat being that Walford's assistance to his counsel would be colored by the vagaries of his illness.

Jaslow's report was more than sufficient for Judge Williams to set a trial date and discard the other reports. It had happened many times before in Dade courts and would happen again, often on much less say-so than Jaslow had provided.

Black and Denaro had decided that they had to force Jaslow to recant when he took the stand. They then devised a scheme to produce that effect. In Florida there is a criminal court rule which provides that witnesses be sequestered from each other and not hear each other's testimony. The rule is invoked by the defense. No Perry Mason types of revelations from the audience.

In this hearing, however, when Yedlin asked if the witness rule was going to be invoked, Black and Denaro quickly said no. As a result, all five psychiatrists scheduled to testify sat together in the front rows of the courtroom, able to hear each other's testimony. The result was, Black delightedly explained afterward, that Jaslow was going to have to listen to his four colleagues and then, facing them, disagree.

They didn't think he would do that.

Especially after seeing the videotape.

* * *

Yedlin objected vigorously to the videotape.

He had never seen it, wasn't able to cross-examine it and had not had the opportunity to prepare for it, he argued. Denaro countered that the prosecutors were not entitled to the tape. The judge ruled that it could be shown.

In the midst of the forty-odd minutes of the tape Yedlin objected. "This is a show, not a psychiatric examination. I'm shocked the doctor would participate in it."

The tape continued to its conclusion.

Dr. Casademont testified, "It was my impression that ... and I have had many hours of contact with Mr. Walford ... he has been functioning under the delusion that he is some kind of envoy from God and has been put on this world for accomplishing some kind of mission. He has always refused what kind of mission that is ..."

On cross-examination Yedlin had to be warned by the judge to control his rising voice. "Doctor, let me ask you this," Yedlin said. "The defendant refused to answer any questions about the event in question, as the alleged murderer of the child; is that correct?"

"Correct."

"Did you run one single objective test [of his mental condition]?"

"I think that—"

"Please answer yes or no. Did you run a single objective test?"

"I would not dare to do it with him."

"Did you run a single objective test?"

"No, sir. I relied on observations that were as subjective as an X-ray or laboratory report, which were the things I heard and things I saw."

"Exactly the things he told you and the things he wanted you to see?"

"Yes, sir," the doctor conceded.

Yedlin sat down, his point made.

But Denaro responded. "Doctor, Mr. Yedlin asked you a very intriguing question: Why you did not give him the Wechsler [Adult Intelligence test] or the Binet [Stanford-Binet test]? Do you deal in such things, or do you have psychologists do that?"

"I have psychologists do that."

"Why didn't you have psychologists go into the cell and administer, say, the Binet test?"

"I could not guarantee the safety of that psychologist."

"Mr Walford may have killed him?"

Yedlin jumped up, shouting, "I object!"

Casademont replied, "I think so."

Denaro swiftly sat down. "No further questions."

Dr. Stillman was next. As he was going through the voluminous listing of his qualifications to testify, Yedlin was cautioned by Judge Williams, "Quit making remarks under your breath!"

Stillman described the occasions on which he had visited Walford. He said he thought Walford incompetent because he could not confer with counsel. "I doubt if he could be contained or could contain himself [in the courtroom]," he told Roy Black.

Yedlin's only questions on cross-examination dealt with why Stillman had not prepared a typewritten report in advance of his testifying. Stillman accurately pointed out that he had initially been hired by the defense team and had been requested by the court to provide a report only a few days beforehand. Yedlin sat down angrily.

Dr. Jacobson reiterated what he'd written: that Walford represented a unique combination of emotions. ". . . a severe dramatic range of fear and anger. I think he's extremely psychotic, impulsive, unpredictable."

He added he believed Walford incompetent for trial.

"I think he would be unpredictable. He might sit calmly [in the courtroom] for some period of time, but I would not think it would be in any way predictable. It could range from relative calm to extreme agitation, depending on whatever was said or happened, what it meant to him and how he interpreted it."

On cross-examination, once again, Yedlin entered the voluntary aspect of Walford's behavior. He asked, too, about how Walford had been able to hold a job, work and travel if he was so unpredictable.

"Didn't he tell you once he knew what happened, but nobody else knew?"

"Yes, he did."

"He was quite happy about that?"

"I don't know that he was happy. He made a big point of it."

"Didn't he feel he had accomplished some sense of triumph, that he knew what happened and nobody else knew what happened?"

"Well, in the way that somebody might be somewhat smug about having a secret."

"So he knew and he refused to say anything about it?"

"Well, I don't know that he knew. He said he knew . . ."

"Just any more than we know whether he's putting it on or not on that tape?"

"I don't follow your question . . ."

". . . We don't know whether he's dancing around there on that tape for our benefit, or he's hearing voices of God, do we?"

"I still don't follow your conclusion," the doctor said.

"Well," Yedlin replied sarcastically, "you know what I'm trying to illustrate."

Dr. Corwin, too, testified to the difficulty he had in interviewing Walford. He said he believed Walford to be acutely mentally ill.

Yedlin limited his questions on cross-examination. He asked Corwin only whether the doctor had been told prior to examining Walford by Black and Denaro that their client was acting bizarrely. The doctor said yes.

Denaro got up. "Any indication that Walford was malingering or feigning this purported psychosis?"

"No."

And then the defense rested, without calling Jaslow. The attorneys knew the state would do that. And it did.

"What did you find when you examined the defendant?" Yedlin asked.

"Essentially I found a patient comparable to what has been described. Although on the date I saw him, he was better put together, better organized, better controlled..."

"What is your evaluation of the defendant, as to whether he is competent to stand trial and aid in his own defense?"

That was the crucial question. And Jaslow began to equivocate.

"I felt...that he did have a major mental disorder, and it sufficiently interfered with his capacity to assist so he wouldn't be considered competent, although he was capable, intelligently, of responding to the questions I posed to him. The underlying schizophrenic process would so interfere with his own concept of grandiosity and his concept of right and wrong, they would significantly interfere..."

Yedlin, in frustration, turned to the report Jaslow had written. "Isn't it true you stated he was capable of assisting his defense, that he desired to respond to the questions placed to him?"

"Yes. He has an intellectual capacity to assist... [but] as far as his disorder, it was so rampant...he took over...he decided how he would respond and when he would respond. I'm sure he would have represented the same picture to his attorneys and to the court."

"He was responsive and free with you, wasn't he?"

"He was controlling..."

"There wasn't any memory loss?"

"No."

"He seemed to have a good understanding about the nature of the proceedings he was involved in?"

"To a certain extent..."

"He controlled the interview?"

"To a great extent."

Angry, Yedlin had one last question. "He's pretty manipulative, isn't he?"

"Yes. He's pretty sharp, in his own way, despite the fact he has this serious mental disorder."

Yedlin sat down.

The final arguments on Walford's competency were short.

Yedlin: "I want to argue that on behalf of the state, that everything we have heard here and seen here, Your Honor, smacks of a carefully rehearsed and built-up situation and script...

"When it comes to one significant area, Mr. Walford says, 'It's my right, and I'm not going to discuss it with you.' Now, Your Honor, is this really the act of an insane or incompetent person, when you view it in the light of what he is alleged to have done? But if you consider the fact that the man is charged with the homicide of the slashing of a nine-year-old child's throat, Your Honor, and what he knows he must face here is probably one of the most terrible crimes that has occurred in Dade County. He can't be particularly unaware of that fact.

"...He can relate to these people. He can speak...if he wants to. He doesn't want to, Your Honor, and in a certain respect, I don't blame him. I wouldn't want to either, if I could dance around my cell, and I could shadowbox and I could howl at the wall and I could be sent to South Florida [State Hospital] with a good possibility of escaping these charges....

"I would much rather do that."

Roy Black took fewer than five minutes.

"In this hearing today, we have submitted numerous witnesses to show the defendant is incompetent to stand trial. That testimony is unrebutted. There was no testimony presented by the state whatsoever....I believe, as a matter of law, Your Honor must find him incompetent to stand trial and commit him to the state mental hospital."

That is exactly what Judge Williams did.

Walford was ticketed for South Florida State Hospital in Pembroke Pines, Florida, in neighboring Broward County, not far from Fort Lauderdale.

Outside the hearing Black and Denaro shook hands, victorious. It had gone precisely according to plan. Walford would now be swept up in the state mental health system, but should he ever return to a trial, he would have one immense factor in his behalf: What better evidence of madness could there be than the necessity of institutionalizing the crazed killer within weeks of the actual murder?

Yedlin complained to the press about the "show." He would have little more to do with the case; it would once again be reassigned to another prosecutor.

12. The Question

Denaro, though, was not satisfied.

The legal victory in his pocket, he felt incomplete; he had to learn, still, what the reason for the murder was. He went back to the jail, alone, and once again confronted Walford. The madman stopped, arrested in the center of the cell, fixed by the attorney's look. He seemed calmer, ready, but for what, Denaro wasn't certain. He kept up his stare for minutes, letting his silence dominate the space between the two men. Walford twitched, and Denaro sucked in a deep breath of stale jail air. He paraphrased from his memory.

"Are ye he who has been sent from above, or shall we seek another?"

Denaro paused, watching the effect the words had on Walford. Any seminary student would remember the phrase, he thought. It was the question that the messengers sent by John the Baptist had asked of Jesus Christ.

Walford shuddered.

Denaro asked again, insistent, demanding, "Are ye he who has been sent from above, or shall we seek another?"

And Walford threw back his head and opened wide his mouth and screamed soundlessly, nothing but air emerging. He raised his arms, as if nailed to his own cross, and his body convulsed. Then he sat, relaxing, staring out at Denaro, arms folded. And he began to talk, explaining. It was, in a way, an immense irony: The attorney who'd so elegantly and eloquently prepared his client's defense, hinging on the inability of the client to converse with the attorney, had discovered the key to unlock that client's memory and tongue. Denaro rested, relaxing, listening, occasionally interjecting a question of his own, thinking all the time: Now I will learn why Arnold Zeleznik died.

CHAPTER 5

The New School

1. The Biggest Hoax

The news that Walford had had his competency hearing and been declared incompetent to stand trial struck the Zelezniks a blow. They hadn't realized that it could happen so swiftly. The blow was doubled by the method in which they learned of Judge Williams's ruling. There was no call from the Dade State Attorney's Office or the Miami police. Instead, they received a clipping from the *Miami Herald*: "Accused Child-Killer Sent to Mental Hospital." The clipping was sent north by Carter's aunt, who lived in South Florida and who had spotted the story, stripped across the front of the newspaper's local section the day after the hearing.

It was not so much the result—though that disturbed them—but the manner of the hearing that infuriated the family.

Betty read a quote in the story from Miami Homicide Detective Carberry. He had said to Joe Oglesby of the *Herald* that the competency hearing was "the biggest hoax I've ever seen. . . ."

Betty saw, too, that Judge Williams had ordered Walford to the South Florida State Hospital in Pembroke Pines. Carberry's partner, Detective Martinez, had characterized the hospital in the newspaper story as "Escape City."

It blistered her heart.

She read that 112 patients had escaped from the hospital during the previous year; that the mayor and council members of the tiny community surrounding the sprawling hospital were demanding added guards for protection and guarantees that the mad child killer would not be allowed to escape. She read, too, that the council was debating establishing armed vigilante patrols on the hospital perimeter to watch for Walford, so that he could be shot down before he fled into the neighborhoods. The citizens of Pembroke Pines were ready to picket the hospital, furious that Walford was to be landed in their midst.

Betty could not rip from her imagination the picture created by the newspaper story. She suddenly saw Walford slipping away from the hospital and running free in the world.

And killing someone else's little boy.

It was a thought beyond nightmare for her, and she was driven over and over again to tears when the vision creased her imagination. Even years later, relating the memory, when she was struck by the sudden fear that some other mother would have to go through what she had experienced, her eyes filled rapidly, and her voice, ordinarily so strong, quavered, barely controllable.

When, hours before Walford was to be delivered to South Florida, state officials bowed to the pressure from the community and changed his assignation to the state hospital in Chattahoochee—in North Florida, outside of Tallahassee—with a maximum security forensic ward, she was barely relieved. The vision that someone else might have an identical agony to hers almost overcame her. She learned of the switch in designated hospitals through the newspaper, too.

These things began to infuriate Carter.

Who had been in charge of Walford's release in Massachusetts? What had been the nature of the competency hearing? What evidence had been admitted? Why had the decision been made? Who had ordered Walford to a minimum security installation? Why wasn't he, Carter, being told anything? What the hell was going on here?

In the direct academic approach that Carter employed, he began to delineate areas of examination. If no one was going to tell him what was happening, he was going to find out for himself. He needed to know about legal madness, the Massachusetts mental health system and the Florida system of criminal justice. Carter retrenched. I must learn, he thought. Knowledge is strength, and he knew he needed that strength desperately.

He began to teach himself about those unfamiliar things, determined to find out what he needed to know.

First the Zelezniks consulted with their close friend Richard Innis, about a lawsuit against the Commonwealth of Massachusetts. He provided the names of several capable firms in Boston that could handle the civil litigation. Not long after the competency hearing in Florida, the family traveled to Boston to speak with lawyers. They had several consultations before sitting down with Evan Semerjian, a lawyer with a prominent, respected firm. It was their introduction to the term *sovereign immunity*.

Semerjian had cautioned the family that the state would probably seek to invoke this doctrine, which, in effect, prevented individuals from suing the state for wrongdoing in its official capacity. The lawyer was outraged by what had befallen the Zelezniks, however, and believed that if he could get the family before a jury, he could persuade the panel that the state had been culpably negligent in its release of Walford. Getting before a jury, he warned, would in all likelihood be a long haul. It would take years, he said. Nevertheless, he agreed to try. On their behalf he filed a lawsuit claiming that the state had acted negligently through its agents, the doctors and administrators at North- ampton Hospital who had released Walford.

The wire services picked up the news. A brief story: "Family Files Five Million-Dollar Suit in Death of Child, 9." Most papers used it as filler or in the news briefs columns.

Back in Philadelphia, Carter now had something concrete to pursue. He immersed himself in studies and tracts on the law and madness. He expanded his research into the area of sovereign immunity and its legal history. His office began to fill with boxes stuffed with documents, treatises, charts and papers on insanity and its intersection with the legal system. He pored over these things, taking notes, marking pages and filling his mind. It was one way of keeping the grief from driving him crazy, he thought in his sadness. Or perhaps he was already crazy and this was helping make him sane.

2. Bobby

He seemed joyless.

He acted lethargic, apathetic, uninterested.

He would not go outside to play.

He could not stand to be alone.

He was fearful, cautious, constricted.

He seemed to lose his child's spontaneity.

He gained weight rapidly, his slender build suddenly ballooning into an unfamiliar pudginess. His world, before the murder so active, athletic, filled with noise and excitement, became quiet, sedentary and passive. He followed his mother around. He followed his father around. His natural urges for independence and to follow his own lead seemed suddenly severed and abandoned.

When Bobby had been a young child, he had had what Carter recognized as an ideation. Little and in his bed in the nighttime darkness, he would become suddenly, desperately afraid of death and dying. "What would become of me if you died?" he would ask his parents tearfully as they tried to comfort the toddler. "Where would I go? Who would take care of me?" There was a plaintiveness in his fear, a little boy's anxiety that had grown out of control. Carter invented a game with Bobby that they played out for the time the small child was plagued by the fears of death. Carter told Bobby to call it simply the Thought. When the fear started to come over him, Bobby would run to Carter and say, "Dad, I'm having the Thought now." Carter would hold his hand and reassure him through the duration, until the fear had passed and he was freed from the anxiety.

As he grew older, the ideation seemed to dissipate, to come less and less frequently, until it eventually seemed to disappear. Until the murder, when it reappeared, more virulent, harder to control. Carter wondered whether Bobby would ever be free of the Thought.

He would not talk about what happened in Miami.

He would not go to other children's houses.

He would not play outdoors unless accompanied by his mother or father.

Even when playing in his room, he would emerge periodically to check on the whereabouts of his parents.

He had always been the quieter of the pair, especially in contrast with the ebullient, effusive, outgoing Arnold. Now, it seemed to Carter and Betty, he was even more reserved, quieter and withdrawn.

When Bobby had been a baby, Carter remembered, he had come down with a serious case of bronchitis and had been hospitalized at Jefferson for four days as the illness reached its peak. Carter and Betty had never really left the hospital throughout his stay; one or the other had been at his bedside whether he was asleep or awake. Carter thought that what was required now was the same kind of devotion; they had to stay by his side until he was able to breathe freely once again.

It was instinctual, their recognition that Bobby was slipping away into a deepening depression. In its own way, their understanding of Bobby's gradual yet distinct divorce from the world was the single greatest catalyst for altering their lives in the aftermath of Arnold's murder. It was imperative that they involve Bobby in action, to force him out of and away from his apathy. Consequently, they engaged in activities themselves. Every task, even the smallest, became a family project. They all would go to the store. They all would go out to restaurants. They all would pile into the car and just drive around Fort Washington and Ambler.

They started taking Bobby to a karate school in Philadelphia at night. He joined a class to learn the rudiments of martial arts. It was good for him to get out, Betty thought, though she and Carter realized that the course was a manifestation of their own fear of vulnerability. They freely acknowledged that getting karate lessons for Bobby was designed to give him an edge; as if when the moment arrived to confront a knife-wielding madman, he would at least have the martial arts resources to buy himself a few seconds. Time enough, perhaps, for help to arrive. What evil is there in that?

His regular school was out.

Bobby was near the end of the New Horizons program the year that Arnold was murdered. Ordinarily he would have transferred into a regular neighborhood elementary school, but it seemed to both parents to be too hard. Bobby was having enough trouble getting up and going to the school where he had been a student for years, where the rooms, the walls, the teachers, the other children, everything were completely familiar. A new routine, a new system were beyond his abilities right then, they thought: too much displacement, too frightening.

Carter came up with the solution.

If regular school was out, well, they would form their own school. He investigated the Pennsylvania laws governing the establishment of a private school and learned what was required in the curriculum by state statute. It didn't seem like much. It was possible, he decided, to charter their own school.

At nearly the same time they found the new house.

Their Fort Washington house seemed to breathe of Arnold in each recess. The idea that they should move, not so much to diminish their feelings about Arnold as to free them from the associations and the instant depression that they caused, occurred to Betty and Carter. They began to search half-heartedly, feeling in part the psychological imperativeness of the move yet equally guilty about it. It was as if there were some sense of betrayal in leaving behind the house where Arnold had grown up and where the two boys had been happiest.

In effect, when the owners of the Fort Washington house, which the Zelezniks had rented for many years, suddenly had to return from abroad, it created an excuse beyond guilt. They had to find something else. It was a practical matter.

They discovered their new house quite by accident. An afternoon family drive through nearby Ambler. Spotting the For Sale sign outside a large, white, rambling old house with a yard and a big tree and an old carriage house garage on a quiet little street a few blocks from the busy thoroughfare of the Bethlehem Pike. Stores and shops were only a few blocks the other direction. It was a neighborhood filled with children, baseball diamonds and old, friendly, lived-in houses, occupied by teachers and firemen and civil service workers. It was unpretentious and middle-class. It was the type of place that welcomes, that makes one feel instantly at home. They knocked on the door, and the owners showed them around. The most unusual feature of the house was a large rectangular room, just off the living room. It was longer and larger than most family rooms. It had many windows, was bright and airy and ran the entire length of the house. Carter saw it and thought: Here's our schoolroom.

They made their minds up quickly, made an offer and purchased the house. Betty, though, hated the packing.

She couldn't bring herself to throw out anything of Arnold's. His clothing, his books, his papers and schoolwork all were packed in boxes and brought to their new home on Rosemary Street in Ambler.

Carter busied himself with setting up the school. A name was chosen: the Renaissance Academy. It was a name selected for its symbolic value as much as any. He found a neighbor who was free to teach languages; he found a teacher with spare time who could teach social studies and geography. A friend of the family was a mathematician and available part time. Carter put it together carefully, balancing all the people, the schedules and the courses. Another neighbor's child was enrolled, so that Bobby would have some company. There was a park close by and, of course, the yard, so there was proper exercise. Swimming lessons were available at a nearby community pool; that, too, became part of the curriculum. Carter added all the courses and activities together and took the proposal that outlined the school to the state officials in charge. It passed muster and was duly chartered.

Bobby was enrolled in his own home.

The large sunroom filled swiftly with books, maps, puzzles, a blackboard and desks. Examples of the two students' work were hung from a bulletin board.

3. "... Never Grouchy, Like Me"

They decided that they needed to create some kind of memorial to Arnold. After the murder they had been swamped with requests from friends questioning what they could do to help remember Arnold. Carter, enmeshed in grief, had merely suggested donating funds to the New Horizons Montessori School, where Arnold had been so happy. The school had accumulated a sizable sum and then had asked Carter what he thought it should do with the money.

Carter hadn't really given it much thought. It was fast passing from winter into spring, and he was just beginning to become wrapped up in the dual tasks of comprehending the legal invasion on which he was embarking and the requirements posed by Bobby. He considered buying books for the school library. Other people suggested purchasing playground equipment. The idea of a scholarship fund was discussed.

The thought of an award came to Carter during a sleepless, depression-filled night. It excited Betty and Bobby when Carter described the idea in the morning.

The family designed a medal together. On one side it carried a likeness of Arnold that Betty had done for a sculpture class. Written on the medal are the phrases *Love Lives Forever, Think Good Thereon* and—Arnold's personal motto—*With God, We Can.* A few months prior to the murder, in a Sunday school class, the teacher had asked all the students to think up a statement that reflected their personal beliefs or feelings. That was the phrase that Arnold had selected.

The award, the family decided, was to go to the elementary school student who showed courage, kindness, concern, love and friendliness. However, as Carter and Betty saw it, the key was for the children themselves actually to make the selection. By involving them in the process, they would be rewarding one of their own. The children in each class at the New Horizons School were asked to reflect upon these various qualities, then to nominate a friend who they thought best displayed the characteristics. Carter and Betty realized that the youngest children at the school would have some difficulty with the concepts, and for them it was more likely to be a popularity contest. The older children, however, who were closer to Arnold's age, understood what was being asked of them much more profoundly. Their nomination essays reflected consideration and gave examples of why they had selected their choice.

The Zelezniks had great problems getting the medal cast. Their first efforts were unsuccessful; many of the foundries they contacted that were capable of performing the task quoted exorbitant rates for a limited series of medals. Many of the businesses were also wrapped up in producing medals commemorating the victory of the Philadelphia Flyers in the National Hockey League's Stanley Cup championships.

The Zelezniks kept searching, and they finally found a man who, because of a tragedy in his own family, was touched by the idea of the award and agreed to do the medals at cost. He was delayed in completing the job, however, and the Zelezniks had to rush to his studio to get the medals and then hurry back to the graduation ceremonies at the New Horizons School where the first Arnold Zeleznik award presentation was to be made.

The first award went to Adam Deutchman, age eleven.

The young boy told a reporter from the *Philadelphia Bulletin* that he had cleaned off his desk at home to make a place of honor for the medal. Adam told the reporter, "He [Arnold] liked writing compositions about the Flyers and he liked baseball. He was never grouchy, like me." His quote ran in an affectionate story in the newspaper the following week.

At the awards ceremony, a typical elementary school affair, jammed with small children racing excitedly about, anxious to start the summer holidays, their beaming parents and relieved faculty, all gathered in the bright sunlight, Bobby, too, was honored. He was given the same medal bearing his brother's likeness and a citation for the "courage and compassion he displayed following his brother's death."

He held the small two-and-one-half inch round silver medal in his hand and said nothing, a nervous, faint smile on his face.

Carter's Obsession

> ...Well, yes, I suppose that is intellectualizing the
> whole thing, but that's just me. And I'm not saying
> here that I'm an intellectual, I'm something else. It's a
> totality...a way of thinking. It's like somebody was
> hammering with a hammer and he doesn't hammer
> right and he smashes into his finger. All right, now,
> the usual thing is to throw the hammer and to get
> angry with the hammer. I have never felt that! Oh,
> well, not never, but this is characteristic of me. I will
> look beyond that hammer. I will say: How come the
> hand is doing that? Why am I swinging the hammer if
> I don't know how to do it?
>
> —Carter Zeleznik, interview on August
> 16, 1979

1. Jack Ruby and the "Preliminary Report"

To get to Carter's office at Jefferson Medical College, one has to walk up a flight of stairs and then down a smaller flight, through an unmarked set of swinging opaque glass doors, down a corridor, past some desks that guard administrators' offices, make a sharp left turn and maneuver past the secretaries who protect Carter and his co-workers from unwarranted intrusion by faculty, students or other visitors. The office itself is small, with a tiny solitary window, marked by the fluorescent modernity that characterizes the entire Office of Medical Education, an island of Formica, white walls and bright colors in the core of the brown brick and worn marble of the medical school. Carter's office is slightly more than a cubbyhole work space; there is room for his desk, a bulletin board, a rolling desk chair, a chair for visitors, a telephone with multiple lines and gray steel file cabinets. The file cabinets are jammed into every available space. On top of the file cabinets are heavy cardboard boxes, filled with other papers, documents and newspaper clippings. The boxes are marked haphazardly. One says simply "Walford." Papers flow from the top. Others say "Sovereign Immunity," "Mass. Superior Court," "Paranoid Schizophrenia."

In the months that grew into the first year after the murder, Carter isolated his inquiry to two specific areas: Walford in Massachusetts and Walford in Florida. However, in following the trail of Vernal Walford in the erratic manner that was the only route open, Carter was forced to expand the areas of investigation. He discovered, for example, that he needed to understand more about the doctrine of sovereign immunity against which they were being thrust in the Massachusetts courts, and he needed to understand the elements of insanity and the law, to comprehend Walford's legal situation in Miami.

He pursued those tasks with exceptional zeal. The boxes and file cabinets in his office swiftly began to fill.

All along he knew that what he was doing was a product of his grief and loss; that did not make it any less worthwhile to him. He understood simply that Arnold's death required action. To sit around, to let other people—the attorneys in Boston, the prosecutors in Miami—take over the responsibility for the two cases was beyond a cop-out, for Carter. It would be a tacit admission that Walford had robbed him not only of his son but of his essence. He thrust his prodigious capabilities into this education.

In one way, it kept Arnold alive for him.

In another, it meant that Arnold would not have died merely as the horrible result of an unforeseeable accident of nature—a terrible coincidence in the split second that God had blinked, or turned His back, or had His attention elsewhere, leaving evil a free rein. Carter became determined to find a reason for Arnold's death, a reason beyond madness. Nothing, he thought, happens in a void. Arnold's death was not a mere happenstance, but the cumulative result of an incredible number of social, psychological and legal factors, flaws and faults. Carter became insistent on learning the truth.

It became more than an insistence, more than a determination. It consumed him.

Not long after they had filed the suit against Northampton and the people at the hospital responsible for Walford's release, Carter and Betty received an anonymous phone call. It was night, the caller refused to identify herself, but she said, "You do it, sue those people! They should never have let that guy loose, and they know it!"

Carter tried to interject a question but was rebuffed.

"No," the caller continued, "I can't identify myself. I'd lose my job. But you're on the right track. Keep poking around. You'll find out the truth. It was wrong, wrong, wrong, and they knew it!"

What was the truth?

Bits and pieces of Walford's behavior began to become clear. They learned about the fight at the Milton Bradley Company plant in Springfield and how Walford had gone to the plant nurse with his complaints about glass in his eye. He had received his layoff notice at about the same time.

The attorney in Boston had hired a private investigator to probe the case. He had traced Walford, discovering, much as the madman's lawyers in Miami had, that the Jamaican had been engaged in all kinds of bizarre behavior following his release from the hospital. The problem, as any lawyer would recognize, was connecting the murder in Miami with the release in Massachusetts. If they were ever able to get their suit before a jury, they had to anticipate the opposition's arguing that Walford had deteriorated precipitously, in a fashion no doctor could have foreseen.

One of the items uncovered in this initial foray into Walford's stay at Northampton was the "Preliminary Report" produced by the hospital in the aftermath of the release and subsequent killing of Arnold.

The report was dated January 11, 1975. It was three pages long. The first page was taken up entirely with a list of the members of the committee of inquiry, the scope of their task, and the witnesses with whom they had spoken.

The committee is charged to determine:

1. Whether any clinical neglect or negligence had occurred and if so what action should be recommended.

2. Whether admission and discharge policies and procedures in force in the Springfield Unit [the wing Walford was held in] were adequate to safeguard patients and public and to ensure adequate patient care and whether they were carried out as required in regard to Robert Miller Grant.

3. If existing policies and procedures were deemed inadequate, to make recommendations for change.

The six-person committee consisted of administrators for the Massachusetts mental health system. It included William Goggins, the assistant superintendent at Northampton.

These were the people interviewed:

Angelina Supan, M.D., the unit physician who had signed Walford's release

Shirley Gallup, M.D., a senior psychiatrist

Marion Miller, M.S.W., acting unit director
Robert Sharon, M.S.W., unit social worker
James Taylor, M.S.W., admitting social worker
Carol Leeming, R.N., head nurse, day shift
Jean Travis, R.N., head nurse, night shift
Louise Flyn, R.N., director of nurses
Jack Bourgeois, day shift attendant
Edward Kubasek, day shift attendant
Paul Gilbraine, advocate, Western Massachusetts Legal Services

The committee had been unable to interview the admitting physician, Dr. Maria Villacorte, because she had been on leave, and the doctor who had sent Walford to Northampton from Springfield Hospital, Dr. William Linson, had been talked to on the telephone.

The "Preliminary Report" did not describe the interviews, nor were there verbatim quotations included. It merely reached three predictable conclusions:

1. The Committee concluded there was no clinical negligence. A staff physician was in charge of the case, saw the patient several times and made the final decision to release him. Although she was not the regular ward physician, who was off sick, this physician works regularly in the hospital and knew the ward and the team. A diagnosis was made, the patient's behavior and treatment was [*sic*] reviewed appropriately and considerable thought was obviously given to the decision to release him. . . . Factors influencing the decision to discharge the patient were that he had signed a voluntary admission and was pressing to leave the hospital, that there was a clinical decision that his condition was not such that he could be committed under existing statutes and that it seemed better to encourage him to obtain treatment in the community than to hold him against his will in the hospital for a limited time. . . .

2. The Committee concluded that the admission and discharge of the patient were carried out in accordance with the policies and procedures of the unit and the hospital in operation at that time. The patient was examined on admission by the officer of the day and the diagnosis and initial treatment plan recorded. . . . The patient was informed of his rights and permitted to change his status from admission under Section XII [involuntary, ten-day observation] to a voluntary admission. . . . The patient received considerable attention from the nursing team as well as being interviewed several times by clinical team members. . . . Opinions of attendants, nurses, and clinical staff were taken into consideration in making the decision to release the patient. . . .

3. The Committee concluded that some aspects of the existing policies and procedures in force at the time of Mr. Grant's visit to Northampton State Hospital were not adequate and should be improved. . . .

This last section suggested that better efforts to contact referring physicians be made, that more frequent staff meetings be held to discuss potential discharges and that appointments be made in community mental health centers for patients being released who had agreed with the aftercare plans established by the hospital. Walford had reluctantly agreed to such a plan. Of course, he had never followed up on it.

There never would be a "Final Report."

The report itself contradicted the statements that had already been circulated in the *Boston Globe* and the *Springfield Union* about Walford's assaultive behavior. The report in no way accurately reflected the actual character of Walford's forty-odd hours inside the old, worn hospital. Indeed, it was a compilation of half-truths, untruths, misstatements, misspelled names and grammatical errors.

But it would take seven years for that to be acknowledged.

Carter, though, knew it from the beginning. He knew instinctively that it was wrong, and he knew it from the meager facts that he'd already accumulated. Over the course of the next years he would slowly, steadily compile more and more evidence that would show that Walford had come to that hospital virulently, dangerously mad and had become worse inside the whitewashed old walls; that in the throes of homicidal psychosis, hearing voices and chanting delusionally, Walford had insisted on leaving and, in fear or folly, been permitted to walk from the hospital, whatever threads prevented tragedy unraveling swiftly.

From Miami, Carter obtained the psychiatric reports that had been prepared for the competency hearing, none longer than a half dozen pages. He read through them methodically, carefully, examining each aspect of the reports.

They outraged him.

A third-year student at Jefferson would have been embarrassed to hand in any of the reports, he thought.

During the course of his readings Carter had come across the Warren Commission's report on the assassination of John F. Kennedy. What interested him most was the section investigating the background of Jack Ruby, the killer of presidential assassin Lee Harvey Oswald. The Warren Commission had prepared an extensive biographical profile and psychological history of Ruby as part of its report. It had delved into virtually every aspect of Ruby's background, from his love of dogs to his underworld connections, to his propensities for uncontrolled violence. Carter contrasted this total, absorbing portrait with the abbreviated, uninformed reports that he had obtained from Miami about Walford. Later he would harp on this discrepancy time and again, not so much to say that Walford should have been investigated with the same intensity that Jack Ruby had been, as to characterize the difference in approach. What angered him about what had happened in Miami was the limitation of the inquiry; it seemed that no one really wanted to know! It seemed that no one was interested in finding out why Walford was there, why he was thinking the way he was and why he'd killed Arnold. Indeed, the only people Carter could see who were taking an appropriate concern in the case were Walford's defense team.

He considered all the things that hadn't been done with Walford.

The doctors had failed to take any patient history.

They had failed to administer any physical tests.

They had not administered any mental tests.

He had not been given an electroencephalogram. Nor had he been given minimum doses of Thorazine, to determine the lowest possible level on which he would regain control. He had been promptly shot up with huge dosages, strait-jacketed by the potent antipsychotic medicine.

Carter wasn't even convinced, initially, that the diagnosis of paranoid schizophrenia was correct. As did the doctors in Miami, he knew that Walford had been a champion boxer in the Jamaican armed forces. There could be organic brain damage. He thought of subdural hematoma, a bruise on the brain. It could produce behavior greatly resembling psychosis. Without an EEG, there was no way to tell. The same was true of temporal lobe epilepsy, a physical condition which prompts violent, aggressive, seemingly psychotic behavior. He was infuriated that each doctor seemed to shrug off the fact that Walford could be interviewed only through bars—as if that were the excuse for not finding out a proper patient history. He was angered that the length of time for the examinations had ranged from one to four or five hours. He felt that was insufficient regardless of one's experience. How could anyone expect to find out anything in an hour?

In short, he thought the reports shabby, uninformed and inadequate.

And there wasn't a damn thing he could do about it.

He wasn't any more pleased with the Dade State Attorney's Office. His reading of the competency hearing transcript brought him to the conclusion that the prosecution had been woefully unprepared. What he couldn't understand was why. How could anyone not consider Arnold's murder an important case? A priority case?

Carter pored over books and journals with titles like: *Readings in Law and Psychiatry; Mental Health and Law: A System in Transition; Forensic Psychiatry, Tactics in Cross-Examination; The Journal of Psychiatry and the Law; The Mentally Disordered Offender; The Mind of the Murderer; Law, Psychiatry and the Mental Health System.* He read such works as *In Cold Blood* and *Compulsion.* He studied the famous cases: M'Naghten, the English case that had given rise to the present-day insanity standards utilized in the majority of states, and Durham, the irresistible impulse standard that was employed in a few other jurisdictions. He read trial transcripts and excerpts from cases from throughout the United States, famous cases, such as the Volbrecht case in Kansas, which contained an attack on the M'Naghten knowledge of right versus wrong standard, and the testimony of Dr. Manfred Guttmacher in the Jack Ruby trial. Guttmacher, perhaps the nation's foremost forensic psychiatrist until his death, had been known for the caution he had employed in his analyses of criminal behavior.

Carter ingested all that and more. He read medical studies on paranoid schizophrenia, psychotic behavior and sociopathy. He plumbed the literature of madness with Dostoyevsky and *Crime and Punishment*.

Throughout the entire learning process, the question in the core of his own mind was: How does this relate to Arnold's death?

He began to see it all as a huge failure of society.

For example, he read over and over again, in critical studies and scholarly, legal tracts, about the inadequacy of the M'Naghten standard on insanity and how psychiatrists, for the most part, felt it was inappropriate to testify in a court of law. The literature of the conjunction of law and psychiatry was wealthy with attacks on the M'Naghten standard of criminal responsibility. While it was popular to attack the M'Naghten rule, however, it was still widely used, the criminal justice system seemingly shrugging its collective shoulders and failing to replace it with something more appropriate. Carter could not comprehend why, given the almost universal disrepute in which the standard was held, given the knowledge that psychiatrists were reluctant to testify in courts of law, why these doctors in Miami had been given such extraordinary power. Why had they been allowed to come in and testify on the basis of what were clearly inadequate investigations, their words emblazoned as if on tablets, uncontradicted, unquestioned?

Why had there been no prepared reply from the prosecution?

Why had the judge ordered Walford to a minimum security facility?

Why had no one contacted him and Betty and Bobby?

What would happen now, with Walford in an institution?

Would they ever get a day in court?

And who was there who would stand up for Arnold?

Sometimes the anger would possess him, and he would shut the door to his office and weep quietly in frustration and grief.

CHAPTER 7
A Ride on a Bike

1. Slow Time

For months the family existed in a twilight state.

Sometimes they felt as if they were playacting, only going through the motions of living, as if their real bodies were somewhere else, almost as if they were watching themselves up on a stage or a theater screen. The connection with the murderous event in Miami was so strong that it sometimes overcame the daily routines, sweeping the Zelezniks up, obliterating the reasoned world around them and thrusting them back into that exceptional mad moment. They would become suddenly depressed, suddenly afraid, struck with an unusual lassitude that bore no relation to the tasks of the day but was rooted instead in the murder in Miami.

Days passed, became weeks, months, a year, then two. The fight to regain a type of normality without Arnold was a constant but evasive thing. They took a trip up to Nova Scotia, for example, the new, diminished family on vacation. They drove north, through the wild coastal regions of Canada, and took the ferry to the peninsula. But the sights, the experiences of the trip barely registered. In later years Betty could hardly describe what they did and saw. She could remember only the absence of Arnold.

There were small things, too. Carter and Betty never ate meat on the twentieth of the month, nor would they eat any dinner. It was a way of remembering that on December 20, 1974, they had gone without dinner.

Betty had trouble controlling her tears.

Sometimes spontaneously the recollection of the loss would simply rise out of her heart into her throat and imagination, and she would sit down heavily, overcome with remorse. She tried to hide those times from Carter and Bobby. Especially Bobby.

It was hard, too, for her to conceal her fear.

There were dozens, hundreds of moments when she found herself alone in the kitchen. Bobby would be upstairs in his room doing homework or reading or occupying himself quietly. She would find herself suddenly transfixed by the silence, captured by a formless, unidentifiable fear, and she would have the overwhelming urge to rush to the stairway and leap headlong up the flight of stairs to Bobby's room, to make certain that he was still there, still alive.

She knew the danger inherent in those moments.

One of the clearest, most difficult of ideas that Betty recognized was that the person who would be crippled the most by overprotectiveness was Bobby. While she wanted to watch over him, guard him and protect him, she knew that that would also lock him in, prevent him from growing up and being independent. That burden, the task of not watching over Bobby constantly, fell mostly on Betty's shoulders. After all, Bobby was within the house the greater part of the day at the Renaissance Academy in the family room. The scope of his play was limited to his room upstairs and the yard, but even there he had trouble going outside at first without Betty present to watch him. Trips, especially those connected with the academy, were always supervised and organized. In a sense, Betty was in charge of the compensation for all this protectiveness. If Bobby was not going to go to a regular elementary school, like so many other children, and be sheltered in that fashion, it was up to Betty to see that he got out and abroad, and, in effect, was able to act like the youngster he was.

So she began a campaign of independence.

When Bobby came to her, wanting to go outside and wanting her company, she would refuse. "No, Bobby, you're big enough to play outdoors by yourself. I'm going to be right here." At first he would cry or stamp his foot angrily or plead with her. Sometimes he would just pause, thinking, then retreat to his own room.

However, the pull of the outdoors was too great for all of his young energy, and reluctantly he began to agree, though he would poke his head back indoors, minutes later, to call out, "Mom! I'm right here!"

She would reply, "Fine, I'm here, too."

Those calls slowly began to diminish.

Betty saw those things as small skirmishes, but successes nonetheless. And if getting Bobby to play outside out of her sight was one victorious moment, she did not hesitate to identify the next. From the front yard to the neighbor's house, from there to the playground, she saw those steps, those small, ordinary, routine expressions of freedom, as great, momentous events. She hid her feelings, however, portraying a solidity, a nothing-out-of-the-ordinary façade that masked the mixture of pleasure and fear she felt.

Bobby put on weight after the murder, his lethargy and loss of action directly attributable to the loss of the brother he'd followed constantly. When Bobby gained a pudginess that was not her son's true shape, Betty finally insisted that he go on a diet. It is a difficult thing to make a nine- or ten-year-old child limit his food and cut out sweets, but Betty remained firm. Slowly but perceptibly Bobby began to lose the weight. Increasingly Betty urged more and more outdoor activity. It worked. Bobby began to look more like himself.

There were setbacks, of course, that carried a knifelike misery. It was Betty's job to turn them into successes. Betty firmly insisted that Bobby join the local swim club. The pool was located only blocks away, all the neighborhood children were members and as a child Bobby had always been a strong, avid swimmer. He was reluctant to leave the house and even more reluctant when Betty explained that she would not be there with him during the workouts.

She prevailed, however, explaining that she would drop him off in the car, then pick him up promptly at the end of the sessions. The orderly routine seemed to reassure Bobby, and he eventually agreed.

The system worked excellently at first. Betty and Bobby would get into the car and drive to the club. She would get out and walk him inside; once there, familiar with the coaches and the other children, Bobby would relax and burst off energetically into the locker rooms and pool. Betty would return to the Rosemary Street house and, keeping a close eye on the time, do housework or work on one of her painting assignments from the Pennsylvania Academy of Fine Arts, where she was enrolled in courses. She would leave herself plenty of time to drive the few blocks to the club, where she would be waiting when Bobby and the other children finished.

One bright, warm day, the kind of afternoon that belies fears and anxieties, Betty took a few extra minutes to finish some piece of work. As she was heading out the door, she was spotted by one of the neighbors, who waved at her, then started over to talk. Betty was caught, poised by the door of the car, half in, half out, trapped in conversation. The neighbor went on, not about anything, really, and Betty began to feel her control dissolving. She kept trying to interrupt—"I've got to go. Bobby is waiting for me. I have to be there to pick him up"—but the neighbor, not realizing the sense of urgency that Betty had about her, kept talking. Finally, at the cost of being rude—something Betty never was—she just cut the neighbor off. "I've got to go!" she said. "I can't talk!"

She piled into the car and hurried to the swim club. She arrived perhaps a quarter hour after the completion of practice. Bobby was nowhere to be seen.

Her first urge was to scream, "Bobby!" Instead, she took a deep breath.

She had to swallow hard, to overcome the sudden images that crowded her consciousness. She fought off the nightmare sense of panic and fear and forced herself to walk slowly, carefully into the club.

No one was about.

She tried her first "Bobby?" then, not raising her voice really, just curious, wondering. She felt her fists tighten and clench when there was no reply. He's here, she thought. Just start looking.

She began to search. Occasionally she would call out. She refused to let her anxiety penetrate the tone of her voice, though with each additional second her nervousness grew.

She found him, hiding behind a partition in a small back room. Tears were racing down his cheeks. She hugged him, then looked hard into his eyes. "You promised," he said, between gasps. "You said you'd be there. You weren't there. I was all alone. I didn't know what to do; everyone went home and you weren't there. I was scared."

Her first urge was to sweep him up, envelop him with her arms and promise that it would never happen again and that she would always be there, to join in his tears and protect him from his fear. Instead, she took another deep breath and held him out away from her.

"Bobby," she said, "listen to me! You know I can't always be everywhere. Suppose the car had a flat. Or I got a phone call from Daddy. Or something else. You're big enough to know what to do. You could have asked one of the coaches to stay with you. You could have borrowed a dime from one of the other boys and called home. You could have asked one of the other mothers to take you home. You could have walked home yourself. It's only a few blocks, and you know the way. You can't always depend on me or Daddy. You have to depend on yourself!"

She looked hard at him, and he nodded.

The two of them then went home in silence.

The next day, when Bobby hesitated about going to the club, Betty bustled him off before he could formulate his objection. She thought: We have to keep going forward!

It was not too much after that incident that Bobby announced he would begin riding his bicycle to the club. On the first day Betty followed him in the car. He waved at her when they reached the pool. The next day he wanted her to follow him again, but Betty refused. "Oh, Bobby, I've got to finish this painting, and I'm expecting a call, then I've got to go to the grocery store. You go, and I'll see you later." She used her most matter-of-fact voice, a little tired, burdened by the tasks, as if it were nothing out of the ordinary.

Bobby stared at her for an instant, wavering, trying to make up his mind. Then he said, "All right," and went outside and got on his bicycle. Betty battled the need to jump into the car and follow him. Instead, she gave a small, carefree wave toward Bobby and watched as he pedaled away, turning and glancing backward only once or twice.

That, Betty thought, is a real victory.

She went back to her housework, a bit nervous, checking up at the clock a bit too frequently, anticipating the sound of Bobby's bike as it finally clattered on the back porch and he announced his safe arrival. Although she knew that it was a victory for Bobby, it would be sometime before she realized that it was just as great a victory for her.

2. The Decision to Fight

The initial stages of the Zelezniks' two legal fights were losses. In Miami, Walford had been held incompetent and shuffled off into the mental health system. In Boston, Superior Court civil action docket number 5706, *Carter Zeleznik, administrator of the estate of Arnold Frank Zeleznik, plaintiff* v. *The Commonwealth of Massachusetts, Angelina Supan, Shirley Gallup, Irving Jacobs, Maria Villacorte and Robert Sharon,* was also running into difficulty. The difficulty was created by delay. The outcome of their lawsuit was, to a great extent, dependent on the results of several pending actions, and they had to await those cases' reaching completion.

Carter liked to refer to the legal doctrine of sovereign immunity as "the rule where the king can do no wrong." For the most part, his simplification was correct. By the mid-1970s the majority of the states in the Union had done away with any type of sovereign immunity. It was a carry-over from the principles of English common law that had been installed in the American legal system decades before. In effect, it prevented an individual from suing the state or the state's agents for wrongdoing when they were functioning within their designed job. It literally immunized the state workers and state government.

The doctrine had slowly, steadily been eroded in many decisions in many states; after all, the right of the people to a court of law is fundamental, and the doctrine flew in the face of that right. However, it was still in effect in

Massachusetts at the time of Walford's release and the Zelezniks' subsequent suit.

After the complaint had been filed, the matter rested while several other related cases were heard. At the same time the Massachusetts legislature was acting to dissolve the rule. In 1973, in the *Morash* decision, the Massachusetts Supreme Court had expressed its belief that the doctrine was unjust and unfair in its application *(Morash & Sons, Inc.* v. *Commonwealth,* 363 Mass. 612*)*. The court recommended that the state legislature do away with the doctrine— but did not abolish the rule by declaring it unconstitutional. The legislature would eventually follow the court's recommendation, but in the initial stages after the filing of the Zelezniks' suit, the doctrine and the legal circumstances surrounding it were in confusion. What had to be achieved first was a clarification of the law and whether the state could apply the doctrine to the Zelezniks' suit.

In other words, they first had to fight to see if they could play the game. Then—if successful, and that was very legally debatable—they would have to go back to square one and begin fighting the merits of their complaint.

Carter thought ruefully: Years. Years. Years. It will take years.

The decision to battle in the courts in the first place, however, preceded all those legal actions. It was a resolution the entire family made together so that when legal setbacks did occur, the family was already prepared to continue and absorbed the courtroom blows with greater equanimity. It was closing in on two years after Arnold's death when the family met in conference.

Carter had accumulated dozens of particles of information about Walford. He boiled it down to what he saw as its essence.

A man comes to the United States illegally. He admits to smuggling drugs. Obtains phony work papers. Obtains an alias. Goes mad. Assaults co-workers. Is diagnosed as dangerous and sent to a mental hospital. Assaults staff. Demonstrates all the classic signs of paranoid schizophrenia. Displays all the signs of uncontrollable dangerousness and savagery. Is released when he insists on it, without any kind of warning or thought of what might happen. Continues to act madly. No one in any official capacity does anything. Goes to Miami and murders Arnold. Then disappears into the mental health system with hardly a murmur from authorities. Is scheduled for a minimum security hospital.

What did they want? Carter thought. For him to escape home to Jamaica so they wouldn't have to worry about him anymore?

Carter, Betty and Bobby sat down in the living room of the Rosemary Street house and surveyed all the documents, all the elements of the situation.

They realized that the criminal action undertaken by the Dade State Attorney's Office was for the most part out of their control. Still, Carter resolved to try to bring some pressure on that office to do something. He said he would have one of the family's close friends, a lawyer, contact the Dade State Attorney's Office and check on the case. He was still infuriated by the psychiatric reports and what he considered the cavalier fashion in which they had been adopted.

Consequently, he announced he would continue to study that aspect. He began to formulate the idea of writing a book about the improper way that psychiatrists were used in the courts.

The real issue, however, was: What could they as a family do?

And where were they to attach the greatest blame?

"They had him; they knew he was dangerous; they let him go," Betty said. "If they only had listened to him, if they'd kept him for observation or I don't know what, then they would have seen what he was going to do. He tried to kill one of the attendants, see here." She held up the *Boston Globe* story which described how Walford had leaped onto the back of an attendant and nearly strangled the man to death. "How could they let him go after that? What did they think would happen?"

"They were afraid of him," Carter said.

"So they just let him go!" Betty replied.

"I think," said Carter, "that in a way they are more to blame even than Walford. They were negligent. He was mad. Both are terrible, but in a way, what they did is worse."

Betty nodded. She couldn't express the anger that welled up in her. Anyone, she thought, could have seen what was going to happen!

"So we have to fight," she said.

"It will take years," Carter said.

"We have years," Betty replied.

"Do we spend the money?" Carter asked rhetorically. "We aren't rich. Our resources are limited."

"How much will it cost?" Betty asked.

Carter shrugged. "Lots. Lawyers always cost lots."

Betty was quiet. Then she said, "We don't have to take some vacations. . . ."

Carter smiled. He reached over and grabbed her hand. "You know," he said, "how much would it cost if we still had Arnold? We should spend that."

Betty's eyes shone with tears, and she nodded.

Carter looked over at Bobby. He hadn't said a word. The worry went through Carter's mind that by continuing to battle in criminal and civil court they would be prolonging Bobby's process of recovery of his own identity, his own childhood. He wondered if it would be wiser to drop everything, to work simply toward forgetting. Would the real cost of elongated legal fights be the loss of Bobby's youth? He nodded toward Bobby and asked, "Bobby? What do you think?"

Bobby was quiet for a moment. He pushed his blond hair back from his eyes. If he was troubled, it did not show in his young man's voice. Ten years old but forthright. "I think we should fight," he said. He hesitated for a second, then added, "Arnold was never a quitter. He would want to fight." Bobby smiled, as if a sudden pleasant memory had struck his imagination. Betty, too, caught a picture in her mind's eye of Arnold on the playing field. He was not the type to give up, she thought. Nor are we.

"All right then," Carter said. He smiled. The whole family held hands for an instant. "We go on with the fight, to the Supreme Court if we have to, but we go on. Together."

At about the same time, in the late fall of 1976, though they did not know it, the clerk of the Eleventh Judicial Circuit, which encompasses Dade County, received the following letter from the director of the Forensic Unit of the Florida State Hospital in Chattahoochee:

Re: Vernal Newland Walford
Committed: 1-31-75
Case No. 75-179-CF-O3

Dear Mr. Brinker:

This information is being sent to you for forwarding to the judge who is currently presiding in this case.

Mr. Vernal Walford was admitted to Florida State Hospital on February 4, 1975. His treatment has been completed and further hospitalization is not indicated. He has been found competent to stand trial.

We are enclosing our complete clinical summary, which indicates he is ready for return to court.

He will be made available for return to Dade County when a duly authorized deputy sheriff with proper court order comes to the hospital to take custody of him.

Please let us know if we can be of further help.

> Very Truly Yours,
> Benjamin R. Ogburn, M.D.
> Director of the Forensic Unit.

Vernal Walford was being shipped back to Dade County to stand trial. A squad of Dade jail guards, the memory of Walford's manic behavior still fresh in their memory, drove north to pick him up, then returned to South Florida with Walford shackled hand and foot. He was placed back inside a security cell, where he stared out at the same institutional green and white painted walls. However, it was not the same man who once had screamed and raved and had shaken the entire jail with his madness. Vernal Walford stood alone, eyes raised, in the center of the cell, beneath the wire-mesh-covered light bulb, next to the commode and the cement pallet that was his bed. His hands shook; the muscles of his face twitched; his shoulders shuddered. His entire body trembled.

No one told the Zelezniks of this development.

CHAPTER 8

"I Saw the Boy Come Running"

1. Pete the Cat, Tark the Shark and the Surfer

By the time Vernal Walford was returned to the Dade County Jail in late 1976, alleged by the physicians at the state mental hospital in Chattahoochee to be competent to stand trial, his first two attorneys had departed the Dade Public Defender's Office for a lucrative criminal law practice. Before leaving, however, Black and Denaro had selected the pair of young lawyers to take over the case. They had also handed over a trial-ready file, containing all the statements, depositions, numerous psychiatric reports and investigative materials fully collated, organized and tabled. To prepare themselves for Vernal Walford, all that the two successors would have to do would be to start reading and plug the videotape into a machine.

That was characteristic of the difference in the handling of the case by the two contending offices, the Public Defender's Office and the Dade State Attorney's Office. While the defense was ready almost instantly, the prosecutor assigned the case when it reappeared on the docket knew very little about it. He had no firsthand knowledge of the event or the investigation. All he knew about the competency hearing was what he read in the transcript. The prosecution file was a mishmash of statements and incomplete detective work. Miami policemen had never been asked to complete some crucial elements. For example, latent fingerprints lifted from the murder scene had never been compared with standards taken from Walford. Blood work. the analysis of samples collected from beneath Walford's fingernails and his stained clothing, had never been tested for comparison with Arnold's blood. No statements from the medical examiner and other key witnesses were recorded. The file did not have current address listings for many of the witnesses, including people who'd been at the Crossways. The search for the murder weapon had never been completed; no weapon was available. There was no information about Walford's background, no documents about his life in Massachusetts and his stay at Northampton. The prosecution did not even have a copy of the now-famous videotape.

The prosecutor assigned to the case was Michael John Korvick, a tall, blond-haired, experienced major crimes prosecutor in his early thirties. It was not even so much a situation where the case was actually assigned to him; he was the chief felony prosecutor working in the division to which the case was allocated by the random docketing system used by the Dade Circuit Court.

A graduate of the University of Miami Law School—as were most of the people involved in the case—Korvick had been prosecuting homicides for some time. He was a successful, effective prosecutor. He had an easygoing, almost quiet style, which contrasted with the bombast and aggressiveness adopted by many attorneys. It was singularly successful with jurors. He was also a friendly, outgoing man; it was hard to understand why he and the Zelezniks grew to dislike each other.

They did, however, with an intensity that was out of character for either party. That dislike ultimately came to affect the case. Korvick saw the family as meddlesome, demanding and not really knowledgeable about the issues and the bizarre medicolegal situation that evolved.

The Zelezniks thought him condescending, arrogant, unfeeling and incompetent. They derisively called him the Surfer.

All that took place later, though, when for a few days it seemed that Walford was going to have to face a jury.

Michael Von Zamft and Michael Tarkoff were the two public defenders recommended by Black and Denaro to take over the case when they went into private practice. The two men, Miami graduates, young but experienced, were enthusiastic at the prospect of handling the case; Walford, in a way, had become something of a pet cause in the Public Defender's Office. Certainly the work that Black and Denaro had begun had a carry-over effect. No attorney following in their wake wanted to become known as the person who had lost the case, after having benefited from the groundwork prepared by Roy Black and Jack Denaro.

Von Zamft, a native of Miami Beach, a reformed "beach boy," as he liked to call himself, was an extraordinarily aggressive lawyer. He was the quintessential battler, a man who so preferred the underdog's role that it was almost essential in order for him to become involved. If Von Zamft enjoyed being the underdog, he was a rabid one. In a courtroom he performed, one second cajoling, the next browbeating, the next eloquent and passionate. He brought an exceptional intensity to the courtroom, a level of emotion that marked his behavior in general. He was quick-witted, extremely fast of thought. He was also a consummate believer in his own ability and knowledge of the law; the judges in the Metro Justice Building would often mutter privately about his steamroller approach. Von Zamft never seemed to care much what the hell anybody thought about him, as long as he was doing his job. A complex man, he contradicted all the gruffness and pushiness with an almost literary appreciation of events. At the time of the Walford case his own father was in a federal prison farm in Arizona, serving time for white-collar crimes. It is difficult to guess how that affected Von Zamft's behavior. But it was never far from his mind.

In his office was a file marked "Pete the Cat." It contained the impossible cases, the unwinnable ones. It was the file drawer in which he spent most of his time.

Michael Tarkoff was similar to Von Zamft in many ways. He, too, brought a florid, aggressive posture to a courtroom. He mingled it with a self-effacing sense of humor; he liked to tell of the client he'd had facing a first-degree murder indictment. The man had never spoken to Tarkoff, not once, not even a pleasantry. During the trial the client wore tattered clothes and his shoulder-length hair in cornrows, unwashed. He said nothing, ignoring Tarkoff and keeping his back to the jury except for the occasional moment when he found time to sneer in its direction. If ever a man looked like a murderer, it was he. Tarkoff, however, proceeded gamely. He shouted; he twisted; he ripped into policemen and medical examiners when they took the stand. He turned the facts backward and forward. He did verbal handstands and backflips and ended his case with a tear-rending plea for his client. Sure enough, it worked. The jury returned with a conviction, but on a far lesser charge than the one the client had faced. The defendant's response was one of surprise. "Far out," he said as the verdict was announced and the prosecutor stamped from the courtroom. "Hey," he said to Tarkoff, "you handle the appeal, huh?" Tarkoff liked to say it was the best compliment he'd ever received.

Shortly after Vernal Walford had rearrived in Miami and been escorted to the security cell in the Dade County Jail, he was met there by Tarkoff and Von Zamft. The two men had researched the case, gone over the documents and seen the videotape. They expected to see the same man, his rippling muscles, his angry, penetrating eyes and a voice freighted with singsong malevolence.

For an instant they stood outside Walford's cell in surprise.

They barely recognized the man within.

His once militarily cropped hair now hung in twisted locks over his ears and headed toward his shoulders. A thick black beard hid much of his face. His washboard stomach now hung over his belt. He was slumped, round-shouldered. His ramrod bearing and muscular precision were gone. In their place were folds of loose skin that seemed to flap when he moved. His eyes were hidden behind thick black-rimmed glasses. He stared out at the two attorneys with mingled docility and curiosity. His voice had lost the staccato edge of anger and conceit that had marked him two years before.

Then Tarkoff noticed Walford's leg. As he watched, it began to twitch, the muscles contracting and expanding rapidly, uncontrollably. For a second he thought of a man who had sprinted a hundred-yard dash and suddenly had to pay for it. The leg tremors seemed to spread; they appeared to take over Walford's body. The two attorneys saw their client's hands quavering, lips smacking and head jerking; he appeared like a fish on a hook, pulled from the water.

The two attorneys watched the once madly tuned athletic body shake uncontrollably. It was as if his entire physique were subject to deep, subterranean quakes that would surface randomly, one instant in the hands, the next in the face, the next in the legs. His eyes rolled, as if out of control. The muscles in his face twitched, palsylike, forcing Walford to grin, frown, screw his nose up, grimace angrily, then tremble. His tongue would suddenly stick from between his lips, smacking. He drooled and then brought a shaking hand to his chin to try to wipe the spittle away.

If the Walford of the videotape had seemed close to some violent jungle animal, this Walford seemed an ugly, bloated, almost benign swamplike creature.

"Mr. Walford?" the lawyers asked in surprise.

"Yes," he replied, his tongue smacking his lips. There was a slowness, a passivity to his tone. "You must be my new attorneys. What do you want? What can I tell you?"

The two lawyers sat down in surprise as Walford told them about the murder.

2. The Voice of God

"So," Tarkoff said to Von Zamft, after leaving Walford at the Dade County Jail. Their minds were filled with the images from the murder, but nagging, too, was the appearance that Walford had made. It so contradicted what they'd expected. Tarkoff couldn't shake the vision of Walford's leg trembling. "What the hell's the matter with him?"

A good question. One that would come to dominate this new Walford's experience in court.

Shortly after Walford's return to Dade County, Circuit Judge Gerald Wetherington ordered five psychiatrists—the same men who'd examined Walford in the days and weeks following the murder—to go back to the jail and reexamine him, to determine if he was actually capable of going on trial for Arnold's murder. That was standard operating procedure; it would be an extremely rare occurrence in the Dade courts for any of the judges to take the word of the state mental system without further checking with any one of the number of psychiatrists who regularly performed forensic evaluations. The state system simply was not trusted; like every system, it was in constant need of bed space, and one way to free beds, it was believed by attorneys and courtroom personnel, was to pump up the court-held patients with tranquilizers and announce that they were ready to stand trial.

The Dade doctors saw Walford in his cell over a several-week period in late November and December 1976. "It was quite a change to see this man in a controlled, pleasant, cooperative state..." wrote one doctor. "When I asked him about some of his prior behavior, he chuckled somewhat sheepishly at times...."

Presumably he didn't chuckle when asked about the murder.

Walford was being given a smorgasbord of antipsychotic medicines. At various times, he was given the phenothiazines, Thorazine and Mellaril orally and Prolixin, a fluphenazine hydrochloride compound—an exceptionally powerful drug—intramuscularly. He was also given Artane and Cogentin, both medicines designed to combat the tremors and quakes. The dosages of the drugs that Walford was being fed were extraordinarily high. For example, he was being given a single shot of Prolixin every week that contained 37.5 milligrams of the drug. The usual large-scale dosage is to give that amount every *two* weeks. Additionally, Walford would get the Artane or Cogentin four times a day and an additional 200 milligrams of Thorazine or Mellaril at night prior to going to bed.

It did not take long for Tarkoff and Von Zamft to discover that Walford's body tremors were the direct result of the substantial, cumulative effects of the drugs. Indeed, each of the psychiatrists who saw Walford pointed out that the Parkinson's type of symptoms Walford exhibited were caused by the build-up of the antipsychotic medicines. Of course, the same build-up was rendering Walford capable of replying to questions and preventing him from hearing voices.

The question for the two attorneys then became what significance the drugs could have on Walford's capacity to stand trial.

The two men began to research the question extensively.

The psychiatric examinations took place in rapid succession. Each lasted somewhere in the neighborhood of sixty to ninety minutes. All the doctors were struck by Walford's cooperativeness and by his responsiveness. He sat calmly, discussing the elements of his past, his behavior and his crime. His tremors ranged from slight twitching to uncontrollable shaking, an erraticism that emerged in the reports. He spoke in the same accented voice but without the rage and the arrogance. He replied to questions but was not spontaneous and did not exactly volunteer details. For the first time the doctors were able to take a history from Walford.

He said he had been born January 7, 1943, in St. Ann, Jamaica.

He was, he said, the sixth of nine children. His father, still alive in his nineties, was a farmer. His mother had died in 1955, but he said he did not know why. When he was ten, he said, he had gone to Kingston, to be reared by an aunt.

He had finished high school, he told the doctors, but completed only a year of college at a Seventh-Day Adventist school. He said he had always been religious, even as a child. He said that he had been dismissed from the private college after his first year because he had been in a fight with another young man over a girl. So, he said, he had joined the Jamaica Defense Force.

He was eighteen and served until age twenty-seven. He had reached the rank of corporal, he said.

He told, too, then that he had become the force's middleweight boxing champion and that in 1966 he had won a silver medal in a sprint at the Jamaican Olympics. After having left the military, he said he had driven a taxi.

He said he had married his wife, Noletha, in 1963. Of her ten pregnancies, he said four children had been stillborn, and one child had died at age two.

The others were alive, he said, ranging in age from age two to thirteen years old.

He had no memory of any head injuries, epilepsy or any other major illness, none, at least, that he admitted to. He did mention that he had broken his thumbs while in military service and once had had an infected toenail. He would not admit to any previous psychiatric history in his family. He denied any cruelty to animals or pyromania but did say that he had wet his bed at night until age twelve. There was no way to determine the reliability of the history he provided the doctors.

"Mr. Walford, how are you feeling?" Dr. Jacobson asked.

"I feel much better," Walford replied. "I was very sick, those days, but now I am better."

"What days do you mean?"

"I was sick when I was arrested," he answered.

Walford sat in the cell. Occasionally his leg trembled and his hands shook, but his voice was moderate, clear, still marked with his Caribbean accent and its singsong, high-low quality. He remained calm, if slightly detached and cooperative. He was not unfriendly. Throughout, he was polite, not evasive. He was not disorganized in his thinking, nor did he jump about verbally, arguing and exaggerating as before. The only tenseness that Jacobson could discern appeared when he asked about Walford's religious beliefs.

"Do you know what day it is?" The doctor asked.

"Yes," Walford replied. "Today is the first day of December. It is 1976."

"Tell me, who has been elected president of the United States?"

"Mr. Jimmy Carter. He has defeated Mr. Ford."

"And the prime minister of Jamaica..."

"Is Mr. Manley."

Jacobson hesitated, taking notes. He knew, from reviewing Walford's Chattahoochee records, that he had been overtly psychotic from his admission up until the beginning of November, when the cumulative effect of the drugs had finally broken down his psychosis. "Do you hear the voices still?"

"No. The voice left me, three, four months back."

Prolixin, the doctor thought. It does away with most voices.

"What is thirteen added to fifty-nine?"

Walford paused. Several quiet seconds passed.

"Seventy-two," he said.

Jacobson wondered what Walford was thinking about. He seemed preoccupied.

"What is one hundred minus seven?"

Another pause.

"Ninety-two," Walford said, incorrectly.

"Minus another seven?"

"Eighty-seven."

"Minus seven?"

Pause. "Seventy-eight."

"What is five times twenty-five."

Silence. Then: "Two hundred and twenty-five."

Walford's body trembled. Jacobson thought of their first meeting. "Do you still read the Bible?"

"Yes. I read my Bible often."

"Tell me about Adam and Eve?" Jacobson thought of Walford's wild sexual interpretation of the apple that had emerged two years before.

"God took one of Adam's ribs and fashioned Eve."

"What does that mean to you?"

"It means that Adam and Eve are made of the same flesh. It is a symbol, put there so that little children cannot understand it."

Jacobson thought again of the elements of their first conversation. "Did white people write it so to deceive black people?"

"No," said Walford. "What do you mean by that?"

"That is what you said before."

Walford shook his head slowly, as if trying to clear an awkward memory, but he said nothing. Jacobson continued taking notes. He would later report to Judge Wetherington that Walford was competent to stand trial, but he would place on his report the caveat that the remission was caused by the chemicals and that Walford remained a very dangerous man.

Dr. Charles Mutter went to see Walford a few days before Jacobson. He took careful notes, quoting Walford on several key points. As with the others, Walford was polite, clear, unevasive and straightforward.

"Tell me," Mutter asked, "when you first heard voices."

Walford hesitated for just the briefest of seconds, then said, "One day, when I was in the prison in Kingston in 1973, I was reading my Bible. Suddenly the thoughts came very fast; one day my body became big, the room lit up and a voice told me He was God! And I had to do what He said. He told me what to read in the Bible.

"I felt like it was a special gift. Or power. I used to go into the streets and catch a bus; we had a little religious service on the bus. I would preach like a power came through me. The power told me to preach. It was like it was some other man's voice."

"And you came to Miami on the marijuana boat?"

"The voice and the power told me that it was all right to come to Miami with those men."

Walford's head shook slightly, perhaps from the drugs, perhaps from the memory.

"When you heard the voice, could you resist? What would happen if you didn't obey?"

"I was too frightened. I felt my body expanding... it physically got bigger and bigger! The voice had complete control! I could not resist what it told me. I must obey! I must obey! I was too scared."

Dr. Mutter, too, would say Walford was competent to stand trial but remained very dangerous.

All the doctors asked Walford about the murder.

He did not hesitate to tell them.

Some detected remorse in his tone.

Others thought he remained confused.

He described what he did, briefly, to the point.

He answered the question, not elaborating.

He did not mention Arnold's piteous scream, or his panicked struggle, or the fear in his eyes when he was caught in that inexorable grip. He related the details of the murder with the same detached coldness that he'd had when he'd inexplicably incorrectly answered Jacobson's testing of his mental faculties with the questions on addition, subtraction and multiplication. It was as if there were no great difference.

"I woke up that morning, and I felt my body expanding. It was growing big, then small. I had a funny feeling that this person was God, telling me what to do. He kept controlling me, telling me where to go, what to do. He told me to go to the airport and tell the people about God. So I went to the airport and began preaching to the people there. It was around noon when He told me to go and buy a knife. I was told I must go and buy a knife. I went to the store. I bought a knife. I returned back to my hotel to eat, I was hungry. I took the food into the hotel room, but I could not eat. I took a few sips of water. He told me to read the Bible. It was Isaiah. My body began to get big again. He told me to take the knife and stand by the door. I waited. Minutes passed. Ten minutes. Fifteen minutes. Then He said, 'Step outside and take what you find there!' I opened the door, and I saw the boy come running. He told me, 'Catch the boy!' and hold him. I did. He said, 'Take the boy to the bathroom!' I did. The door shut, as if He closed it. He said, 'Cut the boy's neck and leave him there!' I did. He said, 'Come on now!' So I followed and went outside. There was blood on my pants, but He said not to mind. At the airport He said, 'Get into the cab!' and I did. But the policeman came then and took me to jail."

One doctor wrote: "...During all this time he was hearing voices and knew what he had done and did feel sorry. He does not still understand why the voices told him to do this. . . . From time to time he thinks of what he has done and he states that he has sad feelings, regretting what has happened. . . ."

He told how, but he did not tell why.

3. *The Three Michaels*

There were two key hearings before Judge Wetherington at which the two defense attorneys and the prosecutor argued over the question of bringing Walford to trial. The first hearing, in early December, went for the state. The second, in January, went for the defense.

After meeting with Walford, Tarkoff and Von Zamft threw themselves into the preparation of the case. They worked nonstop, weekends, nights, readying themselves for trial. They could tell that they would no longer be able to argue, as their predecessors had done successfully, that Walford wouldn't or couldn't cooperate with the defense attorneys. Indeed, now he was not only cooperative but occasionally remorseful. His volatile intelligence perhaps was masked by the drugs, but he was still far more aware than many of the clients the two young lawyers had represented. They also could not argue that he would disrupt the trial proceedings. "God, not man!" had been replaced by a sedate, controlled state.

They thought: We're going to trial.

They poured themselves into the case.

They contacted Evan Semerjian, the Zelezniks' Boston attorney, and he forwarded them copies of Walford's Northampton records. At first they thought it a gold mine of information, but then they recognized that it cut both ways. On the one hand, they would be able to show a jury that Walford's madness had preceded the murder, that he had been hospitalized, that he had been assaultive, that he had behaved psychotically for weeks before the murder. In that context, Arnold's death would be just one more mad act among many performed by a legally insane individual. But on the other hand—and this was a large but—would not a jury see that Walford had already been hospitalized once and then had walked free, only to murder an innocent child? And would it not be an extraordinary leap of faith for the defense lawyers to ask a jury to acquit their client, free him of any criminal court jurisdiction and turn him over to a mental system which would probably release him again?

Von Zamft and Tarkoff knew the answer to that question.

They tracked down the doctors who'd seen Walford in Massachusetts, finding one through the American Medical Association at a hospital in Tennessee. They collected all the witnesses to Walford's madness. They wanted to barrage a jury with a massive sequence of wild, crazy acts, placing Arnold's death in the midst. It was a good defense, they thought, almost a perfect defense.

But one they feared was inevitably a loser.

At the same time Tarkoff and Von Zamft spent hours in the law library adjacent to the Public Defender's Office on the eighth floor of the Metro Justice Building. The question they sought to determine was: Was chemical competency truly competency? Did the state have the right to force a man to take drugs in order to put him on trial for murder?

They were concerned, too, that the drugs hurt their ability to portray the Vernal Walford that had murdered Arnold Zeleznik. They wanted a jury to see him at his maddest and most frightening, the Walford of the videotape, not the pudgy, docile, shaggy-haired man who trembled before them now.

When the psychiatric reports came in, they were uniform: All the doctors said that Walford was competent to stand trial. It was an ironic reversal. In 1974–75, right after the murder, the doctors had been on the defense side. Now they were aligned with the prosecution. The task for Von Zamft and Tarkoff was to manipulate what they were saying so that it cut their way, not the prosecution's.

And the drugs became their sword.

The two men spent hours with medical texts examining the effects of the phenothiazine and hydrochloride compounds and the anti-Parkinson's medications Walford was receiving. They discovered that some of the symptoms Walford was demonstrating were close to becoming irreversible. That became the crack into which they poured their energies.

They found that the amount of drugs Walford needed to render him competent also damaged his liver, stomach and cardio-vascular system. The involuntary facial twitching, in which his jaw would suddenly move laterally and his tongue dart in and out like a fly-catching frog, was close to becoming something he would have for the rest of his life. Similarly he was experiencing greater and greater degrees of loss of control over his body movements. The two attorneys found that it was not an uncommon sight, in back wards of large state mental hospitals, to have patients manifesting all the same symptoms, trapped in a vise created by the antipsychotic drugs and their madness. It was one or the other.

Von Zamft checked the Miami psychiatric community for a doctor to examine Walford and analyze those symptoms. He wanted to find someone previously unconnected with the courts, preferably someone with lofty cre-

dentials, who would impress Judge Wetherington. He discovered his man in
Dr. Brian Weiss of the University of Miami Medical School. A young Yale-
trained psychiatrist and neurophysicist, he was an expert on the effects of
chemicals on the brain. Von Zamft enlisted him and sent him to see Walford.

In the meantime, the first of the two hearings before Judge Gerald Wetherington was held. Wetherington was an exceptionally bright judge, a south-
erner with a thick, good-old-boy accent that periodically dropped away when
he rendered an opinion to reveal a highly informed, trained legal scholar. He
had replaced Judge Williams as chief of the Criminal Division of the Dade
Circuit Court. A few years afterward he would be named chief judge for the
entire Eleventh Judicial Circuit. He was a man of unquestioned integrity and
toughness.

On December 13, a Monday, the first hearing was held in a vest-pocket-
size courtroom on the third floor of the Justice Building. Outside the courtroom, the five doctors scheduled to testify—Sanford Jacobson, Arthur Stillman, William Corwin, Charles Mutter and Albert Jaslow—exchanged
pleasantries and went over their reports and their handwritten notes. Michael
Korvick took each aside, checking to make certain that they were going to
stick with their reports and not waver. Tarkoff and Von Zamft had their heads
together at the small defense table. Their questioning, they agreed, was going
to be directed at the amounts of drugs and what they were doing to Walford.

I sat a row behind them, doing what reporters do, which is wait, doodle,
try to overhear some of their conversation and try to think of the direction of
the story. Mostly, though, I waited for my first sight of Vernal Walford.

The slaying had come to fascinate me.

I had first heard of Arnold Zeleznik's murder in the fall of 1976, a year
earlier, shortly after I had joined the staff of the *Miami News,* the city's second
newspaper. My assignment was the county's criminal courts. I spent my days
wandering through the courtrooms, hallways and corridors of the Metro Justice
Building. I was twenty-six. I discovered that two years after the crime the
murder still had a resonance for the courthouse regulars. Other murders were
contrasted with the memory of Arnold Zeleznik's killing, brutality measured
by a standard created in room 206 on December 20, 1974.

I came to think of it as a crime of absolutes: complete madness intersecting
with total innocence; the barest contact resulting in the most unimaginable of
tragedies.

Within the criminal justice system in Dade County, the crime carried a
unique momentum. The world of cops, courts, crimes, prosecutors, defense
attorneys is a land within a land, a peninsula of society and law that has its

own standards and rules. It is an illusory place, where what is said is part of a drama, where the players have designated roles. It is a truism that criminal courthouses resemble theaters. There are dramatis personae, a set, a scene, necessary dialogue. Memory and action blend on the stage of the court, the difference being that the stakes are higher: life, liberty and future at issue. In Miami, Arnold Zeleznik's murder was recalled with an unusual fervor, less because of the victim than because the killer had had such a singular effect upon the society of justice.

Walford was remembered.

If not his name, then "the man who killed the little boy" was sufficient. As was usually the case, the victims were relegated to the rear of the memory. Walford was the focus, the center of attention for the criminal justice system in Miami.

I had heard all the stories that circulated in the courthouse about Walford. They seemed the stuff of nightmare and fantasy: that he had screamed for thirty-six straight hours; that it had taken eight jail guards to subdue him; that he had been injected with enough tranquilizers to deaden a half dozen men and had raged on, unaffected; that in his cell he had become more animal than man. One afternoon I asked one forensic psychiatrist on his way to testify in a trial if he knew Walford. The doctor, a respected man, had hesitated slightly, mouth open, selecting his words. "He was," the doctor had said slowly, "the craziest man I've ever seen."

So I waited, wondering what apparition would step into Judge Wetherington's courtroom.

He was brought in through a rear door from a holding cell just beyond a soundproofed wall. There were four guards with him, their memories of Walford apparently little affected by his current appearance and circumstances. I looked up as he passed. His head was down, his feet shuffled, he walked with the hesitancy and stiffness of a man beaten severely a day before. His eyes, though, darted through the courtroom until they rested on his attorneys. He nodded to them, without smiling.

He knows the stakes, I thought.

He sat down in the empty jury box, breathing heavily. Guards surrounded him. His eyes were downcast. He seemed more pitiable than evil: unkempt, palsied, ravaged by the drugs. I could see the involuntary twitching and shaking, the lip fasciculation and the tremors that shook his face and body. I thought of the man I had seen in the videotape and the man before me and shook my head. They were two different men.

And then the judge swept in, and the hearing began.

The doctors took the stand, one after the other.

Korvick kept his questioning simple and to the point. He asked what their examinations had revealed and then what conclusions they had reached. Competent. Competent. Competent. Competent. Competent. When Korvick finished his questioning of each doctor, he sat down confidently.

Tarkoff and Von Zamft, taking turns, questioned the doctors about the irreversible quality of the drugs. The experts conceded the point but contended that the amounts were not, as Jacobson said, "out of line." Each doctor candidly admitted that without the drugs Vernal Walford would slowly, certainly, terrifyingly revert to the exceptionally dangerous state that he'd been in at the time of the murder.

The testimony took several hours. Wetherington limited the arguments, and Korvick complied. He remained low-key and fastened to a single conclusion: There was consensus. Order a trial date.

Tarkoff and Von Zamft set off on a different tack. They said that it was unfair to require their client to take drugs that were harming him in order to put him on trial for first-degree murder. It was an Eighth Amendment argument, cruel and unusual punishment. They claimed that Walford was being punished prior to trial and that the drugs, at best, did not make him truly competent, but only masked the real Walford.

Wetherington bought none of it.

"They say he's competent, I'm going to order a trial date," he told the attorneys.

Von Zamft and Tarkoff exploded.

"That's unfair to our client!" Tarkoff said, almost shouting. "They want to kill him in order to kill him!"

"Your Honor," Von Zamft said, his voice on the edge of control, "I won't be party to it! If my client is competent, then I will advise him to not take any drugs. Surely a competent man has that right? To refuse treatment that is not in his best interests!"

"You will do nothing of the sort," Wetherington said. His southern accent had diminished sharply. He stared at the two lawyers.

"I don't see how in conscience I can allow my client to allow himself to be tried for first-degree murder and face the electric chair by taking drugs that are hurting him!" Von Zamft said. He turned toward the defense table.

"Don't turn your back on me," Wetherington said, his voice not raised but filled with exaggerated calmness, each word weighted with anger. "If you give that advice to your client, you will find yourself occupying the cell next to him. Do I make myself perfectly clear?"

Von Zamft sucked in his breath. I could see 100 challenging retorts in his face. He controlled himself. "Yes, Your Honor."

He paused for a second before continuing. He looked at Tarkoff, who was himself gripping the edge of the table. Then Von Zamft smiled, a humorless smile. "We would request an immediate trial date, Your Honor."

"That you can have," Wetherington replied, his voice still cold and angry. He started to flip through the pages of his trial docket,

"We would request next Monday, Your Honor. December Twentieth."

"You want it, you've got it," Wetherington replied coldly.

Korvick, who had been quiet throughout the outburst, jumped up. "That's outrageous!" he said. "Not only do we need more time to prepare, but that is the anniversary of the little boy's murder!" He glared at Von Zamft.

"I'll set a date on Friday," Wetherington said. He, too, was glaring at the two defense lawyers. "This court is in recess!"

I finally got a moment to look up from my pad, where I had been scribbling the exchange between judge and lawyers, and glance to where Walford was sitting. It was difficult to tell whether the shaking in his head was due to the drugs or the knowledge that he was going to face a jury. He grasped Von Zamft's hands briefly, as the guards escorted him slowly, almost painfully, from the courtroom.

4. An Interested Party

No one called the Zelezniks.

Although it was policy in the Dade State Attorney's Office to keep the victims of crime informed about the legal developments, that policy was consistently not adhered to in their case. There is no reasonable explanation for why it wasn't.

Carter learned that Walford was scheduled for trial when friends who had heard the news on a local Philadelphia television station mentioned it in passing. His friend Richard Innis, the attorney who had helped monitor what was taking place in Florida, had also not been informed. When Innis called on Carter's behalf, he learned that Wetherington was considering beginning the trial on the twentieth. The following day the attorney learned that Wetherington had reset the trial date for late February or March.

What the hell's going on down there? Carter wondered angrily.

Doesn't anybody care?

He wrote what could be considered a remarkably constrained letter, under the circumstances, to Korvick:

January 5th, 1977

Dear Mr. Corvick:

I hope that I have spelled your name properly and I would appreciate your informing me about any necessary corrections. I am writing to you with regard to the upcoming trial of one Vernal Walford, who is the alleged murderer of my son, Arnold Frank Zeleznik.... Insofar as I am an interested party to the proceedings, I am concerned with the preparations being made for the trial and my role in it as well as the roles of my wife and remaining son, Robert Carter Zeleznik.

I must, however, immediately express my indignation at not having been kept properly abreast of the developments in this case.... I was shocked to learn [from his attorney] on December 13th that my family and I were expected to be in Miami on December 20th for the trial to begin on that date. December 20th, of course, is the anniversary date of Arnold's death. The short time period also suggested that there would be little opportunity for proper preparations for the trial on your part.

[My attorney] advised me that you personally would contact me either on December 17th or 20th. Until this moment, I have received no communication from you or your office....

I do believe that my family and I should be given the same advance notice of the trial date as the defendant is.... When I spoke with my attorney, he advised me to cooperate with you and your office fully. I intend to do this even though it will be a cause of anguish and emotional upsetment for myself, and more importantly, for my family. However, by the same token, I would look forward to assurances that the case as prepared by your office will be thorough and diligent in all regards.

My observations of the initial competency hearing conducted...in January, 1975, are that it was neither. I am prepared to document my observations in detail and I intend to do so. I fear that the poor showing at the time of the original competency hearing in 1975 may seriously prejudice your own work at this time. Hopefully, with considerable effort on your part now, some of that can be overcome.

...I am prepared to offer my own services in areas where they may be useful. I have made a survey of the medico-legal literature on the subject of the examination of expert psychiatric witnesses.... I have identified a number of sources in this area I trust you are familiar with. It is my feeling, however, that there are grievous conceptual inadequacies in all the references.... I have therefore decided to write my own text on the subject in hopes that it may be useful to you and to others concerned with these matters. I intend to use [the Walford] trial as a means of demonstrating principles to be brought forth in that handbook.... I am also prepared, if you wish, to offer you the opportunity of serving as a co-author of the work as a kind of compensation to you for your efforts. . . . I would personally feel more comfortable having an individual from your profession working with me on this book and I would intend to obtain such collaboration anyway. In any event, I propose to use the upcoming Walford trial as the main vehicle of the work so that it may in time become a classic of how to examine expert psychiatric witnesses in criminal proceedings.

I shall look forward to immediate contact from your office insofar as there is little time left. Indications of a high level of commitment to the preparation for the prosecution of this case will serve to allay my anxieties.

Sincerely,
Carter Zeleznik

Carter's letter prompted a cryptic memo from Dade State Attorney Richard Gerstein to Michael Korvick: "I am disturbed by the contents of this letter. Please reply to it immediately with a copy to me."

A week later Korvick sent this letter to Carter:

Dear Mr. Zeleznik:

I am prosecuting the case against Vernal Walford and I am being assisted by the chief of the Major Crimes Division, Terrence McWilliams.

Terrence McWilliams has had more experience and more success in prosecuting homicide cases involving insanity defenses than anyone else in the State Attorney's Office over the last decade. We are both vigorously and strenuously pursuing trial preparations, which are multifaceted and exist on many levels.

Please be advised that the trial date is March 21, 1977, before the Honorable Gerald Wetherington. Barring something unforeseen, the trial will proceed that week, starting on Monday. Your travel arrangements will be made in coordination with this office, to assure you and your family no inconveniences.

Arrangements will be made with you in the immediate future for a pre-trial conference, at a mutually agreeable date, here in Miami.

I understand your keen interest to be kept properly advised of developments in this case. Prior to December 13, the defendant had been adjudicated by the court to be incompetent for trial and the defendant had been at the state mental hospital. On that date Judge Wetherington, after a full and complete competency hearing, as required by law, adjudicated the defendant competent for trial, although the defendant is presently being treated with an extremely high dosage of psychotropic medication and his body shakes visibly and uncontrollably. The court then set at the defendant's request, a trial date for December 20th, over my strenuous objections. That trial date was intolerable to the state and on December 17th, 1976, at the State's request, the court rescheduled the trial for a date in March.

I agree with you entirely that a trial in the week of December 20th, 1976, would have been inhumane to you and your family, to say the least, and such a date certainly would not have allowed adequate preparation time for trial. It was for those same reasons that the defendant's attorneys demanded such an early trial date.

In speaking with your attorney, I thought I had basically conveyed the same information to him and that he would speak to you accordingly. The last thing I wanted to do was to upset you and your family at that particular time, and I intentionally did not communicate directly with you or your family. I sincerely apologize for any discomfort or grief you and your family suffered, which I may have prevented.

I am interested in your ideas concerning the prosecution of this case and will be in communication with you in the near future.

> Sincerely yours,
> Michael John Korvick
> Assistant State Attorney

I went to see Korvick one morning not long after the exchange of letters. He had the file in a drawer in his desk. He pulled it out and started flipping through the eight-by-ten color glossy photographs of the murder scene and Arnold's body. "Jesus," he muttered to himself.

He showed me Carter's letter and directed my attention to the part in which Carter described the text he wanted to write. "See," Korvick said, "he wants to write his own book." In his tone was a note of distaste, as if he had perceived Carter as wishing to profit off of Arnold's death. At least that was how I interpreted Korvick's tone.

"No, he doesn't, Mike," I said. "He wants to write some sort of scholarly or medical text. What's wrong with that?"

"He'll probably ace you out," Korvick replied. He smiled. He knew of my interest in the case. Every prosecutor I have ever known has enjoyed ribbing journalists about the stories they pursue.

Korvick looked over at the file. "What a mess," he said.

"Why?"

"Not for a story?"

"Well, not now."

"Okay. Look at this. I mean, they almost caught the guy red-handed, right. He refuses to give a statement, but that's okay because they've got him. But nobody does the fingerprint work; nobody does the blood work; nobody interviews all the witnesses. Nobody finds the murder weapon.

"And then look at all the doctors. Everybody agrees Vernal was out of his skull crazy. What have I got to go against that?"

"How about public opinion—"

"In a court of law? How do I get past a directed verdict of insanity? Where's some piece of evidence so that the judge will say, 'Okay, send it to the jury'? I have to be able to provide something to contradict all the doctors. That's the problem."

He shuffled through the papers. "It's a loser," he said. "It was a loser a long time before I got hold of it."

He shrugged.

"No chance?" I asked.

"It was a loser the instant it happened."

I spoke with Edward Carhart, a brilliant trial attorney, who was the chief assistant in the office. Is it fair for the state to require Walford to take the drugs, even if they are killing him, so he can be put on trial? I asked. What is served?

Carhart's reply was typically laconic. "It was a savage crime. A despicable crime. It demands that the jury hear the facts. If they think he should be excused because of his mental state, then so be it. But a jury should hear the facts." I put his quote in a story for the paper.

As the prosecutors saw it, the primary problem was still getting past a directed verdict from the bench. They had to have some evidence to present in counterpoint to the opinions of the doctors lined up for the defense. In effect, the state had to turn Walford's mental state at the time of the murder into a question only a jury could resolve. They never really surmounted that problem, and the doubt seemed to color the entire prosecution effort. "A loser," Mike Korvick had said, and he was not alone in that feeling. Years later Mike Tarkoff would say, "It always seemed to us that the state thought we had a stronger case than we did. It was as if they thought we had the perfect insanity defense, when we didn't. So they just never really argued anything...."

What the defense lawyers saw was a client who'd committed a mad act but knew it was wrong and took steps to flee and avoid capture and detection. Maybe a voice had commanded him to do it, but he still acted guilty as hell, from the instant of the murder onward.

But the state never saw it that way.

Chief Assistant Carhart's strong words were, ultimately, utterly empty.

5. *Tardive Dyskinesia*

Brian Weiss was a slight, dark-haired, bookish man, with the pallor of a psychiatrist, a man who stays in a darkened room too long each day. He went to the Dade County Jail on Friday, January 21, to see Vernal Walford and spent more than an hour talking with him. A few days later he wrote Michael Von Zamft a brief letter detailing his experience.

Walford told Dr. Weiss that he still felt he was right to obey the voice when it told him to murder Arnold.

Then Weiss wrote:

. . . Of particular interest is his physical reaction to the medicines. He has developed extrapyramidal side-effects, necessitating dosage reductions and simultaneous Cogentin administration. Tongue fasciculations and movements, enhanced with finger movements, as well as lip-smacking, shaking of the upper extremities, and occasional involuntary grimacing and mouth movements, all serve to document a mild tardive dyskinesia. This neurological condition will invariably worsen with further antipsychotic chemotherapy and he could become incapacitated. The only treatment is to withdraw all psychotropics at this time, before the condition becomes irreversible.

Perfect, Von Zamft thought. Walford is on the verge of an irreversible condition. The medication is harming him every second it is continued. What judge is going to have that on his conscience?

At the same time Tarkoff found a U.S. Supreme Court case that seemed to provide them the legal leverage they needed. The court had ruled in a Massachusetts case that the state could not require schoolchildren to take smallpox shots against the family's wishes. He saw a parallel with Walford. Clearly it was against his better interests to go on trial, so how could the state require him to take the drugs?

It was something they could argue. Coupled with Weiss's testimony, it might even be successful. They also leaked to me exactly what they were going to do, and I wrote the predictable story: "Do Drugs Make Defendant Capable for Trial?" It ran on the front page of the *Miami News*. A little more pressure on the judge, the attorneys thought.

Korvick was not initially aware of the tack being taken by the defense. Despite his pessimism, he was still laboring to put the case together. He sent out memos to all the forensic specialists and detectives, the medical examiner and the fingerprint men, telling them to complete their work in the case and to get ready for trial. He set up pretrial conferences and got lead Detective Ed Carberry to start checking Walford's background for voodoo activity or anything else that might help. He subpoenaed records from the Immigration and Naturalization Service. He sent a subpoena to the Jamaican Consulate in Miami, requesting their help in obtaining medical, school and army records from Jamaica. The consulate sent back an angry letter saying it wouldn't help at all. He never managed to get any records, if they existed.

As with any trial, especially one as potentially explosive as Walford's, there was a flurry of pretrial motions. The state filed requests for blood, hair, fingernail and handwriting samples from Walford, which were granted. Tarkoff and Von Zamft sent in a batch of mostly routine motions—requests for jury venire lists and so on. Mingled with these was the "Defense Motion to Preclude the Administration of Drugs."

It was their method of getting back into the competency issue. It was set for January 27.

When Korvick started asking questions about the drugs, he would run into the dilemma outlined by Weiss: Walford was caught in an infernal bind. Without the drugs, he would inevitably return to madness. With the drugs, he was being turned into a quaking, vegetablelike nonperson. He was, in effect, being killed by the drugs.

The proper medical treatment for tardive dyskinesia was to cut off the antipsychotic medicines and then reestablish them very gradually, to the point where they did not induce the motor effects manifested by Walford but still controlled his intellectual capacities.

As a prosecutor Korvick was also trapped in a horrendous ethical dilemma. Revenge is not a legally sufficient reason for bringing a man to trial, especially when it costs the man so much. Korvick was left with little outlet. He would again be deserted by the doctors. All would agree with Weiss about the proper treatment of the tardive dyskinesia. To treat Walford properly meant resigning oneself to seeing his competency evaporate in an unrelenting tidal course of madness.

I saw Korvick prior to the hearing. When I started to ask him a question, he simply shook his head in disappointment.

The first witness was Dr. Casademont, the psychiatrist attached to the Dade County Jail. He was questioned briefly by Tarkoff. Casademont said that he had decreased the amounts of drugs given to Walford from the level on which the state hospital had placed him when he'd seen the initial stages of tardive dyskinesia.

"Why didn't you take Mr. Walford off antipsychotics?" Tarkoff demanded.

Casademont shook his head. He, too, remembered the Walford of two years previous. "I don't have the facilities to give Mr. Walford appropriate supervision. . . ."

"If you had the proper facilities, you would have withdrawn the medication?"

"I would have done so."

Korvick sat at the prosecution table. "No questions," he said.

However, Judge Wetherington interrupted. "Now wait a second. Are you telling me that the drugs that you are giving this man is causing him to have this condition, this tardive dyskinesia?"

"Yes, sir," the doctor replied.

"Are you telling me there is an alternative to that?"

"Well, if you pardon the expression, sir, it is a damned-if-you-do and damned-if-you-don't situation."

"What do you mean by that?"

"If the medications are discontinued, it would render this psychotic disorder to return."

Minutes later Weiss took the witness stand. He looked slightly nervous and spoke in a quiet voice that was hard to hear. Von Zamft questioned him. First he went through Weiss's impressive list of credentials; then he asked about his examination of Walford.

"He is suffering from two groups of side effects. One is called drug-induced Parkinsonism, which is an extrapyramidal neurological side effect, characterized by stiffness in muscles, Parkinsonlike tremors. And tardive dyskinesia . . . an irreversible effect of long-term administration of certain drugs. It is involuntary rhythmic movements of mouth, jaw, sometimes the lip-smacking, called a fly-catching maneuver of the tongue."

"What is the outcome of a person who suffers from this?" Von Zamft asked.

"Eventually the person has no control over these muscular movements. He becomes similar to those people who have Huntington's chorea, which is more familiar."

"Is there any known treatment?"

"The only treatment is to withdraw all medications. . . ."

"Have you ever explained to Mr. Walford the consequences of what the drugs he is taking will be?"

"I have talked with him about the tardive dyskinesia. He told me he wishes to be off the medicine if they are going to cause the side effects."

"If he was your private patient, what would you do?"

"I would hospitalize him and take him off the medicine."

On the bench Judge Wetherington appeared deep in thought. He had leaned forward during Weiss's testimony. When the doctor finished, he pushed back, rocking in the black padded leather seat. He turned toward Korvick. "Cross examination?"

Korvick barely stirred. "No questions, Judge."

"Anything from the state?"

"No, Your Honor."

Von Zamft stood before Wetherington. "We would ask the court to order that he be taken off the drugs and sent back to the hospital to be treated properly."

I glanced over at Walford. As before, he was sitting in the empty jury box, occasionally shaking, twitching and jerking. He showed little else, although his eyes stayed on the judge, as if measuring him.

Korvick rose then and said, "Judge, I am not going to even attempt to interfere with what one doctor says he should receive and what another doctor might disagree about. I think it is a matter that should be determined by the doctors. We can't start giving medical treatment or advising it, I should say. . . ." Then he sat down.

Wetherington hesitated, thinking.

He stared out at Tarkoff and Von Zamft as he made his ruling, not at Walford. The defendant was obscured by two huge jail guards, who bracketed him as the judge spoke.

". . . I have told you before that many people come to trial on certain levels of medication, just as insulin restores people with diabetes to acceptable levels of health. In any such case, that is appropriate; someone can stand trial, notwithstanding the fact they are receiving medication.

"However, I won't have somebody receive medications for the purpose of having them stand trial if it constitutes a significant and substantial danger to that person's health. . . ."

The judge fixed his eyes on me and several other members of the press.

"We do not have that type of system over here. We don't do that in this country, and there is no social value significant enough to bring this man to trial at the expense of the substantial impairment of his health, and that is not going to happen as I sit here.

"I will declare him at this particular time not in a position to go to trial. . . ."

I looked toward Walford, but he remained hidden.

Wetherington swept from the bench.

Korvick stood, took a deep breath, gathered his papers and walked slowly from the courtroom.

Tarkoff and Von Zamft shook hands, grinning broadly.

Walford stood and moved gingerly across the courtroom. He paused to shake hands with his attorneys and mumble his thanks. Von Zamft said that he and Tarkoff would come over to the jail to see him, and Walford nodded.

Then, surrounded by guards, he shuffled off through the rear courtroom door, without any outward reaction. I wondered if he realized what was coming. I tried to imagine that first moment of madness, when the cumulative effects of the drugs wore off and the hospital room again filled with an otherworldly bright light and the voice filled him with his inviolable passion.

6. A Visit

Several months later Michael Tarkoff went to see Walford at the state mental hospital at Chattahoochee. Judge Wetherington's final, signed order called for periodic reports on Walford's condition. Tarkoff went up to collect information for one of those reports. He was accompanied by Dennis Urbano, another young assistant public defender, who had some witness depositions to take in Tallahassee. Tarkoff agreed to help Urbano with the depositions if Urbano would come to the hospital with him.

It was raining. The North Florida sky was overcast, a solid mass of gray. The huge walls of the mental hospital were streaked with dark stains from hard rain. This looks like something out of a grade B Hollywood picture, Tarkoff thought. The madhouse rose up on a bluff overlooking a river, its own darkness blending with the gray sky. Tarkoff's impression was underscored as he and Urbano were led into the maximum security wing. Each locked and bolted door, the chained fence and alarm system added to the weight of the impression.

A white-jacketed orderly showed them to a small interview room. There was a small table, where they waited. In a few seconds Walford came through the door. Tarkoff noticed the changes in him immediately. Walford's athletic build was taking shape, the loose folds of skin firming again into muscle, his movements more precise, more controlled. His eyes seemed clearer, penetrating. Walford's voice was direct, not loud, but carrying a distinct severity.

"How are you?" Tarkoff asked.

"I am fine," Walford replied.

"No medication?"

"No, they give me some. It is not much."

Tarkoff noticed that the trembling had greatly diminished. Walford's facial tremors now were about the same as a nervous tic.

"You look better," Tarkoff said.

"There is an exercise area. I lift weights. I run. I work out. It is much better for me."

"Do you remember what happened with the little boy?"

"Yes. I remember."

There was a silence. Tarkoff felt Walford's gaze burrowing into him. He had the sensation that the room was getting smaller, or Walford larger, and he felt choked. He thought then he would not pursue that line of questioning.

"Do you hear the voices again?"

"There is only one voice."

"And?"

"I hear Him many times."

"When was the last time you heard the voice?"

Walford smiled.

"I hear Him right now."

Tarkoff saw Urbano's eyes widen. The young attorney quietly got up from his chair and edged out the door.

"What does the voice tell you?"

"He tells me what to say to you now. He tells me what to do."

Tarkoff saw Walford's muscles tightening and relaxing beneath his sport shirt. No more questions, he thought. Let's get the hell out of here. He smiled and stood up. "Thanks, Vernal. I've got to get back to Miami now. I'll be in touch again soon. Take care of yourself, all right?"

Walford stood. His hands clenched into fists, then dropped to his sides. He nodded and walked through the door. An attendant met him there, and Tarkoff watched as Walford disappeared through a set of swinging doors and down a whitewashed corridor, and it was to the lawyer as if Walford had been suddenly absorbed by a flash of heavenly brightness, encapsulated in a burst of white-hot heat.

Only One Side

There's only one side when you lose your son. . . .
—Peg Mullen, quoted in *Friendly
Fire*, by C. D. B. Bryan

1. ". . . a Rather Slow, Methodical Thinker . . ."

Every three months the computers that kept track of the thousands of defendants who were charged each year in the Dade circuit courts put Walford's
name on the docket sheet under the title "Report re Defendant." These no-
tations would translate into a few minutes of court time; Michael Korvick
would get up and say that the state had no information that Walford's condition
had changed for the better, and the court would head on to the next case.
Walford, chameleonlike, had blended into the system.

The Zelezniks, too, were adrift.

Their hope of seeing Walford successfully prosecuted was effectively shattered following a late April 1977 visit to Miami. It was an extraordinary visit;
Korvick had decided to complete many of the trial preparations despite his
belief that in all likelihood they were useless, and as part of that pretrial work,
he brought Carter, Betty and Bobby down to Miami to meet with him. There
was a lack of vigor in those preparations, though; they lacked the almost
ritualistic absorption and intensity that prosecutors undergo prior to a first-
degree murder trial. His preparations took place in a vacuum created by the
vagaries of Walford's madness. The Zelezniks, utterly inexperienced when
it came to understanding the motivations of criminal court work, walked into
the situation expecting to be caught up in an aggressive atmosphere, in which
the accent would be on bringing Walford to the bar and forcing him to face
the results of his actions. They could not have been more mistaken. The state
was doing nothing to bring about a trial. The prosecution was waiting for the

doctors at Chattahoochee to tell them Walford had once again reached competency. Without that development they did nothing. There was nothing they could do.

Perhaps "nothing" is an overstatement. The state did perform some rudimentary tasks. Michael Korvick stopped me in the hallway of the State Attorney's Office one day and said, "You know, we found the murder weapon."

"Where?"

"Buried, in the landscaping just outside the front door."

He did not seem excited by the discovery.

"A gardener was going through the bushes—you know, scraping and raking away at the underbrush—and he spotted the handle stuck in the earth. He pulled it out and remembered the crime and gave it to the cops."

"Can it be checked for blood or fingerprints?"

"It's been stuck in the ground for a couple of years. There's not much of it left. I sent it over to the lab anyway."

The murder weapon had been discovered precisely where the squads of police auxiliaries had searched. Apparently, as best as could be determined, upon leaving the hotel Walford had reached down and scooped out some of the soft dirt of the landscaping. He had then thrust the knife, blade down, as far as he could into the ground and swept more dirt over the top, so that the entire knife had been effectively buried. The voice commanding him certainly seemed to be knowledgeable about how to flee from a murder scene.

It would subsequently turn out that the lab was unable to process the remains of the knife for blood type or prints.

In contrast with what the State Attorney's Office was doing, or not doing, Carter was enmeshed in the issues of Walford's criminal responsibility. He had thrown himself into analyzing the problems presented by Walford's case and the insanity defense.

The idea of the "book" about the case had mostly been a manifestation of that research, coupled with Carter's grief and his legal impotence. His whole life had been devoted to outlining questions and then aggressively seeking answers; he could barely tolerate the shrugging acceptance of Walford's legal situation.

His frustration was redoubled by his meeting with Korvick.

Betty said later, "They called us up and asked us to come down. They made all the arrangements. Then, when we got there, he acted like he didn't know why we were there. Or why we had bothered to come. It was incredible."

Carter formulated an extraordinary document after the trip to Miami. It consisted of dozens of pages of ruminations, questions, problems and answers that he had gleaned from his studying. It focused on what he expected the trial battle to be, which was the testimony of the psychiatrists, who would maintain that Walford had been mad at the time of the murder. It is the sort of document that a prosecutor might prepare, to anticipate trouble areas in a case. In effect, it was Carter's prosecution of Vernal Walford.

Carter wrote:

The issue involved is whether an individual who does a wrongful thing, knowing it to be a wrongful thing, and who acknowledges this both verbally following the action and by his own behavior before, during and after the action, can be relieved against criminal responsibility on the basis of the particular content of a hallucination which the individual experienced and which he attributes to be the basis for his actions.

Carter prepared a two-page, ten-element tabular presentation comparing common elements of a classic insanity defense against those present in Walford's case. He demonstrated differences in most of the outlined categories.

He also wrote:

Issues for the jury to consider:

1. Do the facts in this case perfectly fit the law?

2. Is the law itself explicit and free from ambiguity, confusion or inconsistency in this area so that it can be mechanically applied to individual cases?

3. Where the law is ambiguous, not explicit, or subject to confusion or inconsistency, what principle may be applied?

4. How may such a principle be applied in this case?

Page after page of Carter's presentation dealt with what he called "Problems." He delineated all the uncertainties about Walford: where he came from; what he was doing in the United States; all his conflicting statements; all the questions about his mental status. Essentially Carter took every element that was known about Walford and questioned the reliability or accuracy of the information. He considered the medical problems, the increased risk of suicide and brain damage and the problems created by Walford's separation from his family in Jamaica, questioning whether that last factor might have had some bearing on the man's behavior and the case against him. He wondered about Walford's statements that five of his children had died. Had they really existed? Were they really stillborn, as Walford had claimed? Or had Walford killed them? What did he feel about the deaths?

Why had no one questioned Walford closely about those alleged deaths? He could not believe that a psychiatrist or policeman, talking with a man accused of the murder of a child, would not leap at the information. Perhaps there had been some link, an out-of-control jealousy or an unresolved anger, something within Walford's recollection that connected with the seemingly random murder of an unrelated child in Miami.

Carter wrote pages of "Assumptions" and backed them up with further questions or statements of fact. He listed thirty-eight separate elements of Walford's behavior, gleaned from the psychiatric reports; he listed eleven areas where there was an "inadequate data base." He wrote an eighteen-item "problem list," itemizing the factors applicable to Walford's incarceration.

He sent all the material to Korvick, along with a four-page letter:

... I understand how emotionally involved persons such as myself and my wife may complicate your own work in preparing for this case, but by the same token, we may have useful insights and perspectives which otherwise would be lacking. In addition to my direct emotional involvement I have a personal commitment to the issues which are involved. I am therefore eager to share the results of many hours of work, discussion with colleagues, and the review of numerous aspects of the literature relating to the issues involved, with you. Hopefully, this information may be of help in your difficult task of planning for the trial. Even though many of the points which I will make will have already been considered by you, I am sending them to give you my ideas.

As you may have observed, I am a rather slow, methodical thinker. ...

That was after the prosecutor had met with the Zelezniks, however. It was not a propitious meeting. Korvick treated the meeting more as an obligation to the bereaved family of the victim than as a means of actually obtaining their views. He asked Betty to recite her experience of searching for Arnold. He went over the line-up in which Bobby had identified Walford.

He outlined the legal situation for them as he perceived it. Walford was in a sort of criminal justice system limbo, in which everything was attendant on the results of his treatment in the state mental system.

He infuriated the Zelezniks with this passivity.

When Carter brought up allegations that Walford had been involved in drug smuggling and perhaps illegal arms sales and certainly had been an illegal immigrant and suggested requesting FBI assistance, Korvick replied that he doubted the bureau would be very interested. When Carter suggested trying to learn more about Walford's behavior in Massachusetts prior to the murder, Korvick countered that it would probably just help the defense. When Carter tried to examine the psychiatric reports for inconsistency and ineffectiveness, Korvick merely pointed to their bottom line: that all the doctors agreed Walford was insane at the time of the murder. Carter, who thought the reports inadequate at best and criminally inefficient at worst, was able to control himself only with difficulty.

Korvick did not seem to care what they thought.

He complained to me later that the Zelezniks were pushy and uninformed. He suggested that part of Carter's frustration was caused by a breakdown in marital relations with Betty. He alleged that Carter had admitted that to him. He scoffed at the studies Carter had done. Korvick saw only those psychiatric reports. Because they were typical of those prepared in the Eleventh Judicial Circuit and because they had been prepared by the squad of doctors most commonly used by the courts, and they did not disagree, he could see no way around them.

So he did not listen to Carter.

Indeed, he warned me that I would have difficulty dealing with them.

2. Two Legal Evils

One of the elements of the criminal case that most disturbed Carter was that the doctors uniformly acknowledged that Walford had understood what he was doing, recognized it as wrong in society's eyes, known it was illegal yet gone ahead and performed the murder because he could not bring himself to resist the voice.

In the months after his meeting with Korvick, months spent poring over the legal literature, it seemed to Carter that the doctors were describing a classic case of the "irresistible impulse" defense. That defense, known as the Durham rule, had been formulated in the District of Columbia by Circuit Judge David Bazelon in an effort to replace the antique M'Naghten standard. Essentially it held that a defendant was not guilty if, because of his mental defect he was unable to resist the behavior he knew was wrong. Named after the defendant in a 1954 case, convicted housebreaker Monte Durham, the rule had been considered a legal experiment until 1972, when it was rejected by the U.S. Supreme Court. In effect, though, the rule remained; it had had an exceptionally wide impact on the criminal justice system, and its influence could be seen in criminal court rules of procedure in many jurisdictions. The Durham rule, however, was actual law in very few locations. Florida was not one of them.

It drove Carter to a point of intellectual wildness. He read and reread and read again the M'Naghten standard of right versus wrong and the ability to conform one's acts to society's norms. He virtually memorized the Florida criminal court manual on insanity.

The more he looked at it, the more he thought Walford was prosecutable. And convictable.

And the more he thought that, the more he saw no one doing anything about it.

After the April 1977 trip to Miami the family returned to Ambler and settled back into the uneasy routine of recovery. Bobby joined a Little League team, Betty continued with her art studies and Carter poured himself into his work. In his office the boxes of documents continued to multiply, some marked "Walford," some marked "Sovereign Immunity," each a testament to frustration.

The news out of Boston was just as bad as that from Miami.

The lawsuit against the doctors at Northampton and the Commonwealth of Massachusetts continued to be pinioned to the doctrine of sovereign immunity. Although a special master named by the trial court that had reviewed the dispute between the state and the Zelezniks had decided in their favor, that decision had promptly been overturned by an appellate court. Then, in 1978, the Massachusetts legislature passed a Torts Claims Act, which did away with the doctrine, but the act was retroactive only to the 1977 *Whitney* decision [*Whitney* v. *City of Worcester*]. The Zelezniks' suit predated *Whitney*. For them, the doctrine was still intact.

It sometimes seemed to Carter that he was ensnared by two routinely accepted legal evils: sovereign immunity in Massachusetts and the M'Naghten rule in Florida. The literature of the law was pregnant with scholarly writings and opinions decrying both doctrines. It was as if all the lawyers were sitting collected, shaking their heads and murmuring about the wrongs implied in each rule of law, yet nothing could be done about it. A bilious, red-hot frustration overcame Carter at times, and he flushed with frustration. It seemed so elementary to him: Arnold had been killed unfairly, and his family deserved a forum to assign the blame in that death.

Perhaps in his tenacity, his persistence that went far beyond what others would muster, there was a compensation for his own feelings of guilt and grief. Be that as it may, he steadfastly refused to quit.

Betty, too, kept on. In her own way she posessed an inner strength that carried her forward. While Carter pondered all the subtleties and details of their dual impasses, she felt a huge, unwieldy, immense sadness. It worried and angered her that Arnold might have died in a vacuum—a single, horrible moment, duly registered and reported in breathless terms by the newspapers and then evaporating, absorbed by the next tragedy. Arnold meant more than that. She was determined that Arnold's death would not become a mere shrug.

Bobby, too, reached conclusions. He felt Arnold's loss with an intensity that only siblings could understand. When he trotted out onto the baseball diamond and Arnold wasn't there, when he picked up a ball and there was no one to play catch with, the moments weighed on him.

He saw the frustration of his parents, as well. He aligned himself with them, as was natural, but he also became acutely conscious of the difference the loss and absence of Arnold had created between his family and others. If he thought the legal fights to be part mission, part obsession, part grief for his mother and father, then that was okay, because all those things were valid.

More than valid. Essential.

It was a difficult formulation for a young boy to make, but Bobby made it nonetheless and never wavered.

All these feelings—Bobby's, Betty's and Carter's—were hidden amid the days, weeks, months and years that settled onto the family. No one, it seemed, paid any attention to them. They did not know when, or where, they would find an outlet, a forum for their feelings, but the pursuit continued.

It was into that fight that I stepped.

3. An Exchange of Letters, a Meeting in Philadelphia

I was haunted by images from the case.

There seemed to be so many mysteries attached to the slaying of Arnold Zeleznik: How had Walford become the way he was? What was to happen to him? What had driven him to Miami? Why had he been compelled to seize Arnold from that hallway?

On the opposite plane, I considered the situation that had befallen the Zelezniks. They had been victimized by a singular savagery. It belonged in a realm of can't happen, won't happen, couldn't happen. I did not think it possible to conceive, even to let the thought enter the consciousness, that one's healthy, intelligent, mature nine-year-old child could be seized from the hallway of a pleasant, modern, middle-class hotel in the few seconds that one's back was turned and be violently, remorselessly executed in accordance with the dictates of some twisted imagination.

It was beyond random chance.

It was horribly, tragically unique.

Crimes sometimes appear to be conspiracies of chance. An X factor here, combined with a Y factor there, and abruptly all the actions fall together into an invisible, unbreakable, deadly equation. Arnold Zeleznik's murder was such a cruel quotient. I could not imagine a greater blow than that sustained by the Zeleznik family. The death of any child is a special grief, an agony of emotions. Had Arnold died of childhood leukemia, I thought, the family could have railed against the intransigencies of modern medicine, so sophisticated yet so inadequate, but at least they would have had the opportunity to try to save him and in that effort would have lain some relief.

I considered those parents crippled by the death of a child in war. Suppose Arnold had been given those extra few years to rush to the verge of adulthood, only to have it ripped away by bomb or bullet. Again, though, I saw outlets: acceptance in the flag-draped rituals of military death or perhaps attacks on the evil that is war.

There were other accesses to agony. Arnold could have been happily playing outside like so many other nine-year-olds, and been hit by a car as he chased a ball into the street. He could have been struck by lightning. The Zelezniks could have found comfort in that most commonplace and effective explanation of the sudden: It was fate. It was God's will.

(Betty, her eyes filled with tears but with an edge of anger carrying her words, said a few months later, "How could Arnold's murder have been God's will? What God would do that to a child? What God would put us through what we have experienced? I don't believe God, any God, would. Not for an instant.")

But the death of Arnold Zeleznik fell outside the parameters of reason. Illness, war, accidents all are a part of daily life. One can pick up the morning newspaper on any given day and read the litany of tragedy, violence and death that is our heritage. I thought how often I had contributed to that daily recitation; I had written of so many deaths, people shot, people drowned, people stabbed, people strangled, people ripped apart in cars, by bullets, by each other. There is a shared common knowledge that pigeonholes any death and ultimately leads to a type of acceptance and understanding. But the distress the Zelezniks had been trapped within seemed different.

How could anyone survive what had happened to them?

In the fall of 1978 I wrote Carter a gentle letter inquiring about the possibility of interviewing the family. He replied in October:

I have just received your letter. I appreciate your courtesy in writing to me rather than in phoning me "out of the blue" insofar as the letter itself produced a remarkable stress reaction on my part. Suddenly I was again overwhelmed by feelings and thoughts which virtually crushed me four years ago.

My immediate impulse is to want to talk to anyone who has a legitimate interest in what happened in Miami. I would be happy to tell you about my son, Arnold, in hopes that you could sense the beauty of that child and the profundity not just of our loss but of the world's loss. I would also like you to meet our remaining son, Bobby, who is doing well in school, in swimming, in baseball, playing the cello—but who has scars that I can discern. I feel he has been the strongest of all of us.

However, as you understand, there has been litigation concerning what happened in Miami, not only in Miami, but also in Boston. I have forced myself, consequently, to control what I say on this and related (and sometimes unrelated) matters in order not to prejudice justice in those suits. Eventually, I feel, it essential the full story be told. . . .

Carter wanted desperately to tell his story but felt constrained by the potential prosecution of Walford and the lawsuit in Massachusetts against Northampton and the state mental health system. Letters flurried between us and his Boston attorney. Tentatively we agreed to meet, not exactly for an interview, but more for a feeling out. It would be in Philadelphia after the Christmas holidays.

Carter's voice flooded across the lounge area at Jefferson Medical College, a strong "You must be John," and I was seized by his powerful handshake. He was tall, slender, gray-bearded, but with wide shoulders that spoke of hidden strength. Betty, seemingly half Carter's size, dark-haired, open-faced, was instantly concerned: "Have you been waiting long? How was the drive? Were you able to park? Oh, I knew Carter should have told you about the visitors' lot across the street. . . ."

Behind her hovered Bobby.

He was shy, caught at that difficult age, twelve going on thirteen. He was slim, blond, with a small smile that seemed to crease his face with difficulty. He shook my hand firmly, then retreated after a few words of welcome.

In the faculty dining room we ate sliced roast beef and made small talk: the weather in Philadelphia, the weather in Miami. The newspapers in Philadelphia, the newspapers in Miami. The food. The holidays. The economy. Gas prices.

I asked Carter about the lawsuit in Massachusetts. "Accountability," he said. "That is what it is all about. The money doesn't mean anything. It's just a figure we put on it to get their attention. Accountability is the issue.

"You see, I don't really blame Walford. . . ." I saw Betty nod in agreement. "Madman. They had him. They failed to perform any type of rudimentary examination and let him go, just like that. It was a breakdown, a whole moral, physical and intellectual breakdown. It was indicative of the way we're heading in this society. That's why it's essential to force them to admit their responsibility. The hospital is to blame. The doctors are to blame. The state is to blame. The system is to blame. Accountability."

I asked Bobby about baseball. Favorite team?

"The Phillies," he said.

"Bobby would like to be a professional ballplayer," Carter added.

"It's all he talks about in the summer," Betty said.

Bobby's head was down. He pushed the food with a fork.

"That was what Arnold wanted," Carter said. "Even when he was little, it was all he could talk about. Growing up and becoming a major-leaguer." I saw Bobby's head hang a notch lower. Carter gently wrapped an arm around Bobby's shoulders. "Not everyone gets to be a professional ballplayer who wants to be one. Sometimes I hope Bobby will go into the law.

"You see, we are currently hung up in the courts on the doctrine of sovereign immunity. Now that's a legal term that means basically that you can't sue the king, or in this case the state, for doing wrong. I expect we may have to fight this all the way to the Supreme Court. My guess is that it may take years.

"It's not unimaginable that it will take fifteen or twenty years. And in that time Bobby, if he doesn't become a ballplayer, may become a lawyer. And wouldn't it be something if the first case he had in front of the United States Supreme Court was his brother's lawsuit?"

Carter delivered the speech in a warm, affectionate manner; the arm stayed around his son's shoulders. He did not see Bobby's eyes fall and his back bend as if greatly weighted.

And there, I thought, is the biggest battle.

Carter's initial reluctance to be interviewed dissolved later that year with the defeats in the Massachusetts courts. We spoke on the telephone in late August 1979. It was eight months after we had first met. They had decided to go ahead and be interviewed, Carter and Betty said. They offered to put me up while we talked. There seemed to be excitement in their voices, almost a sense of release.

There was no doubt in my mind that they hoped what I eventually produced would help focus attention and outrage on what they felt were the dual legal injustices they had suffered. Carter, who would ultimately become very press-wise, saw my participation as a means of bringing their story to the public eye. There was absolutely nothing wrong with that, of course. They also hoped, I believe, that by talking with me, they would be able to synthesize some of their feelings and bring some subterranean grief to the surface. At one point Betty turned to me and said, "This all seems so therapeutic." I think, too, that by talking with me, they felt it would help Bobby not to be afraid of his feelings or be constrained by them. Carter and Betty both believed strongly that feelings in the family should be aired; to hide a thought was to be crippled by it. Talking with me, they hoped, would bring them out of whatever shells they had created.

4. Someone to Throw Strikes To

Betty started apologizing a few blocks before we reached the house and continued, despite my protests, right up to the time we walked through the door. The house was a mess, she said, Carter has this pack rat quality that accumulates things and can't stand to throw things out, she wanted to straighten up, but. . . . I kept telling her not to worry.

The Zelezniks' home mimicked their lives; it was a wild museum, filled with baseball gloves and legal transcripts piled onto painting supplies and sketch pads, with books everywhere. The furniture was simple and haphazardly selected, arranged so that there was space to talk and space to move about freely. They did not live in a particularly large house, and the accumulated stuff of their lives filled it to the bursting point. It was a house of extraordinary comfort and ease; there was a palpable friendliness about being surrounded by all the papers and paintings. Betty was right; it did reflect Carter's pack rat quality. It was not a fragile home or an ordered home, a rigid home. One of the things I came to admire the most about Carter, Betty and Bobby was that in all the times I visited them, they never tried to hide the way they lived, the feelings they had, the emotions they felt. They never served me a meal different from one they would have eaten themselves or tried to put one light on something when another was real. From the beginning it was as if they said, "Here is how we are. Accept us as we are." I was so accustomed, from my newspaper stories, to finding things not to be as they seemed that it was almost relaxing to be with people who didn't try to make me see black when the world was red. They never complained over any question I asked, regardless of how personal. They never complained when the time required to produce this work stretched from one year, to two, to three, to almost five. They never demanded, never denied. They never asked anything of me. They were always open.

When Betty and I talked, she sat on the couch in the living room, making a few nervous gestures until she relaxed and ignored the notes I was taking and the tape recorder going on the table between us. Bobby would come in and out, listen, watch, get bored, get up and leave, return, add a few sentences or a comment, get up and go, come back—in short, act like the restless young man he was.

I noticed changes that reflected the eight months since I first met him; he was at that age where one should never take one's eyes off a boy, for fear that while one does so, he will have grown six inches, his voice will have dropped two octaves and he will have started shaving. Bobby seemed much more grown, much less shy. He was indeed taller and thicker, with an athlete's young build, wiry, muscled, quick.

Betty answered readily. Occasionally she had to pause; there were moments when the heavy sadness seemed to fill the room.

"One thing I learned, growing up, was that I think children should and can take whatever is going on. Whatever a fact is. I think that I learned that you can't turn your back on a fact, a true fact. If it is a fact, you should be able to face it. But to turn your head on it doesn't change the fact.

"We raised Arnold and Bobby that way.

"They knew that whatever they did was a reflection on them. Indirectly on us, but directly on them. By doing something wrong, they may hurt us, but in the meantime, they're hurt more than we are because whatever a person does, they have to be responsible for. And they have to take the consequences of it.

"I think I've been much freer with my memories than other people. I used to talk about it, Arnold's death, all the time: what it meant to us, how much it changed us, what we've had to go through. I remember once I was talking with a friend, who'd never really said anything, and I just started talking about it, about how sad it made us when Arnold was killed. And she was so surprised that I could, and she said, 'Now that you've brought it up, I've got to tell you how badly I have felt about it.' You see, I would never plan when I would talk about it. I would just emote.

"It's always there, you see."

Betty cried for an instant.

"There has been no finger to point towards anyone. Arnold was perfectly healthy and happy. He didn't want to die. He didn't do anything to deserve it. There was no reason for it to happen."

She dried her eyes. "I'm sorry," I said, but she shook her head. "Tell me about coming back...."

"I had the awful feeling of leaving someone behind. We were suddenly so incomplete.

"It didn't last," she said. "Oh, it was a long time, more than a year, maybe two. It still hurts; that's always there. But you have to go on."

She smiled then, but it was still mingled with tears.

Betty got up and showed me a large painting she'd done of the two boys. They were dressed alike in blue and grinned out from the canvas. She showed me, too, a bust of Arnold that she'd sculpted, which had been the basis for the relief on the award medal. She walked over to the corner to a bookshelf and pulled a round blue hat from beside a stack of photo albums. "This is the conductor's hat the men gave him," she said. A faint smile rippled her face at the memory. "He was so proud of it. Parading around, calling off the names of the train stops. . . ." She returned the hat to the shelf and stepped to a table against a wall of the living room. The table held a large, round mosaic. I stood next to her. There were two figures in the center, a dark-haired boy and a blond-haired boy, both dressed in baseball outfits. They were caught in the midst of play, swinging a bat, catching a ball; on the backs of their jerseys were the numbers 10 and 9. "Those are the ages Arnold and Bobby would have been when I did this," she said. Betty stood frozen by the edge of the table, staring down at the brown and tan shades of the clay, her eyes filling rapidly with tears. She looked up at me, biting her lip. I could see her struggle for composure for just an instant; then she dabbed away at the tears and smiled a bittersweet small smile. "Sorry," she said.

"You don't have to apologize," I replied.

She nodded. "That's true. I don't."

Carter arrived home later, making a joke about my brother's Italian car, which I had borrowed to drive to Philadelphia. I offered to sell him the piece of junk on the spot. He laughed and declined. Betty, Carter and I resumed seats in the living room, and we immediately began discussing the murder again. It was a characteristic of Carter's; so close were his feelings and thoughts about what had happened that he could go literally in an instant from jokes and repartee to an exceptionally intense level of memory. At first it threw me, as if I thought there should be some appropriate scene setting first, but then, I wondered, why? Who cares? What propriety is there after your child has been murdered? The three of us continued to talk. As before, Bobby floated in and out of the room.

"You see, John, there are so many principles involved in this thing. You cannot separate it and see it as distinct. I keep talking about society, about the direction of the nation as a whole and connecting it with Arnold's death. It is hard to simplify, but let me try to show you what I mean. For example, if we did not have this nationwide drug problem, then Vernal Walford wouldn't have been smuggling narcotics into the United States and wouldn't have been here at all. So why do we have this drug problem? Because of the behavior of the government? Because there is some inherently weak moral fiber in our society? Possible. Possible.

"You go on a little bit. Why was Walford released from Northampton?

Well, outright incompetence is one answer. They were afraid of him, of what he might do to them, though how he could do much more is questionable. But it isn't so simple as that. That's much too easy an explanation. You have to examine all the factors that come to bear on the situation. What was happening to our mental health delivery systems in late 1974? That's right: deinstitutionalization. A long, grandiose word to describe putting people out on the street without controls, without care. It was the policy of the government, misguided, mistaken. And it colored the decisions made in Walford's case.

"So we have a situation arising where a dangerous man is in a hospital where the official policy is to clear them out, get them out of the wards, back into society. And you couple that with the physicians at the hospital. What kind of doctors usually take state mental hospital posts? Right again. Foreign-trained doctors.

"Now, there are many fine doctors educated at fine universities outside the United States. Goodness, we at Jefferson see them all the time. But there are also some who don't know much and can barely speak a word of English. And you tend to find them in places like Northampton.

"Again, what have you reduced the question to? One of national policy, state policy. Society's dilemmas. Arnold died; Walford killed him. But sometimes I think of him only as a wild animal. Now even a wild animal kills for a reason: fear; hunger; to protect itself. They could have found that out about Walford, too. So when I say I don't blame him, that's not exactly correct. I certainly don't want to see him rewarded! He carries one sort of guilt. But many other people, other systems carry just as much.

"Walford was, in so many ways, symptomatic of so many ills we have in this country. Of crimes, of drugs, of illegal immigration, of deinstitutionalization, of government's failure to take responsibility.

"Responsibility. Responsibility. I keep using that word. I consider the state of Massachusetts to be morally responsible. That's why we filed suit there."

Carter made a face. "Sovereign immunity. They hide behind it. First they say it's no good, it's wrong and it's offensive. But that doesn't stop them from using it to their advantage. I think that they are cowards. The attorney general of the Commonwealth of Massachusetts and his staff. They know that the doctrine has been discredited and can no longer be employed. But that doesn't stop them from citing it in our case because they have been lucky enough to win some court decisions. It is both ethically and intellectually dishonest!" He slapped the ball of his fist into his open palm. "Just plain, old-fashioned dishonesty."

When Carter hesitated, I asked, "Would that really be it? Suppose the state of Massachusetts, I don't know, the governor, the attorney general, someone, got up and said, 'We're sorry. We shouldn't have let him go. We screwed up. It was our fault. Our policies were in error, and we're damn sorry,' that would be it, you would be satisfied?"

Betty began nodding her head vigorously.

"Yes," she said. "Just an admission, I think that's all we really care about. Isn't that right, Carter?"

Carter, too, nodded. "Yes. That at least would be a part of it. An important part. There would have to be a commitment on their part to make sure something like this doesn't happen again. But most importantly, I think you have to have an acceptance of responsibility. That's what I want them to do.

"And you have to assume the consequences. If it looks like rain but you don't take your umbrella with you and it starts to rain hard, well, you're going to get wet. It is as simple as accepting that consequence. I don't think of this as punishment, merely as a logical result."

"And Walford?"

"John, it's not much different. Accepting consequences."

Carter paused, thinking.

"I guess I'm a very strange father. If my child did something wrong, he would have to suffer the consequences. When Arnold did something wrong, he did. He always stood up, looked me in the eye and took what was coming to him. I don't want to hold the state of Massachusetts to any higher standard than that I held my son to.

"I talk about the Supreme Court and taking the lawsuit there. You see, I think the government, the system, in Massachusetts was malicious in its behavior. The hospital was malicious with their phony positive probe of the release. It was as intellectually dishonest as Watergate. I think the doctrine of sovereign immunity is malicious. I think their invoking it, discredited though it may be, is malicious. And I cannot believe that the highest court in our land would allow a group of people to act so maliciously. If it were to allow that, it would mean to me that there is no society, that you have destroyed society, law, fairness."

Carter sighed deeply. He put his head back and took in a great draft of air, then expelled it slowly.

"I have finite resources," he said slowly. "I'm not the richest man in the world. I don't have the most time, energy and so forth...."

"How much?" I asked. "Time? Dollars? Energy?"

"Lots."

He put his chin down on his chest, thinking.

"Thousands of hours. Thousands of dollars."

He paused.

"I have put in, if you like, an equivalent amount of all those things which I would put into fathering a child."

Again he hesitated.

"I believe that I had two children and I still do. I feel my life is still divided between the two children."

I turned to Betty. "Do you feel the same way?"

She didn't hesitate. "Yes. Absolutely. In a way, because Arnold's life was cut so short, I feel we have this responsibility. There is no way, really, to know what mark a child will make on the world. I guess we feel that we have to make this mark for him. To experience it for him."

Carter nodded in agreement.

Betty said, "We have been advised by various people that we're just wasting our time—"

"Most people," Carter interjected.

"But I don't think that. And with the money part, well, we'll go as far as the money lasts."

"I remember," Carter said, "when Jim Shanks [a reporter with the *Boston Real Paper*] was here after we filed the suit, he said, 'There's no way you can lose this.' Well, I see a way. The way is when the person who's making the decisions is the one you're trying to work against, then it's awfully hard for them to be straight in this. That's the Massachusetts courts. After all, they're a part of that state's government, too."

"Don't you think," I asked, "that what he was referring to was the issue of liability, when put to a jury of twelve people? Then you won't lose...."

"But it's getting to that point. And if the U.S. Supreme Court says that it is more important to protect the sanctity of the Massachusetts doctrine of self-immunity than to secure the rights of an innocent child..."

Another deep breath.

"Well, let's just say that is not something that will present the American way of life in a favorable light to the world."

Carter went to one of the crowded bookshelves and pulled out a stack of photo albums. Bobby joined us, and we all looked through the pictures. Carter and Betty kept up a running narrative.

"Here's Arnold, before Bobby was born, just walking a little. Omigosh, I look so pregnant! And here we are at the beach, I guess my sister took this one. See, that's Carter without the beard. He grew it after Arnold was killed, the next summer. He was so surprised when it came in gray...."

"See, Bobby." Carter nudged Bobby's ribs. "Look at the muscles on your old man...."

"Not that great," Bobby said.

"Not that great! Not that great! Why, you..." He grabbed Bobby, and the two of them wrestled, laughing, for a minute.

She pulled out another set of photos. There was a shot of Arnold and Bobby sitting with a store Santa Claus. The two boys are grinning on either side of the red-suited man. "This was taken December eighteenth," she said. "It's the last photo we have of Arnold. We always used to do that, each year, have the boys pose with a Santa Claus. I guess it seems a little trite, but it was one way we measured their growth, year in, year out. The next year Bobby had to be taken alone. I don't think he liked that much." She looked over at Bobby, who didn't reply. "Isn't it funny what parents remember and what becomes important...?"

After Bobby had gone to bed, we continued talking. I asked Carter and Betty about the experience in Miami, and they went over the murder and finding the body.

"The police got there quickly?"

"I suppose so," Carter replied. "But the Friday afternoon traffic slowed things down. They couldn't even get the ambulance in. I guess the only thing you can say is what if they had got there sooner, the rescue squad, started an IV, heart resuscitation, adrenaline, perhaps—"

Betty interrupted.

"No, Carter, there wasn't any chance. I picked him up. I knew.... There was no chance."

Matter-of-hard-fact, no-arguing, no-debate, no-room-for-doubt finality tinged her voice.

"Arnold was dead. I knew it when I touched him."

Husband and wife looked across the room at each other. There were tears in their eyes; but they continued talking, and the conversation went on far into the night.

"In a way," Carter said at one point, "I think Arnold saved his mother's and brother's lives."

"How so?"

"Well, suppose he and I had continued on, instead of me turning back. Who would have been next down the hallway? Betty and Bobby. What chance would they have had against the madman? Remember, he was a champion boxer. So sometimes I think that Arnold took the brunt for all of us...."

His voice trailed off then, and again he dabbed away tears.

The next afternoon, after some sleep and more talk, we took a break. Carter was back at Jefferson, and Betty and I had filled tapes and notebooks. Bobby came in, tossing a baseball in a glove. "Have an extra?" I asked. He smiled.

"Sure." He found me a battered infielder's glove. "I really liked that one," he said, "but I got a new one for this season." He showed it to me. We went out into the backyard, paced off about fifty feet and started to toss the ball back and forth.

"You pitch?" I called.

"And shortstop."

"The glamour positions," I said.

He laughed. "I guess so."

Bobby went into a windup and fired the ball. It stung the palm of my hand.

"Not bad." I fired the ball back, and he grinned again as he bent to dig it out of the dirt.

Back and forth the ball went. Bobby's throws were hard, direct, with pace, slapping into the leather glove. Mine sprayed about, and he smiled as he twisted and leaped to spear the ball. After thirty minutes or so I gave up. "C'mon, Bobby, let's call it quits. I'm getting to be an old man."

"You're not that bad," he said.

"Thanks. I can use encouragement like that."

He smiled again. It was a smile that seemed measured, difficult.

"Do you get to throw the ball much?"

"Not too much. I wish I could do it more. The problem is my dad's not too good at it," he said, "and sometimes my mom tries. But she's worse, and she can't really catch the ball if I throw it hard...."

But I knew that wasn't the real problem.

CHAPTER 10

High Courts, Low Courts, Gains and Losses

> Arnold has made his peace. It is we who are his
> survivors who have yet to make ours.
>
> —In the Supreme Court of the
> United States, spring term, 1981,
> Carter Zeleznik, pro se

1. "A Nice Person Who Love People..."

The Zelezniks never were what I expected.

Sometimes, at the start, I was unsure who had been more damaged by the murder in Miami. Walford, certainly, was shipwrecked, his mind tethered by the drugs and his madness, but initially I thought that the Zelezniks were made just as mad by the act.

I thought there was a wildness, a crackpot quality to some of what Carter was saying, particularly when he would condemn all society with his round-about, cyclical reasoning. With so little prompting, Carter would launch into this grand scheme, assigning the blame for Arnold's death to all of society's weaknesses and frailties. We all were to blame, he would argue, hands clenched with intensity, just as we all were to blame for the war in Vietnam or the weakness of the nation's economy or the national preoccupation with drugs and alcohol or the failure to control handguns. He equated those things, seeing Arnold's death not only as a specific blow to himself but also as a symbol of a more universal evil, an evil within all of us.

When Carter rambled on, in those arguments, he would draw parallels to some of the great social trials of history. More than once he mentioned Watergate, again using it as a symbol of lawlessness and government gone wrong. He said the same spirit was abroad in Massachusetts, with its immoral application of the doctrine of sovereign immunity. A number of times he had spoken of Dreyfus and how French society had been shaken by that famous trial. Perhaps, he said, our society should be shaken by the death of a harmless little boy in Miami. He spoke with passion about those people willing to stand up to fascism, especially in Nazi Germany in the years prior to the onset of the Second World War. He cited instance after instance where men had stood up and fought for what they believed in: Concord and Lexington, Harpers Ferry and Gettysburg, the Freedom Riders, Miss Jane Pittman and Martin Luther King, Jr.: "I Have a Dream." He talked of the Scopes Trial, the French Revolution, the Battle of Britain and Churchill: ". . . we shall fight in the fields and in the streets, we shall fight in the hills; we shall never surrender."

His arguments threw me.

At first I thought they were merely the surface manifestations of his huge unconscious grief and guilt. But that was only to see things psychologically, not politically. It took me a long time to realize that it was not unfair for Carter to see Arnold's death as symbolic, and it took me years to recognize that there was indeed a great measure of truth in what Carter was saying. However, I had to witness the callousness of the systems of justice to appreciate what Carter felt.

In addition, if Carter saw the death of his child as an event of magnitude comparable to the Dreyfus Affair, well, what evil was there in that? To him it surely was; indeed, an event far greater. Ultimately I came to agree with him, and I, too, wished that society's complacency would be shaken by Arnold's last cruel moments in Miami.

The Zelezniks defied categories.

Covering the criminal courts, I had witnessed a pitiful parade of victims. I always placed them into two divisions: those, heads bent, seemingly wrecked by what had befallen them; those, teeth bared, on the constant edge of anger because of what they had suffered. The Zelezniks didn't fit into either grouping. At times they bent with the weight of the memory of Arnold's murder, and at times they ground their teeth in frustration over what ensued—but they went far beyond these emotions in the sorting out of their lives after Arnold's slaying.

Still, I wondered: Why did Arnold die?

As I flew back to Miami after visiting the Zelezniks, I saw two answers: Something had happened within Vernal Newland Walford; something had happened within society.

I followed many false trails.

On the jacket of a portion of the Chattahoochee medical records obtained by the attorneys in the Public Defender's Office, there was a notation from one of the social workers who had spoken by telephone with Mrs. Noletha Walford of Penn Street, Kingston, Jamaica. She was quoted as saying, "He is a nice person who love people and always want to help them."

Noletha Walford also wrote to the men representing her husband. She addressed the letter to Phillip Hubbard, who by then was no longer the Dade public defender but had been elevated to a seat on the Third District Court of Appeal.

Dear Mr. Hubbard

Hello to you sir, I have received a copy of your letter telling me about what you have been doing for my husband Vernal Newland Walford. Thank you very much sir. There's nothing I can do to help him, I have five kids to take care of with the help of my mother. Please give my regards to all the people who have been helping on my husband's behalf. My thanks to them, sir.

Mr. Hubbard I would like to come and look for my husband. I have an aunt living in the states for years and she said I should try and get a letter from you or the doctors in charge of my husband. Please sir, could you send me a letter I could take to the immigration office here in Kingston in order to get a visa.

Thank you very much Mr. Hubbard.

God bless you. I look forward to your reply.

> Very truly yours,
> Noletha Walford

There was no reply.

Efforts to find Noletha Walford at the address in Kingston that she provided were fruitless. One investigator was told that she had obtained a Canadian visa and emigrated to that nation, but it could not be confirmed, though Walford had mentioned that that was where she was in one interview with a psychiatrist. As far as I could determine, she had had no further contact with anyone connected with her husband's case.

Similarly, efforts to contact Carl Walford in the Hartford-Springfield area were unsuccessful. I sent registered letters. I called on the telephone. An investigator knocked on the door of the only address I had. No answers, no replies. The bugaboo of all journalists.

Meanwhile, Walford was occupying his time in the mental hospital, receiving minimum individual therapy, group-oriented therapy, recreational therapy and job training. Mostly, as can be determined from his records, he was riding a mental merry-go-round driven by psychotropic drugs.

Periodically the authorities at Chattahoochee would send first Judge Weth-

* * *

erington, then his sucessor, Judge Wilkie Ferguson, cryptic form reports documenting Walford's "progress":

... Interaction with staff and peers is appropriate and socialization skills are good. It appears Mr. Walford is suffering from Schizophrenia, Paranoid Type (Chronic) with an underlying Explosive Personality (DSM II 295.3 and 301.3). Presently Mr. Walford presents as a pleasant and polite individual who is somewhat suspicious. His thought processes remain disorganized, with fragmentation of associations and persecutory delusional beliefs. He reports hallucinatory experiences of a grandiose, religious nature. . . .

Twice, in November 1977, and in July 1979, Walford was shipped from the state mental hospital in Chattahoochee back to the Dade County Jail, considered by the doctors at the hospitals sufficiently competent to stand trial. On each of those occasions Walford was once again interviewed by the same doctors who had seen him from the beginning. Each time they found that Walford, although lucid, was in a poor state of what was called chemical remission. That was to say, his schizophrenia and the external manifestations of the disease—his bizarre behavior and disruptive nature—were being controlled to a limited degree by the antipsychotic medicines.

But in 1977 the voice remained with him.

"Do you hear voices?" Dr. Jacobson asked.

"I hear a voice. Sometimes, when it is faint, I hear many voices, but it is mostly one voice," Walford replied.

"What does the voice say?"

"It tells me things. It tells me answers to your questions. It tells me what to do. It tells me what to say. It tells me great things, of which I had no knowledge! I have learned about ancient times. It has put me inside the Bible."

"Who speaks to you?"

"He is our Father. Hallowed be His name."

"What drugs are you currently taking?" asked Dr. Mutter.

"I need more. I still hear the voices, but not as strong as before. They come from God. Sometimes they frighten me. Sometimes the dreaming will cause me to awaken frightened. I never dream of the boy, but think maybe that it was wrong or that it was right. The voices are talking to me all the time. They know much more than I do."

"Do you ever think about going on trial?"

"If it comes up, I will go. I am not scared. I have a feeling inside of me. I fear not man, because he can kill the body, but God can kill the body and the life!"

* * *

Walford in 1979 had almost reverted to his December 1974 state. He was well groomed, bearded, and wore clean, simple street clothes. He had lost more weight and gained more muscle tone. The authorities at the Dade County Jail would not let the doctors enter the cell with him; they wouldn't let anyone into the cell with him. "He is on the verge of becoming dangerous again..." Dr. Weiss wrote.

Walford paced again, unable to stand still.

Sometimes he would chirp birdlike sounds.

During some interviews he would stride over to the commode to confer with God before answering certain questions.

Throughout the conversations Walford once again punctuated his discussion with allusions to the Bible and quotations from the Scriptures.

"Who is it you talk to?" asked Dr. Mutter.

"The Heavenly Father. He says, 'If I tell you what to do, do it!' As he told Abraham."

"Can you disobey the voice?"

"His powers are so much greater than mine. I cannot do that!"

"Why did you kill the little boy? Why did you make the sacrifice?"

Walford stopped, considering.

"I was told not to be afraid. He told me, 'I am with you.' So I was not afraid."

"Why would God want to kill someone?"

"He has, many times! Sodom! Gomorrah! He visited plagues upon Egypt and upon Pharaoh!"

Dr. Mutter wrote afterward: ".... He feels he is completely possessed by a spiritual force that has the power to destroy at will and he is subject to the whim of the voices that control his mind and thought.... I am quite puzzled he was released from the hospital in his present mental state."

Walford was calm when Dr. Jacobson went to see him.

"What's on your mind?" the doctor asked.

"I think of God with my mind. All the day long, all the night long. And I love God all day, all night! I pray and I give thanks to Him for the pleasure that He has given me in life! He granted me life and I thank Him."

"What else do you think of?"

"I think only of God, our Heavenly Father."

"Do you think you have been sick?"

"You cannot make me think I am sick!" Walford's voice rose sharply. "God is with me!"

"Do you miss your home in Jamaica?"

"I think only of God!"

"Do you think you can stand trial?"

"God is with me. He talks with me day and night!"

"What does He say?"

Walford waved his hand, dismissing. "We know what we know!" he replied.

Jacobson later wrote: ". . . the defendant is convinced that he is right and that his way is the best way. There are few internal restraints which could control him in stressful situations."

On neither occasion, in 1977 or 1979, did Walford come seriously close to trial. As before, no one from the Dade State Attorney's Office ever contacted the Zelezniks about any of this, and as before, all the reports made by the various doctors held that at the time of the murder Walford was psychotic and therefore failed to meet the M'Naghten test for criminal responsibility. What emerged from those examinations was the treadmill quality of Walford's illness. The amount of drugs necessary to control completely the violent aspect of his schizophrenia would also begin to destroy him physically, with a slow, steady, inevitable return of the tardive dyskinesia. The medical course open to Walford was continued drugs—but not in huge amounts. Enough to keep him from murder, not enough to be murdering him. It was the classic existential dilemma, an infernal Catch-22. Walford, it appeared, was destined to ride the edge of his madness forever. "Prognosis, guarded, long-term outlook poor, this man is capable of extreme violence."

The obvious question was: What was to be done with him?

2. A Table of Probabilities

Sometime before Arnold's murder Carter had come across a pamphlet. Much of Carter's work in the Office of Medical Education dealt peripherally with accreditation, and he was closely aligned to the Chicago-based Joint Commission on the Accreditation of Hospitals, the private foundation that studied and rated the care and procedures employed by the nation's hospitals. Carter had once been offered a job with the commission, but had turned it down to remain at Jefferson. It was a simple matter for him to make some telephone calls and determine that Northampton State Hospital, from which Walford had been so precipitously released, had always had great difficulty meeting the joint commission's standards. Actually many state facilities had that trouble.

The pamphlet came up in other research, however, and after Arnold's murder Carter turned to it. It was called *Probability Tables of Deaths in the Next Ten Years from Specific Causes*. It had been published by the Health Hazard Appraisal team at Methodist Hospital of Indiana in Indianapolis in 1972.

The pamphlet took various age and ethnic groups and measured the chances of death for each from various causes. For example, according to the tables, a white male between the ages of sixty and sixty-four, had 13,759 chances from a control group of 100,000 of dying of arteriosclerotic heart disease. That ranked it as the primary cause of death in that age group, whereas motor vehicle accidents ranked ninth, with only 400 chances out of 100,000. The primary cause of death for a black male, age twenty-five to twenty-nine, was homicide, with 1,395 chances out of 100,000, far outdistancing motor vehicle accidents and heart diseases, the next two categories listed. Carter's tables were for the year 1968, the last year examined.

Before the murder Carter had examined the category of white males, ages five to nine. The primary cause of death was motor vehicle accidents, three times higher than the second-ranked cause, drowning accidents.

Homicide ranked sixteenth, with only 5 chances out of 100,000.

That was how little chance Arnold had had of becoming a victim. Carter showed the tables to demonstrate the caution that he and Betty had shown. In cars and around pools they had always been watchful and careful. The boys had worn seat belts. They had taken swimming lessons and drownproofing courses. Carter had studied what threatened them and taken steps to prevent anything from happening. Except the unimaginable.

3. Winners and Losers

When the Massachusetts legislature did away with the doctrine of sovereign immunity and passed the Torts Claims Act in 1978, the Zelezniks' lawsuit against the state was effectively emasculated. Despite the recommendation from the state's highest court that it make its decision retroactive to 1973, the legislature chose to establish 1977 as the cutoff date. The Zelezniks' attorney, his case trapped within that hiatus period, went to court again, fighting only to be allowed to go to trial.

But without success.

In 1979 they lost on the trial court level in the Suffolk County Superior Court. The same year they lost their first round on the appellate level.

In November 1980 they lost their bid for a rehearing on the appellate level. The Massachusetts appellate court likened the Zelezniks' petition to a decades-old case. It was a divorce case, and in that instance the court had called the matter a "frivolous action." The word frivolous is one that is bandied about frequently in courtrooms, generally by one side attempting to demean the opposition, to draw attention to the opposition's utter inadequacy. As it seemed to be applied to the Zelezniks' suit, however, the word infuriated Carter. His voice became hard, harsh, rigid with fury.

"It enrages me! How can they call the death of a child frivolous?"

He took a deep breath, struggling for control.

"Who are these people to say such things? Have they no feelings? They are despicable."

His hands quivered slightly, and he pressed them together, to hold them in place.

In January 1981 the Supreme Judicial Court for the Commonwealth of Massachusetts rejected any further hearings on the suit.

That was, the attorneys told the family, the end of the line.

The impact of the decision was immediate. Carter had always believed that the case would have to go to the U.S. Supreme Court, and now that was the only step open to them. What he had not anticipated was the reluctance of the attorneys to take the case there.

In Boston, Evan Semerjian explained to Carter that any further appeal carried a foregone conclusion. All the decisions had gone against them; they had no constitutional right and no constitutional issue to present to the nation's highest court. They had no precedential cases to argue, no decisions on which to construct a case. It would be unethical, he explained to the Zelezniks, for him to take a case to the highest court, knowing those things and knowing the inevitability of failure. He refused to take the Zelezniks' money and their case. He was out.

Carter took his problem to a friend, a prominent Philadelphia lawyer, who examined the record. He told the Zelezniks they were wasting their time.

Carter contacted an attorney and law professor at Harvard who was expert in the field of sovereign immunity. After twenty hours at $75 an hour, the lawyer told Carter to call it quits.

During all that time Carter was under considerable time restraints. A response on the last and hardest ruling was necessary within ninety days.

He simply would not accept that it was over.

Betty and Bobby, too, felt agony over the decisions of the courts and the subsequent dispersal of the lawyers. They were suddenly completely, absolutely alone. The lawsuit against Massachusetts had been such an important aspect of their reconstruction as a family. For all they knew, Walford was lost in the Miami criminal justice system; he was totally unreachable, but Massachusetts was not, they had thought. It gave them a focus, a place to put their feelings. From the start they had been willing to spend years fighting. Now it seemed they were not even to have the luxury of a champion to fight in court for them.

Carter spent restless nights. He paced through the bedroom, upstairs, downstairs. Sometimes he sat in the darkness; sometimes he lay in the bed, twisting under the strain of the situation. In its own way it was almost as if it meant abandoning Arnold.

Finally, one morning he announced, "I will do it myself."

And Betty and Bobby cheered.

4. Friday the Thirteenth

They would not have cheered, however, if they had had any knowledge of what was happening at almost the same time in Miami with Vernal Walford.

Back in 1975, Michael Von Zamft had been named to the Florida Supreme Court's Criminal Rules Committee. The committee was a large body of prosecutors, public defenders and private attorneys who met periodically to review and revise the *Florida Rules of Criminal Procedure*, the handbook that governed the behavior of most criminal cases. Von Zamft, expert in issues involving insanity—as well as the death penalty and other areas—was a forceful member of the group. Near the latter part of the decade he brought with him another young assistant public defender, Barry Weinstein. Weinstein was one of two attorneys in the Dade office in charge of mental health law.

One of the rules undergoing review was 3.210, the subsection that dealt with incompetency and insanity. Von Zamft and Weinstein pushed for a new standard. First, the definition of incompetency was to be made significantly more precise; doctors examining defendants were to be required to reply to specific questions on a defendant's capacity for assisting counsel. That revision would have no effect on Walford's case.

But the other revision the two lawyers pushed through would.

Under the new rules of criminal procedure, a lawyer representing a defendant who had been consistently incompetent to stand trial for a five-year period, without substantial probability of becoming competent in the foreseeable future, could move to have the charges against his client dismissed and have him handed over to the state mental health system under the provisions of Florida's Baker Act, the law governing involuntary confinement of mental cases.

Under the new system the criminal case no longer existed, and the only control on the erstwhile defendant was the views of the doctors in the mental hospitals treating him.

Some of the prosecutors on the rules committee wanted the rule to incorporate a continuous ten-year period of incompetency, but they were outmaneuvered in committee by Von Zamft and Weinstein.

Of course, those other committee members didn't know that the two men represented Vernal Walford. When January 1980 rolled around, the new rules governed Walford's case. He had been incompetent for five straight years. It became a matter only of waiting for the right moment, before Von Zamft and Weinstein took the matter up in court. The right moment would be defined by Walford. In 1979 he had been dangerously psychotic. According to the cyclical pattern of his behavior, he was due to enter a lesser state of rage, as his drug dosage was slightly increased.

At the time no one was in charge of Walford's case in the Dade State Attorney's Office. Michael Korvick had left the office for private practice. The case file was in the office's vault. No one was aware of the effect the rules change would have on his case. When, late in 1980, Barry Weinstein filed a motion to dismiss charges, it took the office completely by surprise.

Two new prosecutors were assigned the case. Arthur Berger, a tall, bald, intellectual appellate attorney, and Robert Kaye, a longtime prosecutor and chief of major crimes for the office. Shortly thereafter he would be named by Governor Bob Graham to a spot on the Dade Circuit Court bench. Kaye brought in Berger to see if there was anything they could do to fight the application of the new rule.

They came up with a plan: not a good one, but something.

They told Weinstein that the state would agree—*stipulate* was the legal term—to all the psychiatric reports filed over the half decade the doctors had been examining Walford. It would stipulate to a not guilty by reason of insanity verdict in the case. Under those provisions, though the first-degree murder charge would be effectively eviscerated, the judge would still retain jurisdiction over any release contemplated by the physicians at the mental hospitals.

It was slim control at best but, they thought, better than none.

Weinstein agreed to the deal.

On February 13, 1981, Walford's case was set.

It was a most unusual hearing.

The judge in the case was the new Criminal Division chief, James Jorgenson, a devout former policeman, soon to become an appellate court judge. The hearing was scheduled for 2:00 P.M. and was held in a courtroom empty of spectators. The only people present were the two prosecutors, Weinstein for the defense, the judge, the clerk, the bailiff, the stenographer and a squad of ubiquitous jail guards, who surrounded Walford.

Kaye got up and read quickly through the pile of reports, citing the opinions of all the doctors that at the time of the murder Walford had been insane. "The state at this time is willing to stipulate to the contents of those reports . . ." Kaye said.

"The defense will stipulate to the contents of the reports dating back from 1975 to the present, Your Honor," Weinstein said.

"On that basis," Jorgenson replied, "the court will find and adjudicate the defendant not guilty by reason of insanity."

A few seconds later Jorgenson committed Walford under the provisions of rules 3.217 and 3.218, whereby he would retain jurisdiction over any release.

"The court finds the defendant still represents continuing danger both to himself and to the community in general . . ." Jorgenson said.

He looked over at Walford, who was sitting quietly, his eyes darting back and forth, absorbing the action in front of him.

"Vernal, do you understand what's going on?"

He stood. "Yes, Your Honor."

"We are going to send you back to the hospital. Do you understand that?"

"Yes, sir," Walford said.

Jorgenson turned to Weinstein. "Counselor, are you fully satisfied with these proceedings and that your client understands?"

"Yes, Your Honor, I fully do," Weinstein replied.

There was one great irony in the hearing: In order to hold the proceedings, it was necessary for Walford to be declared competent to stand trial. That was part of the deal. After six years of battling competency the defense agreed to accede and admit Walford was competent.

Walford shook hands with Weinstein and was escorted back to the Dade County Jail. He was not a free man, exactly, but he was certainly a great deal closer to freedom than he had been for years.

In all, the trial of Vernal Walford took twenty minutes.

* * *

I did not call the Zelezniks right away to tell them of the news. I waited to see if someone from the state would bother. After two weeks had gone by, I wrote Carter, Betty and Bobby about what had happened, describing the hearing, the latest psychiatric reports and the maneuvering by state and defense. Almost immediately I got a lengthy letter back from Carter:

...I had not an inkling of what was going on in Miami with regard to Walford, but I am not at all surprised. I expected something of this kind—as early as the evening Arnold was murdered. I can remember tearfully admonishing the detectives who came to see us in the hotel that if they were going to let this man get away because of a technicality...they would have done a disservice to justice, or words to that effect. Perhaps one of them may remember better what I said. It doesn't really matter, but I expected that after a time, the "authorities" would like to brush the matter aside and get on with new and more exciting things.

I am not suprised that I was not contacted. I find it difficult to accept the idea that it might have been a "mistake." When I wrote to Mr. Korvick who was then handling the case, I was struck by his insensitivity and self-centeredness. I also communicated to him some critical comments with regard to how Walford had been "examined" and how the law was being interpreted. I think that district attorneys prefer more passivity in those they deal with. Given the "new law" (applied retroactively, of course), there might have been no options, but I am concerned with the apparent superficial nature of the "trial." I wonder about Walford's actual mental status, how significant the hallucinations were, what he had to say about himself and what he did, how seriously mental status examinations were conducted, and so forth. It is obviously cheaper for the state to do what it has done, later to discharge him, then to deport him to Jamaica, where he is likely either to be killed or to kill someone else, unless he decides to revisit this country.

My feelings. Some anger. Some expectation and consequent resignation. Some (more) tears. The tears are always the hardest to explain and they come when I may not always be prepared for them. Yet I pity those who are unable to cry when there is need for crying. I'm not certain that Bobby is able to cry and that bothers me but I can't make him and I don't try to do so. Perhaps he does it when I'm not around or maybe he will do so later. I do not believe in holding in everything.

My anger is less toward Walford than toward the unfeeling bureaucracy that to my mind is more responsible for these things. I am not convinced that human society is viable. We may indeed have an atomic war that ends it all. We have shown our willingness, if not our eagerness, for that. However, I see a greater possibility of our going out with a whimper and not with a bang. It comes from lack of feeling, lack of faith in essential social values, lack of leadership, lack of dignity and lack of commitment to common goals. We are long in procedures. Our technology is great. But I see no direction. I think the bees will outlive us.

If we gave them the chance, so would the Canadian geese.

About two months after the "trial" I went to see Bob Kaye in his office. He complained about the new rule, not knowing the history of its creation. He described how the state had been forced into a corner; the only way it could retain any kind of future control over Walford was through the not guilty by reason of insanity scheme that had been accepted by the defense.

"It was a big mess," he said. "Tragic."

"Have you been in touch with the victims?" I asked.

He put his hand to his forehead. "Oh, my God, no, I forgot to do that."

"I heard from them recently. . . ."

"Are they angry?"

"I don't think they know much about it. They are concerned with their lawsuit. . . ."

"I'll write them right away. Have you got their address?"

"Yes. It's simple. Carter Zeleznik, associate director, Office of Medical Education, Jefferson Medical College . . ."

"Oh," Kaye said, scrawling down the address, "I didn't know he was a bigwig."

He never wrote.

As usual, no one ever contacted them.

But by then they were swept up in their own fight.

5. A Light Brown Jacket

It was late May, a brilliantly bright, warm early-summer afternoon in Philadelphia. I sat with Carter in his office as he spoke about the defeats in the Massachusetts courts, his words somehow underscored by the boxes of documents cramping the tiny room.

"You see," Carter said, "I had been told by all these competent lawyers that I couldn't win. 'You should quit,' they said. 'Settle with Massachusetts if you can. Write a book.' One, my friend, told me that this was an obsessive neurosis. 'Give it up,' he said. I wanted him to take the suit on. He said his firm would require five thousand dollars up front. But they didn't really want the money; he said he thought it would be unethical to take it. He kept saying, 'We want you to give up.'

"We had been friends, you see, but now we were speaking somewhat coldly. . . ."

Carter paused, thinking.

"They said we were just chasing windmills. One told me that we had less than one chance in ten thousand and to quit. They told me our chances were nil. Well, they aren't nil, but they might be small." He smiled then. "Very small." He waved his hand, dismissing the concept.

"Well, perhaps it is obsessive. Obsessive, yes, but a neurosis, no. A neurosis, by definition, is self-defeating behavior. I'm not sure this isn't constructive.

"Sure, there are times when I say maybe no, maybe let's forget it. Then I say no!"

Carter leaned forward in his chair and punched one fist into his open palm, forcing the words to gather momentum in the small room and reverberate, as if with the force of an echo.

"The issue is not whether you're going to win or lose, but whether you think you're right!

"Maybe I've intellectualized my emotions. I doubt we'll be able to beat the odds. The Supreme Court gets four thousand cases a year and hears two hundred. That's five percent. Of those, half are suits brought by the government. That leaves one hundred cases out there. Long odds.

"Well, I realize the egocentrism involved in my even thinking, hoping, praying, I can beat the odds. But"—and he hesitated, to add emphasis to what he was saying—"you can't walk away from crucial issues."

He thought, then added, "You would be walking away from life."

After the Zelezniks had made the decision to write their own appeal to the U.S. Supreme Court, Carter obtained all the transcripts and records and spent a harried, intense week in his office at Jefferson and at home, late into the evenings, constructing the legal brief.

Betty and Carter—luckily an expert typist—did the typing in one day. Carter had obtained the rules governing submissions to the Supreme Court from one of the attorneys who had rejected handling the appeal. A printer ran off the forty-seven pages of the brief in a few minutes. At home, Betty and Bobby helped assemble the necessary forty copies, binding them together themselves in a light brown cover. On Saturday, March 28, the three of them drove to Washington.

It was windy, blustery, typical early-spring weather, that time when nature seems indecisive, fickle and out of sorts. Betty stopped, arrested at the base of the wide steps leading up to the great, dark Supreme Court building, her heart catching with a sudden memory. For an instant she saw the four of them, on that snowy day more than six years earlier, on the same steps; in her mind's eye she saw Arnold dashing ahead with little-boy exuberance toward the front doors and beneath the carved motto. Then she shook the memory from her head, though her eyes filled briefly with tears. "Just the wind," she murmured, and she followed Carter and Bobby up the steps.

Carter deposited the copies of the brief on the clerk's desk. "Here we are," he said. "Forty copies."

The clerk glanced at them quickly. "These won't do," he said.

Carter's mouth dropped in surprise.

The cover was the wrong color.

It had to be white.

The print size was correct, but the spacing was wrong.

Carter had placed the "Questions Raised" section behind the jurisdictional statement, on page 3. Now it had to be at the beginning, although there was a table of contents that said what page it was on.

The corrections, they were informed, had to be made by the following Tuesday.

Like anything in the legal world, it seems, there was an out. Carter had to file a pauper's petition, which, when presented to one of the justices, would give him a sixty-day extension. (Justice William Brennan granted Carter's petition on Monday.)

Carter said afterward, "I didn't like filing the pauper's petition, but of course, if I'd had to pay to get the corrections done by Tuesday, that is precisely what I would have been."

When the clerk explained the rules changes to Carter, he said that four or five of every ten papers submitted to the High Court were rejected because of improper format. Carter also learned that the rules had been changed after November 1980 and that Carter's brief had been correct under the old rules— which his attorney had unwittingly given him.

There was a lawyer from the Texaco corporation in the clerk's office with Carter. He had flown in from New York that morning to paste into his document a paragraph which had to be on page 3 rather than page 1. Carter turned to him and said, "Well, 'equal justice under the law,' provided all format requirements are met...."

They had all laughed at that.

The clerk of the United States Supreme Court rejecting Carter, Betty and Bobby's appeal because the jacket was the wrong color turned out to be one of the best things that happened to the Zelezniks. It was so petty, so outrageous, so ridiculous in comparison with what the family had suffered that it became something of a rallying point, symbolic of all that had happened to the family in the embrace of the law. The newspapers and television would love it.

First of all, as Carter acknowledged to me, it bought them some time. Carter was able to send out the copies of his brief to friends for comments and revisions. He attached a cover letter to the document:

Well, because we now have a little (not much) time, I am sending copies of the rejected version to friends for their reaction. I wish Arnold's grandfather were here to have helped in the preparation of the appeal or even to argue it should the occasion arise. I think he might have been pleased that we have proceeded on our own as we have thus far anyway. And I hope the same can be said for Arnold, himself.

Incidentally, because of the time problem, this now has to be a petition for a writ of certiorari rather than an appeal. So, wherever it says "appellant" I have to put in "petitioner" and wherever it says "appellee" I have to put in "respondent." I am sure there must be some other tricks they didn't tell me about.

I really doubt that the Supreme Court will be interested in a case involving a little boy, but in the event that the Court even agrees to hear the case, this would be national news and should they decide in our favor, this would be unprecedented national news. I would not advise anyone to sit by the television awaiting it. . . .

Carter's brief cited twenty-nine cases he thought relevant, including the *Morash* (1973), *Whitney* (1977) and *Vaughn* (1979) cases from Massachusetts, which controlled the Zelezniks' suit. He cited the Fifth Amendment and the Fourteenth Amendment to the U.S. Constitution and U.S. and Massachusetts codes. He also cited four law review articles, the last of which was entitled "The Myth That the King Can Do No Wrong."

The two "questions" Carter hoped to raise with the Court were:

1. Is an all-embracing and absolute doctrine of sovereign immunity which fails to take into account the merits of any particular case in which state employees have acted negligently and wantonly, and for which no justification is provided or is even acknowledged to exist, in violation of constitutional requirements for due process and equal protection?

2. Is a combination of judicial decisions and a legislative enactment which creates multiple classes of litigants with regard to their right to sue the Commonwealth of Massachusetts, again with no justification offered or possible, in violation of constitutional requirements for due process and equal protection?

* * *

But the real key to the entire brief, which Carter managed to file in time, without errors in jacket cover or form, was actually found in the final paragraphs Carter wrote:

The lawsuit against the Commonwealth of Massachusetts is Arnold's last testament and legacy to the world in which he lived and which he loved. Arnold has made his peace. It is we who are his survivors who have yet to make ours. The wrong which was done to him cannot be undone, but the conditions which led to it are still in need of correction.

Although it has been held that statutory entitlement to sue for the wrongful death of another is not itself a fundamental or constitutional right (*Parham* v. *Hughes*, 99 S. Ct. 1742) it should be understood that monetary compensation could not produce adequate redress in the present situation in any event. What is sought is the right to litigate, to put the Commonwealth of Massachusetts on unequivocal notice that its right to act irrationally and arbitrarily and in violation of the United States Constitution is subject to challenge and that its negligence is subject to disclosure in a court of law.

Even, therefore, if the United States Supreme Court in its wisdom were to permit suit only for the purpose of demonstrating publicly the truth of the allegations made by the petitioner without any opportunity for a monetary award to be obtained, Arnold's last possible constitutional right, that of being heard, would be assured.

The motivation for this suit lies in the notion that in a free society, the citizen has not only the right to protest injustice, but the obligation to do so, the power of the government to prevent that protest in a court of law notwithstanding. Nay, given the power of the government to prevent that protest from occurring in a court of law, the obligation is made the more compelling.

Arnold Frank Zeleznik, if squarely confronted with a situation which would have called upon him to sacrifice his life for the well-being of others, would have done so without hesitation as so many others have in fact done, although he would have wanted to say good-bye and "I love you." He would have done so because he was a child of compassion and of courage. But neither he, nor any other person should be called upon to sacrifice any right, least of all their lives, to no good purpose or to a negative purpose such as the protection of the incompetence, negligence and irresponsibility of a state and its functionaries.

They were brave words, written with tears blurring Carter's vision.

CHAPTER 11

A Story Worth $10 Million

1. "...I Have No Rights"

In his office Carter and I continued to talk about what had befallen Walford in the criminal justice system. I said, "You know, Carter, it would not be possible for Walford to buy the kind of representation he received. Roy Black and Jack Denaro are two of the highest-paid, most respected criminal defense lawyers in Miami. Denaro even has a nationwide reputation. Von Zamft, Tarkoff—they aren't that far behind. Barry Weinstein was a specialist. A million bucks couldn't buy that kind of help."

Carter nodded. He rubbed his forehead for an instant.

"It bothers me. Not that they did such a superb job for him, but in comparison with the state. The system can afford to have its rights protected, can afford to obtain appropriate justice, but it seems that Walford's help was so disproportionate to what we received. I recognize, in a sense, I have no rights.

"There should be some attention given to the rights of families affected by these decisions, however. But again, just as in Massachusetts, the issue is accountability. In a way, the state prosecutors don't owe me anything. But they do owe it to society."

"And if Walford gets out?" I asked.

"I have a responsibility to have shouted. To have made some noise."

Carter thought for a moment. It was characteristic of him to take the few seconds to order his thinking.

"I see this not as Walford the man, but Walford the set of procedures."

Hesitation.

"I see the whole insanity thing as...well, insane."

Hesitation.

"It is as if they have contempt for a child's life."

Again he paused.

"I don't feel personal hatred or animosity. I guess Walford is a victim, too."

But he didn't know then what I knew.

Betty, smiling, clasped my hand warmly, instantly solicitous, as always. A flurry of questions: "How was the flight? How's your wife? When is the baby due? Ohhhh, you must be getting excited! Don't forget to send us pictures. Is she feeling okay?" Her eyes were alive, excited.

"Wait until you see Bobby," she said. "He's getting bigger and older and—oh, you'll see."

"No more Renaissance Academy?" I asked.

She shook her head. "It was quite a decision," she said.

Bobby and the neighbor's child, the sole students of the school Carter had established, had been graduated that spring in a small ceremony. He was fourteen now and ensconced in the ninth grade. It had been a hard time. I remembered asking him, before the graduation, what he was going to do.

"I'm not sure," Bobby had said.

"What options do you have?"

"Well, there's private schools and public high. I guess we could continue with Renaissance...."

"What's your preference?"

He'd shaken his head. "I just don't know."

I'd thought then how hard it must be.

Carter and Betty had not forced the issue. They had understood that Bobby had to come to his own conclusions. Whatever soul-searching he did, he did alone, in his room. He opted for private school. He took tests, did excellently and was accepted at the Penn Charter School, a prep school of considerable reputation. Betty said that Bobby had simply walked into the school on his first day quietly, with determination and without looking back. The transition had been swiftly absorbed in the newness of the school, new students, new friends, hard work. His grades were superior; the Renaissance Academy prepared its students well.

Carter, Betty and I stood in the lobby of the Penn Charter School waiting for Bobby to emerge from the throng of jeans, work shirts, slide rules, tattered textbooks, lacrosse sticks and energy that flowed around us. There is a unique tone to the core of a boys' school, a mixture of voices easily mingling the awkward transition from youth to young man. The sounds enveloped us, dozens of snatches of conversation, all aided by that particular excitement that comes with the impending end of the term; boys talking baseball, Latin, tests passed and flunked, term papers and summer vacations, trips abroad and girls and next year's courses. Carter, Betty and I stood out in that crowd like beached whales.

Bobby seemed to materialize from the mass of racing, strutting, strolling boys, almost as if he had separated from a living, constantly shifting mass, and maneuvered over to us. He shook my hand, and we instantly launched into baseball conversation. His blond hair seemed indecisive, not certain whether to be wavy or curly; it was pushed back from his forehead in an exaggeration of tangles. His eyes met me squarely. I noticed that instantly. Perhaps it was familiarity, but I thought that he had grown up more than a notch in that year of school. He was taller, too, and wiry, with an easy, coordinated grace. He waved at other boys. His face was open, smiling, his eyes alive. His shoulders were square, and I searched his appearance for the weight that I had first seen, the day he and I had first met. It's somewhere, I thought. But it's in its place.

When we got a few seconds alone, I asked him, "Bobby, when you think of all that has happened, what do you feel?"

He hesitated, not uncomfortably, but searching for a precision. Like his father, I thought.

"I feel sometimes that I am different. Different from the other guys."

"How do you mean?"

"Well, there were some guys that got a few six-packs of beer and went down in the woods to drink them. And then they were going to drive home. Now I guess they were going to be all right, but I wouldn't go. It's as if I have to be a little more careful. I feel a little more responsible. It's not that I think I'm special or more important or anything, because of what's happened, but different. Maybe I know a little more. I'm not sure."

I could see his eyes mirroring the sorting out that he was attempting with his emotions.

"Do I make any sense?" he asked.

"A lot," I replied.

That evening Carter, Betty and I sat and talked. As usual, Bobby floated in and out of the living room, occasionally joining in, then disappearing to his room. He had studying to do.

"You know," Betty said, "in Miami we were never considered at all. We were treated very badly."

"I think," Carter said, "that it is society that suffers. A prosecutor has an obligation to society. There was no evidence that the prosecutors in Miami recognized that right."

Both seemed resigned by what had happened.

It was not an event that caused them to explode with anger or dissolve in tears. I suppose they felt an inevitability about the manner in which Walford had avoided criminal responsibility.

"I suppose Walford is a victim of the system, too," Carter mused, repeating his earlier comment.

"He didn't act that way," I said.

"Ohhhh," Betty said. "You went to see him?"

"Yes."

Her face changed then, a sudden wind shift, from a grudging, frustrated acceptance to a fearful fascination. She moved to the edge of her seat, bringing her hands together in her lap, expectant. "What did he say?"

"Does it matter?" Carter said. He seemed suddenly depressed, as if deflated.

Betty answered swiftly. "It matters to me."

There was a second's silence, and she leaned forward.

"I want to know what he said," she demanded.

2. What He Said

The North Florida Evaluation and Treatment Center is located a few miles outside Gainesville, Florida, a short distance past a prison farm. It is an area of rolling pastures broken up by stands of high pines and tendril-laden weeping willows. The facility was built in the mid-1970s and currently houses about 200 men. It is considered maximum security; a social worker there said there had never been a successful escape from the institution.

There is a small sign that says NFETC by the side of the county road that runs out of Gainesville and a modest black macadam street that heads across a wide field. Cattle graze in the sunlight. No buildings are visible from the road.

A few hundred yards down the street there is a large sign that says any person bringing weapons, controlled substances or liquor into the facility will be prosecuted. A little way farther there is a foot-wide yellow line painted across the macadam and a sign that says any person crossing the line implicitly gives his consent to be searched. Standing on the line, one can just make out the low-slung complex of gray and off-white cement colored buildings in the distance. The facility sits flush in the center of a field; a green wall of trees rises up behind it.

As I drove toward the buildings, the sun reverberated off the hood of the car, blinding me. The heat was insistent, uncompromising, angrily filling the still air.

Inside, I was asked to sign a paper agreeing that I would reveal no patient's identity other than Walford's. I was escorted into the center by a young woman, one of the social workers assigned to Walford's unit. He was housed in Building 13 in a pod with eight other men. A guard, located in a bulletproof glass office, operated an electronic sally port and let us step from the center's lobby into the grounds.

The compound was ringed by a fifteen-foot-high chain-link fence, topped with several rows of barbed wire, curled back on an angle to prevent anyone from climbing out. We walked down a street within the compound, surrounded by the inmates, milling about freely in the sun and heat. It was close to 100 degrees away from the shade. All the buildings were numbered; there were dormitories and therapy rooms, bleak in their similarity. It had the appearance of a small, functional gray-cement community.

Two men were playing a guitar. One was showing the other how to form chords, encouraging him. A few notes seemed to climb up into the cloudless blue sky. "I just don't understand why you would want to talk with Vernal," said the young social worker. She had a slight southern accent. "I mean, I don't understand why you think his case is anything special."

I did not reply.

Another young woman joined us. She, too, was a social worker, and the two of them wanted to sit in on the interview. A doctor's office, a small cubbyhole off of a recreation area, had been set aside for the interview. All three of us took a seat and waited.

Walford arrived, unescorted, a few seconds later.

His handshake was loose, uninterested, but his eyes were intense.

He stood six feet, but slightly stooped. His hairline was receding from the front, but his hair was long, wiry, pushed directly back and curling over his ears. He wore a thick, bushy mustache. The hair on both his lip and his head was tinged with gray. He wore brown-trimmed thick eyeglasses but sometimes peered over them, giving him a slightly inquisitive, oddly distinguished look. He was chunky, a roll of stomach protruding over a pair of new blue jeans. He wore a white sport shirt, freshly laundered, and new desert boots. His arms were thick and powerful, a stevedore's muscles.

He sat across from me, our knees nearly touching, our faces only a yard apart.

His left leg trembled slightly, and he pushed his hands together tightly.

He fixed his eyes on mine, his glance unwavering, though he rocked back and forth in the chair. His lips occasionally smacked together, but not in the pronounced fashion I had seen so many years earlier.

I introduced myself and started to make a quick explanation of what I was interested in, but he interrupted me sharply, with an abrupt hand motion.

"What I want to know, man, is what is in it for me?"

They were his first words.

His speech was direct, uncluttered. The Jamaican accent was slight, mingling easily with Americanisms.

"What do you mean?"

"I want to talk about money. I am broke, you know, I need money. How much is in it for me?"

"What were you looking for?"

"I think it is worth fifteen grand."

I laughed. "I haven't made anything off this. Perhaps someday, but not so far. I certainly don't have fifteen thousand dollars."

Walford did not laugh. "You're not telling me the truth."

"Yes, I am."

"You are not. You think this is some joke affair? You have the money, I know. You cannot just fly up here, dressed in a suit like that! You're holding back. I cannot do that. I am stuck here. It costs money, I know that. So you think of this as just a joke affair!"

I wasn't smiling either, then. "I do not think of it as a joke."

"I have to suffer so long, all these years in the hospital, in the prison, man. You're greedy, man! I know they pay money for these stories! This is a reality story, not made up."

"That's not the way the publishing world works."

He shook his head. "You come up here with a cock-and-bull story about no money. Your part of the deal sounds funny! You're just greedy, man! I know the story! Only me! I was the one there; no one else knows the way I do! You are a fool; you're wasting my time. This is reality, not made up."

"I'm sorry . . ." I started, but he interrupted.

"I was the one there, but they will get all the money. I know about that man! He is suing them in that state Massachusetts for four million dollars! He will get four million dollars! And I won't get anything!"

"I think he'd rather have his son. And he will lose the suit."

"You don't know! He will get it. Four million!"

We glared at each other in silence.

"All right, Vernal, you don't have to tell me anything. But I cannot pay for the story. I am on the staff of the *Miami Herald* and the paper does not allow people to pay for their stories."

"Oh, I know about that *Gleaner* paper! You think I'm a fool. I know that they must pay; how do you think they make their money? You think anybody can come in with a story and just put it in the paper? No, they pay! I know about that *Gleaner*! You telling me a cock-and-bull story, man. I will tell my story somewhere else!"

I paused, angry.

"Vernal, tell me, do you see a line of journalists out there waiting to hear your story?" I waved toward the front of the compound.

"Oh, there are many, there are others interested."

"Vernal, I'm going to write the story anyway."

"Then I will sue you and get all your money."

Again we stared at each other.

After a moment his voice retreated from the edge of our argument. He seemed reflective for a second. "You know that hospital in Chattahoochee? They sent me a bill for fifty thousand dollars, man. Where do I get that money? I have no money. I'm broke."

"What do you think they'll do about it?"

He paused. "I guess they can come and kill me."

He sounded discouraged. I tried a different tack. "What about Massachusetts?"

"You know that hospital, they put me in with no charges; that's why they had to release me."

"You were hit in the eye."

"Yes. It broke my glasses."

Then he held up his hand, as if to cut the both of us off. "I want to be paid," he demanded.

I shook my head. "How much do you think your story is worth?"

He sat back rigidly. "It is worth ten million dollars!"

I shook my head again. "We're not getting anywhere," I said. I closed my notebook.

He stood up, his eyes wide, filled with anger. "You wasting my time, man," he said.

He stepped toward the door but stopped and turned. "How much you got with you? How much can you come up with right now? Right now! How much?"

I thought for an instant about the $35 I had in my wallet. I looked at him. He'd settle for that, I thought. Then I thought again. I'd be damned before I would hand him one cent so that he could tell me about murdering Arnold Zeleznik.

"How much you got?" he demanded.

"No," I said.

He looked at me. "I have suffered. In prison for years and years. This is my story, man, and I have suffered. My attorneys, Black and Denaro, they say it take fifty thousand dollars to get me off. Instead, I get the public defender."

"But you got off," I replied.

He shrugged. He stepped toward the door.

I stood up. "Well, Vernal, if you change your mind, you know how to get in touch with me."

"Yes. If my mind changes." He scowled and clenched his fists.

"Money talks, huh, Vernal?"

"That's right!"

He strode from the room. The interview was finished. I turned toward the two social workers, who had watched the whole angry exchange silently. "Ten million dollars," said one. "Maybe we ought to increase his dosage a little. That seems a bit grandiose."

"Was that right about the bill from Chattahoochee?" I asked.

She nodded affirmatively. "That was the angriest I've ever seen him," she said. Her voice had a tentativeness about it; for the first time I wondered if there had been some danger. It is probably not a wise practice, I thought in retrospect, to argue with homicidal psychotics.

I collected my notebook, and we walked outside. It had been dark in the office, and for a moment I was blinded by the flash of the sunlight reflecting off the buildings. As my eyes adjusted, I saw Walford, perhaps fifteen or twenty feet ahead, turn and stare back at me. The anger in his eyes mingled freely with the waves of heat rising from the black tar street. As I watched, our eyes met, and he seemed to snarl at me. Then he turned on his heel and purposefully stepped off into the unforgiving sunlight, disappearing around a corner, marching restlessly away.

3. Betty

Betty sat back hard on the couch. "He wanted money," she said.

"Well, he wanted some money. Fifteen thousand, ten million, or maybe thirty-five bucks, it was hard to tell."

"And he thought that all we cared about was getting rich."

I nodded.

Tears formed at the corners of her eyes.

"All the money in the world..." she started to say, but then she stopped. "No one could pay us back for our loss," she said. This was a simple, declarative fact. She shook her head and gathered in a deep breath. I could see her considering what she was going to say. "You know"—she looked at me—"it's such a common instinct, but I never felt like I wanted to get my hands on him and kill him myself. I always thought that he was more of an animal, I guess, and that he didn't, in a way, know what he was doing. I mean, I didn't think that he should be excused for what he did, but that his craziness should be considered.

"But he seems so..." She groped. "I don't know, greedy. Evil. To think we just want the money! Oh, God! How cruel."

She paused.

She had paled; now she was regaining her color. "You know, one attorney told us that Walford would have had a better lawsuit than we do." She shook her head, as if to clear a compacted nightmare. "I suppose, before, he never really seemed real. He was just a name on a document, a description, someone somehow disconnected with us. But now he seems, I don't know, alive. He thinks about us!" She shuddered.

Carter had put his head into his hands and remained uncharacteristicly quiet throughout Betty's reaction. I watched as he, too, inhaled deeply, ordering himself. He leaned back in his chair, eyes skyward momentarily, sighing.

"Would you want to see him executed?" I asked.

Betty paused. "It's hard," she said. "There is a hateful part of me." She gathered herself again. "I remember, once I was at my art class. Now most of the people there knew about Arnold and what had happened, but some didn't. It was during a drawing session, and we all were talking as we were sketching. The subject of the death penalty came up, and there was this one Swedish girl, an art student, and everybody was expressing their views. And I remember, she started to talk, and she said, 'I can't understand your system. Like that man who killed the little boy in Florida. What right has he got to live?' And everybody got quiet because they knew. And I said, 'That was my little boy,' and I started to cry, and so did she and many of the people in the class. But I said, too, 'I don't see how it rights any situation,' and I guess I still feel that way. I don't see how taking another life corrects anything. It's hard. I mean, right now, listening to what you said, I hate him. But still, I don't see how taking his life solves anything."

Betty nodded her head up and down.

Carter spoke then, his voice slow, deep, rumbling up from his emotions, deliberate.

"One thing Arnold's death taught me," he said, "is that you have to have a reverence for life, for all living things on this earth. You can't gain this reverence by hatred. You can't gain it by demeaning life. . . .

"You can't become what you hate."

4. ". . . A Son Who Was Nice and He Died"

In the morning Carter, Betty and I drove over to the New Horizons Montessori School. We got there early and watched as the children began to flow into the old brick building. Carter was vibrant, excited; there was something about children that brought out an extraordinary sense of enthusiasm in him. He waved and bent down and talked with the children in the playground area before classes started. Dressed in old tweed jacket and tie, his gray beard and hair mussed by a warm and gentle wind, Carter seemed part Pied Piper, part grandfather. The children flocked around him, laughing and hanging on his words. He had the ability to talk to the children on their level without sounding condescending or boringly adult. Betty watched with me. "He's like that," she said without introduction. "He just seems to bloom." She laughed richly.

It was the seventh year of the Arnold Frank Zeleznik award.

Carter and Betty introduced me to the faculty, who all seemed overjoyed to have them there. We went from classroom to classroom, handing out mimeographed sheets of paper for the students to fill out. The papers asked these questions:

1. "What is a good thing which a child can do to make this a better world?"
2. "What child at this school do you think should win the Arnold Frank Zeleznik Award this year?"
3. "What did this child do that makes you think he or she should get the award?"

Carter would sweep into the classrooms, wait impatiently while each teacher gave a small introduction, then gather the children around him. He sat comfortably at chairs designed for children. In the first classroom we were instantly surrounded by third graders. Carter began by asking them about a recent overnight program they had been on to a camping ground. The voices washed over him with excitement.

"I liked the bonfire!"

"I liked the ghost stories!"

"The night walk was scary!"

"We ate fresh fish!"

"I liked the marshmallows!"

A chorus of assent to that comment.

Carter held up his hand. "What are we going to do this morning?"

Hands shot up around him. He pointed at one.

"The Zeleznik award!"

Carter nodded. "Right. This is the school where it started. Does anybody know why?"

Ethan, age nine: "Because"—he paused, looking around him at the other students, then continued—"you're giving the award to the nicest person in the school because you used to have a son who was nice and he died."

Carter nodded again. "That's right," he said. "Tell me, what are some of the good things children can do?"

All the hands shot up.

"You should help somebody if they have a problem!"

"You should keep the world clean!"

"Don't kill animals!"

"If another kid is hurt, you can help him!"

"You can share things!"

"Right, right, right, right, right, those are all good things," Carter said as the list rolled out of the young voices around him. One child's hand went up again. Carter nodded toward her.

"How old was your son?"

"He was nine," Carter said. His voice stayed the same.

"How did he die?" another child asked.

"He was killed . . . by a crazy man," Carter said.

"How did he kill him?"

Carter hesitated. "Let's not talk about the bad things; let's talk about the good things in life."

"Excuse me," asked one small girl, peering down at the mimeographed paper, "I have a question."

"Yes, dear?" Carter said.

"Are there some special answers?"

"No, honey," Carter replied. "There are no right answers and no wrong answers."

CHAPTER 12

Tick . . . Tick . . . Tick

1. "Are We Rolling, Rob?"

Carter truly believed that the petition he had written would be heard by the U.S. Supreme Court. He would not say it in any public forum; on the contrary, he would cite the statistics and the odds against success. He would say that the best legal minds he could find had uniformly told him that he had no chance and that, really, he held out no hope. Inwardly, however, deep beyond any public statement or pronouncement, Carter believed that the nine members of the highest court would hear his plea.

He thought of them as parents and grandparents; he thought they would instantly recognize that what the family was seeking was not the opportunity to make money through a lawsuit, but the opportunity to assign blame for Arnold's murder. How could they deny him that? No matter how coldly and analytically he researched the issue, he could not bring himself to the harsh realization that the nine Supreme Court justices, charged, in his view, with upholding the rights of all citizens, would not come to his aid. In the equation Carter's emotions produced, he saw his plea as the rights of the individual, on the one hand, and the rights of the bureaucracy, on the other.

It was Arnold, his innocent child, versus an antiquated, despised rule of government. Seen in those antilegal, simplistic terms, Carter, in that fantasy realm of hopes and dreams, believed the choice was obvious.

He asked me repeatedly, "Do they actually read the suits?"

He felt that no jurist could fail to see that in any measurement the rights of the family of a murdered child were far more important than those of some huge, unfeeling state government.

He asked, "Is there any way you can find out for certain that the justices actually read the documents submitted?"

I replied that there was no way I knew of to determine absolutely who read what. I told him that I suspected the briefs were reviewed by law clerks and summarized for the justices but that despite the overwhelming number of suits filed, the Supreme Court took great pains to examine each application carefully. I said I did not think that Carter's brief would be lost in any judicial crack.

"If they read it," he said, "they would see."

One of the intriguing aspects of the lawsuit was Carter's insistence upon bringing the government of Massachusetts to trial. Many attorneys had told him that he could always proceed against the individual doctors and social workers at Northampton; it would be an easier suit to argue. Additionally, they would not necessarily be blanketed by the doctrine of sovereign immunity, though they had already invoked the same right in court documents.

Carter refused.

The doctors at Northampton were part of a system, he said.

It was a system created by bureaucracy, incompetence and insensitivity. It was a system predicated on the erroneous applications of disproved theories, such as deinstitutionalization. The people forced to perpetrate such a foolish, misguided, mistaken and inherently evil policy were victims, too, in Carter's mind. However, they were culpable victims. He wanted them in the dock—but beside the state of Massachusetts. That is why the people at Northampton were listed in the lawsuit alongside the state, intrinsically entwined.

There had been virtually no publicity about the Zelezniks' fight against Massachusetts until they opted to take their arguments themselves to the Supreme Court. An occasional story had appeared in the local *Ambler Gazette*, but nothing which sought to document the extraordinary efforts in which the family was engaging.

In Miami what news there was focused on Walford. His acquittal was missed by both the *Miami Herald* and *Miami News*. The *Philadelphia Inquirer*, the city's leading paper, and the *Philadelphia Daily News* carried virtually nothing about the family between 1975 and 1981.

However, the decision to go themselves to the highest court changed that bleak picture. A reporter from the *Ambler Gazette* wrote a lengthy front-page article about the family, illustrated with one of Betty's drawings of Arnold. That attention prompted further attention: A local radio show became interested; a local television station contacted the family.

There were so many external details in the family's story that made it a natural. They had been so abused, not merely by the murder in Miami, but at every turn by some bureaucracy. They were articulate; they were open; they were able to describe in detail the impact of all the small plagues that had been visited upon them. All that was powder for the media. The wrong-colored jacket on their brief, for example. The failure of the Dade State Attorney's Office ever to tell the Zelezniks what was happening with Walford. The word frivolous seemingly assigned by the Massachusetts appellate court to their lawsuit. In one reply brief, the Attorney General's Office had written of the murder of "Robert Zeleznik..." in Miami. They had gotten the date of the murder wrong. And there was another quotation, in another reply brief, that would be quoted over and over again: "No psychiatrist... has any test, method or expertise for predicting future dangerousness. The art of psychiatry is just one step from the art of black magic."

These foolish words would eventually be ridiculed before an audience of millions.

Carter had always recognized the importance of becoming allied with the news media and he, Betty—and Bobby, too, though to a lesser degree—gained a substantial understanding of the way they worked. Carter had an instinctive way of striking the right chord. Perhaps it was just the quality of their story; after all, not once did Carter or Betty have to pretend in their emotions. It did not make much difference who asked them about the murder and the fight against Massachusetts. Their response, whether spoken for the first or five hundredth time, was always directly from the heart. In a way, they gained from the process. It was not that repeating it so much diminished the potency of their loss. But the strength of the loss was somewhat humbled by the familiarity that grew through expressing it so many times. They were consistent; they were steady; they were thoughtful and expressive.

The tears, every time, were real.

One day that spring Carter and Betty went to the studios of the National Public Radio affiliate in downtown Philadelphia. They were led through a maze of small offices and sound chambers to meet with Ric Peters, who had seen some of the local stories that were beginning to emerge about the Zelezniks. There was some small talk, a warming-up time, as Peters went over a few cogent details. Then Carter was taken into a black-walled, soundproofed radio studio. Betty sat in the adjacent control room, behind the sound technician and engineer, watching Carter through a large plate-glass window.

"It's exciting," Betty said. "Too bad Bobby's at school. He loves this stuff." She gestured at the banks of lit dials and meters on a board before her.

Carter and Peters took seats before the microphones. There was a voice check, and Peters gave some last-minute instructions: "Keep close to the mike, just relax and don't worry. We're not live, so we can do it again if we mess up." Carter nodded.

Peters turned, pointing at the engineer. "Are we rolling, Rob?" The engineer held up thumb and forefinger in the universal sign. Peters swung back toward Carter. His voice changed from a jocular friendliness into that studious, practiced radio station tone. He gave a brief "Our guest today is..." introduction, then said, "All right, Carter, why don't you tell us what happened to cause this case to drag on for years and years...?"

Peters didn't need to have warned Carter. All his responses were direct, to the point.

"You're seeking five million dollars?" Peters asked.

"The point is to bring out in a court of law the responsibility. One cannot establish the cost of a life. The money part is not the central issue. This doctrine of sovereign immunity discourages people from acting responsibly.

"Everyone else is liable for the way they act. You are. I am. The federal government is. Why not the state of Massachusetts?" Carter said.

Unsaid was the name Vernal Walford.

Peters asked, "Why did you start this?"

"Well," Carter answered, "it started out as grief work, to alleviate the sadness, the depression, the despondency. But it has become more than that." He paused, ordering his words.

"Sure," he continued, "I'm a Don Quixote. But I don't think that chasing windmills is such a bad thing after all."

After a half hour of conversation Peters motioned to the engineer, making a chopping action with his hand. He took off his headset and shook Carter's hand. "Terrific," he said. "There's more, much more, here than I can use. You handled yourself well."

Outside, Carter shrugged. "Perhaps it can help," he said.

The biggest help, however, came from a man named John Tarquinio at WCAU-TV, Channel 10. The television station had a public affairs program called "Alive at Five." It contacted the Zelezniks and arranged to do an interview with the family in their home. Reporter Bill Baldini, producer Bill Wagner and a camera crew showed up, and put together a lengthy—for television—feature on the family's legal struggle. It was an exceptionally moving few moments, not the ordinary fare for television news stations. Ultimately the impact of the interview would be widely felt. Tarquinio, the public affairs director of the television station, was a friend of Don Hewitt. Hewitt did not have as well known a name as the people who worked for him, but within the news business he carried great weight.

He was the executive producer of CBS-TV's "60 Minutes."

The Zelezniks were about to become a national story.

But they had to sustain another blow first.

2. Two High Courts

The U.S. Supreme Court began its fall term on October 5, 1981. On that date it announced the cases the justices would be reviewing. Carter's petition was rejected in a single-sentence announcement that Carter angrily suspected was produced by computer. It said simply that the Court refused to assume jurisdiction in the matter.

As all the lawyers had warned them, they had lost.

But this loss was irrevocable.

At that point their only legal avenue was to return to square one, in the Suffolk County Court in Massachusetts, and sue the doctors at Northampton individually. The likelihood of any settlement with the state was probably gone, but that had never been Carter's intention. Early in the suit, the State Attorney General's Office had made a tentative settlement offer of approximately $25,000. But the state would not at the same time make a statement accepting responsibility. It would not publicly acknowledge that Walford's release from Northampton had been erroneous and had resulted in Arnold's death. After brief discussions Carter, Betty and Bobby had turned the offer down flat. But that had been years earlier, in 1976.

Carter plunged into a black depression.

Betty, too, was ensnared by doubt and discouragement.

Bobby, in the midst of schoolwork, the exciting beginning of the new school year, was confused. He understood the importance of what they were seeking; he believed in it; he believed in his father. It saddened him to see Carter so despondent. It was incomprehensible to him. His studies, especially American history, stressed the rights of the citizenry, the access to the courts. It was impossible for him to read about *Marbury* v. *Madison* or, for that matter, to remember *Jaworski* v. *Nixon*, and not think that something was mistaken. The courts had always stood up bravely for what was right, and now here they hadn't. To a fifteen-year-old, the equation was simple and direct. Bobby watched, worried and anxious, to see what his father would elect to do. He knew only one thing for certain: Carter would find something.

When I spoke with Carter during those few months, he seemed bitter for the first time. Rancor, sarcasm and unfettered anger clouded his voice. Carter stated over and over again, "I don't believe they read it.

"I don't believe they bothered at all.

"I don't believe they ever saw what I wrote."

For the first time all the many instances in which Carter had talked of accountability and responsibility seemed worthless to him, the words giving him an acid taste. He said, "How can I as a parent teach these things to my child when I don't see anybody, not even the Supreme Court of the United States, standing up for them?" The fantasy of standing before the nation's highest court and expressing his anger and hurt and loss had had a powerful effect upon Carter. Now, suddenly robbed of that dream, he was adrift.

"I just don't know what we're going to do," Carter told me that winter in a telephone conversation. I had no suggestions.

It was an agonizing solitude for the three of them.

Suddenly all the hopes and aspirations had been dismissed. They had placed so much of their recovery into the anger against the state of Massachusetts. The fight had had such a symbolic strength; it had been their way of screaming to the world that they had been unfairly damaged and robbed of someone they loved. It had come to dominate so many emotions for them. What they couldn't understand was: They were the wronged party. Why was the system of justice so weighted in favor of the madman killer and the incompetent state government? It was beyond unfair. They tried to reach within themselves to make some meaning out of it, to reach some kind of understanding. Suddenly, with a one-line refusal, they had been cut off, abandoned, alone with their questions and their frustrations.

Betty thought of it as some horrendous sentence. It was almost as if they were the guilty ones and were going to have to pay with their lives, imprisoned forever by a conspiracy of wrongs, the world turned upside down.

They did not know what to do.

Into the morass of depression, however, rode the proverbial cavalry to the rescue: "60 Minutes."

Tarquinio, at WCAU-TV, had sent Hewitt the tape of the "Alive at Five" broadcast featuring the Zelezniks. Hewitt had jumped on the story with alacrity. It was assigned to Norman Gorin, a veteran producer, and Morley Safer. Gorin, an engaging, friendly man, with a sense of rumpled familiarity about him that contradicted the slick image of television news, mirrored his medium: That instant was when he wanted to do things, in a second was a frustrating hindrance, and tomorrow an impossible delay. That insistence was coupled with a jocular sense of humor and a persistence about obtaining a story. To Carter, Betty and Bobby, it seemed that no sooner had Gorin called the family to set up the interview than he was at the door, trailed by huge lights, cameras, yards of black electrical wiring, sound technicians, microphones on booms and, of course, the famed Mr. Safer.

And just as swiftly it became clear to Carter that what had failed in one forum might well succeed in another.

3. The Lost File

Gorin sat in my study, and we talked about the Zelezniks. He pored over many of the documents I had obtained about Walford and picked my memory for details, perceptions and observations. He took notes, listing whom to talk with and how to find them.

He had already taken the precaution of reserving rooms at the Crossways, telling the desk clerk that he wanted room 206. That was a backup procedure; he anticipated that the new owners of the hotel would allow them to film in the L-shaped hallway. That proved to be true, though the Best Western hotel chain, which had purchased the Crossways, obtained a signed statement from Gorin that the hotel would not be identified in the broadcast. Researchers from "60 Minutes" were also busy tracking down the doctors who had been at Northampton and had okayed Walford's release. All the people whose names had filled Carter and Betty's conversation for so many years were being contacted. Those directly involved in the release, and still facing the potential of legal action, were refusing to go on camera. Gorin and I joked about the impact of a call from "60 Minutes"; even the innocent break into a cold sweat, I said, and he laughed.

We talked for several hours. Gorin was an extremely quick study; he picked up names and roles instantly. He knew the direction in which the show was heading; it was the direction defined by the Zelezniks' ire.

The following day he and I met at the Metro Justice Building in downtown Miami. He needed the videotape of Walford and whatever other photographs he could obtain. I told him that I didn't think the defense lawyers would hand over any stills but that the videotape was used for training. It would be available.

It wasn't that simple.

Barry Weinstein, still representing Walford despite having obtained the acquittal, objected strenuously to letting Gorin copy the tape. The matter was put down for an emergency court hearing. From my files I took the transcript of the original competency hearing for Walford in which the cassette had been introduced as evidence. Accompanied by Assistant State Attorney Jose Quinon, who knew almost nothing about the case, we went before Circuit Judge Arthur Snyder.

Weinstein argued that allowing "60 Minutes" to have the tape would violate Walford's privacy. He said it would focus undue attention on Walford. He stopped just short of saying that the publicity of a "60 Minutes" broadcast would probably keep Walford in the mental hospital longer and abort efforts Weinstein was making to have him released and deported to Jamaica.

Gorin, stepping to his feet, unfamiliar and not an attorney, explained that the tape was evidence and had been shown publicly once. Why not again?

Judge Snyder watched about twenty minutes of the tape. He read the transcript. Then he ordered the tape attached to the court file and copies made available to the state and "60 Minutes." A technician in the state attorney's office copied the tape that afternoon.

The photographs were a different story.

Jose Quinon had no legal objection to giving copies to Gorin and me. The problem was, he didn't know where they were. When he had ordered the file of case 75-179 from the State Attorney's Office vault, it had not been there. Clerks had searched the area unsuccessfully. It was, perhaps, the most fitting symbol of the manner in which the case had been handled by that office. The file, with all the statements, transcripts, evidence and reports, was lost.

4. On Camera

The broadcast, as Gorin envisioned it, would use Carter, Betty and Bobby as its core. Safer would do a narrative description of the murder, walking through the hotel from the swimming pool to outside room 206. There would be a moment of drama as he opened the door to that suite and stepped in, his path the same as that taken by the Zelezniks. The show would then take off on its primary thrust, the inappropriate release of Walford from Northampton.

None of the hospital authorities would go on camera.

Nor would anyone from the Massachusetts Attorney General's Office.

Documenting what had happened was not overly difficult, however. Nurse Carol Bombard and hospital orderlies Jack Bourgeois and Edward Kubasek were not only available but anxious to talk. They were the three who had watched Walford explode during a ward session and try to attack Bombard. The two men, with the help of other patients, had wrestled Walford into a security cell—a twenty-minute fight that saw them bruised, battered and shaken. Kubasek had been nearly choked to death. Afterward they had heard Walford threaten to kill others; they had heard him chanting, and talking to his God. They had known he was dangerous and assaultive. They had wanted to see him transferred to the Bridgewater mental facility, a maximum security institution. They had not been listened to. The three had objected vigorously when Walford had been released; they had (not by name) been quoted in the local papers describing the event in the days and weeks directly after the murder in Miami. When "60 Minutes" contacted them, they were ready, the recollections of Walford still remarkably fresh in their memories.

Gorin also lined up a brief interview with Dr. Abraham Halpern, the distinguished president of the American Academy of Psychiatry and the Law. He was to comment on the "black magic" allegation made by the Massachusetts Attorney General's Office in a legal brief.

A title was assigned to the broadcast. It was called "It Didn't Have to Happen..."

The only change the camera crew made in the living room in which the Zelezniks sat with Morley Safer was to shift the location of the large painting Betty had done of the two boys. The crew wanted the painting on the mantelpiece in the center of the room, not in the corner it ordinarily occupied. The painting served as a backdrop for the conversation; as the camera moved between Carter, Betty, Bobby and Safer, it crept in and out of the picture, a subtle counterpoint to the words being spoken.

Carter, the primary spokesman as always, did most of the talking. He listed all the things that had happened, from hearing Arnold's cry for help to the wrong-colored jacket. He described the frustrations suffered in the courts. He told of writing the American Civil Liberties Union but never even getting the courtesy of a reply, of contacting the American Psychiatric Association but hearing that it couldn't get involved. He coughed back tears once or twice.

Safer asked: "... Why are you going ahead with this? I mean, are you not inflicting even more pain on yourself with this?"

"We don't live in a pain free world..." Carter began, but Betty interrupted.

"Well, at the time we made an agreement that we would go as far as we could and use as much money as we had. We felt at the time, if we had to sell everything that we owned, we would do it in order to get to the Supreme Court, which I at the time thought would listen. We have not used all of our money. We have a little more and we can continue to go on...."

"But," Carter said, his sigh audible, "if I could be convinced that there was justice done, that there had been no negligence, I would never have entered the case, or I would stop. What I see is one cover-up after another. And I feel that Arnold would want this...."

"I know, I don't believe for a minute that you're doing this for the money," Safer said. A few seconds later he turned to Bobby, and asked, "What do you feel about this, this crusade, if I can call it that, that your parents have embarked on?"

Betty and Carter did not know what Bobby was going to say. He had never really articulated to his parents whether he thought it was worthwhile or not. He had supported them, accompanied them, but Betty especially had noted a type of closeness, perhaps concealment. They had not coached Bobby about what to say to Safer.

"Well," he said. His voice was steady, direct. "I'm definitely for it. I mean, I agree with what my dad has said, and I've tried to help. It's kind of hard for me because I don't really understand it as much as they do. But I certainly try to give them the support I can, I guess, morally or mentally. I definitely agree with it, and I would like to see them pursue it, and maybe, if it comes, then I would pursue it when I get older and when I feel more comfortable with the situation. . . ."

"What I'm asking," Safer said, "really is: In a sense, are you not sacrificing your lives, your own lives, with this obsession, I guess some people might call it . . . ?"

"Yes, it is an obsession," Betty replied, "and I think we are sacrificing our lives. I feel sorry for Bobby because he has to go along with us, because he doesn't have any choice, but—"

Carter interrupted. "Yes, he has a choice."

"He has a choice, you say you have . . ." Safer started, but now Bobby interrupted all of them with a rushing torrent of words.

"I have a choice, but I agree with it . . . the paragraph that my dad read [the summation of his brief] that's exactly the way I feel, too. It's as if he gave up his life, and it was, in a sense, senseless, because he's not getting anything for it and the world is actually losing something because it is a cover-up. Or not a cover-up, but . . . and if something isn't done, it was just a wasted life! And that would . . . and my brother's life was an important life! He was a fine person who would have made something in this world! So just to let it go on, just to let it drop, would not be correct, and I would certainly would like to give something to try to make something out of it. There has to be a good point in it! Though that sounds maybe morbid or something. But you have to try to find the good point, even if it's going to be hard and tiring and painful!"

Bobby leaned back on the couch, as if exhausted, and for one of those bright moments in every parent's life, Carter and Betty filled with an inexhaustible pride.

CHAPTER 13

"All I Have to Say"

1. A Phone That Won't Stop Ringing

The "60 Minutes" broadcast was on February 28, 1982. It was the first segment of the show. It was viewed by more than 33 million people. I had flown north to watch the show with Carter, Betty and Bobby. They were excited and more than a little nervous before airtime. Carter was apologizing beforehand. "Television can't do that much," he was saying. "Even Gorin told me that they couldn't hope to get every facet of this down. It may be superficial, but I hope it will have some impact. People will write, I hope." Betty was on edge, excited, as was Bobby. They were worried about how they would appear, what would be said. It was a type of delightful worry; as Betty said, they were, after all, ordinary people who had, by virtue of the one event, been separated from the common mass. It was a separation she would have preferred not to have had, but it was there nonetheless.

She hadn't really known how to behave in the weeks after the crew had completed filming, waiting for the show.

She felt it was somehow inappropriate to go around saying, "Be sure to watch '60 Minutes' on Sunday. We're going to be on." It would have seemed wrong. Ultimately she told very few people. One person she did tell was a young black woman who was in an art class with Betty. The young woman had become very upset about the Atlanta slayings and spent a good deal of time talking with Betty about the fear and frustration she felt over those brutal, senseless murders. After a while Betty had told the young woman about Arnold's murder. The young woman had brought in a green ribbon for Betty the next day. The ribbons were symbolic of the loss felt by the black community. Betty had worn the green ribbon until the case was concluded by the arrest of the man subsequently convicted of some of the murders, Wayne Williams.

The contradictory feelings had always troubled Betty. There had been the desire to hide away with her grief and memories in the days after the murder and periodically thereafter, and she had fought against it, replacing it with an insistence on restoration. And now there was another feeling. "In a way," she said of the "60 Minutes" inquiry, "I feel guilty getting so much attention. There's so much violence, so many people victimized in the world." She paused. "It's hard to think of yourself as so important that other people would be interested in what you say." She was like a moth, both attracted and hurt by the flame.

Carter sat in an easy chair, Betty and Bobby together on the couch. The familiar stopwatch face appeared on the television screen. Betty gave a small, barely perceptible start when Safer appeared, sitting next to one of the mock magazine covers that the show used to introduce their story. The family was silent throughout the broadcast. Bobby watched silently, his attention centered on the small screen of the family's television set.

"This tragedy did not have to happen..." Safer said.

The camera followed Safer as he walked through the murder scene. He stood outside Northampton, in the snow. The old, tired-looking brick walls rose up behind him. The camera trailed the correspondent inside the now-empty and abandoned Springfield Unit. Safer picked his way amid the broken glass and rubble that littered the hallways where Walford's angry voice had once reverberated. Still following Safer, the camera focused on a small port-hole in one door; Safer explained that inside was the seclusion cell where the drugged, strait-jacketed Walford had screamed to his God. It was through that tiny opening that the doctor in charge of the unit had interviewed Walford the day after the attack on the nurse. Walford had then insisted on his freedom and demonstrated how improved he was. Still afraid to be in the same room as Walford, Safer explained, the doctors had okayed his release, fewer than forty-eight hours after his arrival at the hospital.

Psychiatrist Abraham Halpern was interviewed. The correspondent read him the "black magic" quotation from the Massachusetts attorney general's brief. Halpern responded directly: "The statement by the attorney general of the Commonwealth of Massachusetts is ridiculous and preposterous. There isn't a psychiatrist in the United States who is responsible and even minimally trained who would have released within forty-eight hours a severely psychotic and delusional patient. It could not have happened except in the face of extreme negligence."

Carter's image came on the screen. The camera panned to Betty and Bobby, sitting on the couch in the same seats they occupied as they watched the show. Suddenly Bobby was alone on the television, talking of finding some meaning in his brother's death. As Bobby watched himself speaking on the show, Betty leaned over and gave him a small pat on the leg.

Back to Carter. "The state of Massachusetts is off the hook...."

Then Safer was alone, back on the set. "Vernal Walford was acquitted of the murder of Arnold Zeleznik by reason of insanity. He is now in a Florida state mental institution."

Tick, tick, tick went the stopwatch, and the show cut to a commercial break.

Carter's eyes were red. "They did a good job," he said.

There was a second's rest, and all three took in deep breaths. Carter exhaled suddenly and laughed, the mirth of a man suddenly relieved of a great worry.

"How 'bout it, Bobby, they do a good job?"

"Yeah."

"You looked good," Carter said to Betty.

"Ohhhhh..." she said, shaking her head. Her eyes, too, were filled, but she was grinning, and her words were rushed with excitement. "I must look really bad because I thought I looked just pathetic...." She was laughing and crying at the same moment. She turned to me. "It's funny, but it does enter your mind, how you look. I guess, because of the cameras—"

"I had no idea where the cameras were," Carter interjected.

The phone rang, and Carter jumped up.

"It went fast," Bobby said.

"I think they did a substantial job for just fifteen minutes," Betty said. "I had never seen those photos of Walford." She stopped, thinking. "Knowing something and seeing something are different."

"I thought it was good," Bobby said to me. "I liked it when the people who were in it were strong in what they said."

Carter hung up. "Those photos," he said. "He was just a caged animal."

I asked Bobby if seeing Walford had stirred his recollection. "That was the way he was. I can still see him, his face, his hands...."

The phone rang again. Carter jumped up again.

"Does it scare you?" I asked.

Bobby shook his head.

Carter hung up with the words "Write a letter to Norman Gorin, producer, '60 Minutes,' CBS-TV, New York. Thanks for calling, let's get together soon."

"That was..." he started. The phone rang again.

He spoke for a few minutes, then hung up, having given the same address. In a moment it rang again. It was a former neighbor, someone the Zelezniks hadn't seen in a decade. After that a former colleague called. Then another old-time friend. One of the anthropologists who had accompanied Carter to Ethiopia before his marriage called. At one break in the onslaught Carter turned to me and asked, "John, can you think of another developed country in the entire world with our level of inhumanity and violence?"

The phone rang. I looked at Betty and Bobby and said, "Saved by the proverbial bell." We all laughed together.

On the phone, Carter was saying, "Right, excellent. Thank you." He hung up and said, "That was Joan. She's already written her letter."

"What did she say?" Betty asked.

"Oh, how could it happen and why didn't the Supreme Court do their duty . . . and good for her, I say."

He laughed out loud, a short release of tension.

"Good for her good for her good for her," he said.

2. The Next Day and Some Other Days in Massachusetts

The next day, a Monday, Republican Senator David Locke, the assistant minority leader, rose on the floor of the Massachusetts State Senate and said that the "60 Minutes" broadcast had raised serious questions about the performance of state officials and the responsibilities of the commonwealth in the release of Walford from Northampton. He suggested to the body of men and women that the Senate fund its own investigation of the issues outlined by the show and of the release of Vernal Walford. There was considerable support for this suggestion.

Later in the week Democratic Senator Patricia McGovern, a forthright former public defender with an abiding interest in the mental health delivery systems, went to the majority leadership in the Senate, requesting to be put in charge of the investigation, assuming that it was to be broad enough in scope and properly funded. She received those assurances and was given the task. "Massachusetts is off the hook . . ." Carter had told Safer in the broadcast. Well, Massachusetts was voluntarily putting itself back on the hook.

Suddenly many people were interested in what the Zelezniks had to say.

The Associated Press and United Press International were covering the formation of the inquiry committee out of Boston. The *Boston Globe* reporter who years earlier had written stories quoting Kubasek, Bombard and Bourgeois about the release, was back in touch with the Zelezniks. She traveled to Ambler to meet them and wrote a series of articles about their situation. Other reporters from Massachusetts papers also joined in interviewing the family. A reporter from *Boston* magazine spent a weekend with the family. Television stations, too, filmed the three of them, especially when they went to Boston to meet with the committee. The *Philadelphia Inquirer* finally discovered the story; a lengthy news feature was written by reporter Emily Lounsberry and ran on the front page. Another reporter, Martha Woodall, began preparations for an even longer magazine piece on the family, which was scheduled to run in the *Inquirer*'s Sunday magazine. "60 Minutes" was inundated with mail from around the nation, decrying what had happened to the Zelezniks. Betty had said to me that she was scared that CBS wouldn't get a response. Her fears proved groundless.

It was an extraordinary conversion. In the course of minutes the Zelezniks went from almost total anonymity to the center of a great deal of publicity. They did not alter their style much to accommodate this wave. Carter, Betty and Bobby kept repeating the same things they had been saying for the past seven years. The language didn't change, only the means of expression. Suddenly, finally, it seemed people were listening.

In Boston, Senator McGovern put together a staff. She chose as director a young man with whom she had previously worked, Gregory Torres. The two of them envisioned a two-headed investigation; first a specific inquiry into the circumstances surrounding the admission and subsequent release of Vernal Walford from Northampton; then a second phase investigating the overall commitment and release procedures employed by the Massachusetts Department of Mental Health.

Greg Torres was a tall, dark-haired, black-bearded man in his early thirties. An occasional broad *a* slipped into his conversation, contradicting his background as the son of an immigrant from Nicaragua. He was a tenacious, aggressive investigator, a man equally at home using his considerable charm or punching out direct, angry, hard questions. Since graduating from college and obtaining his master's degree in government, he had worked in a number of jobs closely connected with Massachusetts state government; he was an expert at the particular interwoven nature of Massachusetts politics. The opportunity to probe the mental health system was one he embraced readily.

Setting up the inquiry took longer than originally envisioned. The opening sessions were set for June 21. Prior to then, however, Greg Torres was deeply enmeshed in what had happened in November and December 1974. Carter had traveled to Boston to meet with the committee before the open hearings were conducted. He carted with him all his boxes, all his documents, depositions, statements, investigations, clippings and opinions. He met with

Torres early one morning in the late spring. Torres had been unsure what to expect from Carter. What he got was the synthesized, controlled fury of seven years of stored anger and outrage. The two men had entered a small interview room adjacent to the committee chambers to start talking. Torres, scratching notes, reading papers as Carter shoved them across the table, listened for hour after hour as Carter delineated his experiences and formed his arguments. More than once Carter's eyes filled with his memories. In his direct, linear style, Carter ransacked the history of his torment. This happened; this happened; this happened. Wham, wham, wham, down on the table slammed the documents of Carter's obsession. All the words spoken so many times— accountability, responsibility—filled the small room, hanging alive in the still air. Lunch passed, ignored. The two men ("eyeball to eyeball," Torres said later, laughing) stayed in the room throughout the day and into the early evening, until they were exhausted and the boxes of papers were exhausted.

Gregory Torres went home that night and looked down at the sleeping form of his own newborn child and wondered: Would I be any different?

3. Bobby's Question

When the open hearings of the inquiry committee convened in June, they intended to hear from more than thirty witnesses. A wide, high-ceilinged room not far from the Senate floor had been set aside for the committee. The members sat at a bank of chairs behind a wide wooden desk. Witnesses took seats just in front of them at a table laden with microphones. One major problem arose almost instantly: The committee had no enforceable subpoena power, and several key witnesses, the people at Northampton who had made the decision to release Walford, were reluctant to testify. After all, they still faced Carter's lawsuit. Preliminary documents had been filed in the Suffolk County Court to sue them all individually. Carter and his attorney had availed themselves of the only open legal avenue. Greg Torres explained this dilemma to Carter; the inquiry would proceed without the witnesses. After all, depositions and other court-related statements were available, though some of the impact, obviously, would be lost. Carter talked over the situation with Betty and Bobby, and the three of them swiftly agreed on the proper course. They dropped the lawsuit and publicly agreed not to refile it.

It was an important decision. It effectively placed all the family's hopes in the single forum of the legislative inquiry. However, the Zelezniks had never liked the idea of pursuing the individual doctors; it was the common-wealth that they were after. Now they were to have their moment, in front of the press, the television cameras and lights and the public.

They made the most of it.

Betty testified first. The transcript of her statement runs twelve pages. She hesitated just once to brush back tears.

"I would like to preface my remarks by describing the scene which took place over seven years ago. Ours had been a very close family and, I judged, a loving one. Arnold was dead, having been murdered by Vernal Newland Walford. We were distraught. Arnold's younger brother was crying and saying over and over again, the following: 'I don't hear Arnold's voice in my playing anymore. I don't have anyone to play with and why did it have to be Arnold? Why? Why?'

"I submit that the purpose of this investigation is to answer Bobby's question at last and completely."

Betty went on, describing the "investigation" that the hospital had done of its release of Walford. She described how infuriating it was, how the family would not have been subjected to the years of litigation if only the people in charge had admitted their error. Then she read the letter that she had received from Arnold's teacher, Terry Young, in the days after the murder. There was utter silence in the hearing room.

"What was wonderful about Arnold was that he wanted so much from life and that he was willing to give so much to life to get what he wanted. . . .

"Arnold was neither bashful nor bold; he knew his place and he accepted himself for what he was. He was a proud and good child. . . ."

Betty then described the events of the murder.

". . . The only good thing that was, that might have been, was that it was sudden and Arnold's suffering was brief. He had lived life with the courage of a youngster who was both cautious and trusting. And this is how he died. . . ."

Betty groped for control as she described the funeral. Senator McGovern asked if she wouldn't want a break, but she shook her head and plunged forward, quoting Carter's letter to himself.

". . . he was in death as in life, a beautiful boy. Since that time and in some ways for the rest of our lives, we have been grieving our loss and Arnold's loss and the world's loss. On January 2nd, 1975, Carter finally returned to work. Bobby and I rode with him to the train station. Carter left for the train with a heavy heart. As he did, Bobby said to me, 'When Arnold left, he left us his courage. Now all we have to do is use it.'

"And we've striven ever since then to do that. That's all I have to say."

* * *

Carter's statement was lengthy. The transcript ran more than seventy pages. He attacked the mental health system and the system of justice. "The system failed..." he said over and over. And then he asked why. He approached the hearings with the same dogged, detailed style that had characterized his own inquiries from the start, more than seven years earlier. He didn't say anything appreciably different from what he had told me or told Morley Safer and Norman Gorin or had written in his legal brief. The words negligence and incompetence rolled out onto the table before him, underscored by the clicking sound of the stenographer's dictation machine, taking down every word. He spoke on, oblivious to camera lights, to anything but his task. When he finished, he rose, a man drained.

Bobby was as short as Carter had been long.

Looking slightly uncomfortable beneath the lights and wearing a jacket and tie, Bobby took his place at the table before the committee. He had a sheaf of notes before him, and he tried hard not to rush, concentrating on speaking directly and clearly. "For the record, please, state your name," said Senator McGovern.

"I am Robert Carter Zeleznik."

"How old are you, Robert?"

"I'm fifteen."

"Fifteen? And do you live with your parents?"

"Yes."

"All right. And your family has indicated you would like to make a statement at this time."

"Yes."

"Why don't you go ahead, please?"

"Okay. I'm speaking to you as a brother of Arnold and it's difficult for me to do this because he was such a close friend of mine, such a wonderful person. I think of him as a model child and as a model person and also as a model brother. This was because he had been nurtured with a set of ideals. I call them human ideals, because the bottom line of each of these ideals would be that these ideals would enable him to help society, that they would be a benefit to society.

"One of his typical ideals was that of responsibility. He knew that it was okay for him to make a mistake. However, he also believed that when he made a mistake, it would fall incumbent upon him to make reparations for his mistakes and to take measures to prevent them from happening again. In this way the world would be better than it would be before he made the mistake.

"This committee is now confronted with the chance to redeem the tentative responsibility held by my brother. The hopeful outcome of such action by this committee would be in decreasing the chances of anything like this ever having to happen again. If this were to be, if this were to happen, the mental health profession would be better off than it had been when he was alive; hence my brother's death would not have been a useless sacrifice. He would be dead, but his ideals would live and they would still benefit society and that is what he had always hoped and that's what I hope.

"And that's all I have to say."

Bobby stood up, looked the committee members in the eyes and then turned and walked slowly to the pew where his mother and father were sitting, dabbing at the tears in their eyes. However, this time, perhaps for the first time in a long time, they were not tears of discouragement or tears of frustration or tears of anger, but tears of a different sort.

CHAPTER 14
Jack Denaro's Mystery

Oh, God said to Abraham, kill me a son,
Abe said, man, you must be putting me on.
God said no, Abe said what
God said you can do what you want Abe,
But next time you see me coming you
Better run...
Well, Abe said where do you want this
Killing done?
God said, out on Highway 61....
—Bob Dylan, "Highway 61 Revisited"

1. *"...No Man Acts for No Reason"*

I still did not know why Arnold Zeleznik had died.

Carter had channeled what he considered the reasons for Arnold's death into the investigation of a system; he had always seen the murder as part of a whole series of events, which had begun months earlier when Walford had first been smuggled into the United States. In his mind, so many people could have prevented the murder, and he came to feel that they were equally responsible. Walford, he thought, was a grenade passed carelessly from hand to hand, with a mindless ignorance of the danger. When he exploded and Arnold fell, were not all those hands that had sought to avoid any connection with the event as guilty as Walford? In a sense, I broke with the Zelezniks at that point. I could see their fury with the hospital and all the people who had had a chance to prevent the murder. I saw it as reporting on the emperor's absence of clothing. After talking with Greg Torres and being impressed with the sincerity of his effort to determine why Walford had not been kept in the hospital, I felt that the truth would eventually emerge. It was only a matter of ordering the facts. However, the legislative inquiry in Massachusetts would answer only the question of why Walford had been available to kill Arnold Zeleznik. There was a further why that remained within the killer himself.

I was still fascinated by the man who had performed the murder, perhaps, in an unusual way, even more than by the Zelezniks. I considered many times what I might have said, or might have done, when he and I had been face-to-face. What combination of words might have triggered him to respond instead of to argue?

I replayed all the things, in all his incarnations, through all the varying degrees of psychosis and lucidity, that he had told the psychiatrists. I tried to picture him in my mind's eye, as he had described himself, standing behind the door to his room, waiting, knife in hand. I wondered how it must have felt, with his rigidly taut body, muscles stretched to breaking, to think that he was uncontrollably contracting and expanding. Was the heavenly light in the room blinding or illuminating? Was the voice loud and insistent, or was it soft, gently cajoling, seductively persuasive? Did it whisper into his ear the command to open the door and take what he found there? Or was it a shouted order, issued amid the clash and rage of battle?

Something did not ring true.

Something, I thought, was missing.

And so I went to see Denaro.

The first time I had contacted Jack Denaro, he had been reluctant to talk about the case. He'd said he still felt that in some ancient way, Walford remained his client, and until the murder charge was resolved, he thought it wiser not to talk about his participation. It was not exactly a client-attorney relationship that kept him reticent, but a different kind of ethic, one fashioned in the superheated atmosphere in the Dade County Jail when Denaro had asked Walford, "Are ye he who has been sent from above . . . ?" That obstacle had been removed, though, when Walford had been declared not guilty by reason of insanity at his twenty-minute "trial" in February 1981. Denaro and I met sometime later in his office overlooking Biscayne Bay. In his wiry, intense way, Denaro wheeled back and forth in his chair at his desk, gesturing occasionally with his hands, peering at me through tinted glasses.

"You know, the mystery possessed me for a while," he said. "And this, like any other murder, was a kind of whodunit. Only this time it was a whydunit. I kept looking at the facts. He's in the hospital in Massachusetts and gets out. Then his behavior becomes stranger. He is fleeing from something. He comes to Miami. Then, after the killing, he just exploded! He became a rabid dog with a dialogue that revolved around the Bible.

"You see, no man acts for no reason. There's always a reason there. It may be grossly insane, but it makes sense within that context. There must be a reason. And that was the mystery. Finding out the reason."

There is disagreement in the medical profession on the exact causes of schizophrenia. Some physicians believe that it is organic in origin; others, psychological. Heredity seems to play a major factor; the child of a schizophrenic parent has a substantially greater risk of developing the disease. There are schools of thought that contend that the disease is affected by sociocultural background. Others believe that it is caused by chemical imbalances within the brain. Some people want to treat it with traditional psychiatric therapy; others, with different drugs; still others, with a combination. Although the disease follows broadly-defined paths, it maintains a highly individualistic character; schizophrenics do not necessarily behave alike in similar circumstances. The disease is found in all cultures; although studies differ, in the United States it affects as much as one percent of the general population. It contributes more than twenty percent of the admissions to mental hospitals, and at any given time close to half the beds in the nation's mental health facilities will be occupied by schizophrenics.

Paranoid schizophrenia, while not uncommon, affects far fewer people than simple schizophrenia, and the majority of the paranoid schizophrenics seen by physicians pose the greatest danger of harm to themselves. It is rare, luckily, for a paranoid schizophrenic to become dangerous to others. The combination of assaultiveness and rage that Walford experienced was extraordinarily rare.

I looked at much of the literature of paranoid schizophrenia. There were dozens of examples of schizophrenia, paranoid type. The descriptions of men or women deluded into thinking that God or their next-door neighbor or the Russians were listening in on them were numerous, but those examples told me little about Walford.

It wasn't as simple as saying with Freudian smugness, well, Vernal Walford was abused and tortured as a child, creating in him the necessity to develop a delusional system to protect himself from the terror, and when those feelings of anger and inadequacy eventually surfaced in Miami, Florida, he killed a little boy to compensate, and so really, psychologically speaking, he was killing himself.

There were no pat answers.

No easily followed patterns of behavior.

No real access to the emotional road map that led eventually to room 206.

Carter always railed against the psychiatric reports performed in Miami. I asked him many times why he was so upset with them; as always, he responded that they failed to perform elementary tasks and provide basic information. Eventually I came to see that what angered him was that these men had never seemed to consider why Walford had acted. They had been concerned only with finding out what he had done and then fitting it into the admittedly unworkable framework of the M'Naghten rule. Even when they had learned that Walford heard voices, what they had wanted to know was what the voices said. That was important, of course, both legally and psychologically—indeed, I too wanted to know what the voices said—but no one ever found out why he heard the voices. I thought of the moment of relative lucidity when Walford had casually mentioned the deaths of his own children.

Even for those men assigned to probe the workings of the mind, Walford remained an enigma.

2. A Newspaper Story

Denaro:

"I would go, day after day, and talk with him. He was giving information, but I could tell he was still holding back something. Something was there. The mystery of why he did it was still there. I knew it. I could feel it in my gut."

I thought of the letter.

Shortly after the murder, Walford had sent his girl friend-landlady Lucille Fernandez a letter. It was written on plain white stationery with the title and address of the mental hospital across the top. His handwriting flowed furiously across the ruled lines of the page.

> Dear L Fernandez A100819
> I miss you
> only for the time but I know
> that you did just what you had in
> mind to do a nother nab because
> is the same way you treat your
> husband. Fro Befor me because
> if you remember I told you that
> you are going dead but you take
> it for a joke if is one day
> befor I depart from this

world I am going to kill you
belive it or not because you
treat me like a dog but I
am just with my judgement
that is why I did not kill
you long time because
you keep preacuring me
so much that I think about
every time but it is the living
God that save you from me
So when you see me again
you know serturne that
I would treat you better than
any man that you every have
in your life but through
the love of money you
put me out without thinking
but is only a matter of
time because if I don't
kill you and your *child*
God knoweth that I
am not right

Sign Walford

Lucille Fernandez had scrawled across the letter: "I see from this letter that he is right back where he was when he left the state hospital in Mass."

Denaro:
"The hospital. Being baptized in the church up there. He told Lucille Fernandez he was going to kill her daughter! He had a true irresistible impulse to kill a child!

"There was nothing he could do to prevent it! He told her he had the desire to kill her child, so he left immediately. And that brought him to Miami. He was fleeing that homicidal impulse. He was trying to get away, back to Jamaica, trying to escape from the demands his mind was placing on him. Then we see him at the airport, preaching. He has obviously made up his mind to kill because he goes and buys the murder weapon. The decision to sacrifice a child was formulated. But where did that come from?"

After his release from Northampton, as Lucille Fernandez had told the defense lawyers, Walford had become involved in the Alden Baptist Church in Springfield. The pastor who'd baptized Walford a few days before the murder was the Reverend Miles Crawford. Crawford told Greg Torres and the investigators from the Massachusetts Senate inquiry that Walford had taken an unusual interest in the pastor's ten-year-old daughter. Once he had been spotted watching the child as she got off at her school bus stop and had followed her home. Another time she had been playing close by Walford in the pastor's office when Crawford had realized the desk separated him from his child and the madman. His eyes, showing sudden panic, had locked with Walford's. The Jamaican had grinned, a manic, evil smile, and said for the pastor not to be worried, he wasn't going to do anything to the child.

I thought of the Bible open on the bed. He had been reading the Book of Daniel. Daniel, the last of the Old Testament seers and prophets who foresaw the coming of the Savior; the interpreter of dreams and revelations in whom the Holy Spirit resided. Daniel, tossed by jealousy into the lion's den for his prophecies and preaching. I thought of the crowds that had flowed past Walford in the airport, heads turning at the sound of his voice raised with the Word as it coursed electric through him. I saw all the people hurrying away, quickstep, ignoring his message. How all those sudden stares and swiftly averted eyes must have infuriated him. In the lion's den, I thought.

Denaro:
"He goes to the kitchen and comes out with the plate of food. Remember, they found it on the bureau, untouched. It's then that he spies the little boy. He goes into the room, sets the dinner down, grabs for the knife and opens the door and seizes the little boy."

Standing by the door, listening to voices? Open the door, and take what you find there. No, I thought. That was delusion, the mind's memory playing tricks. That was how Walford wanted to remember it, as a miracle provided by God. I thought of Abraham, hand stayed by the angel, his eyes averted from the throat of his own child to where he could see the ram, horns tangled in a nearby bush. A sacrifice was supplied. Vernal Newland Walford, no less than Daniel or Abraham or Jesus Himself in his own mind, wanted to believe that God had given him his victim. It was part of the justification process that Walford had undergone afterward. Even at his most bestial, snarling self, Walford was still human and still knew that what he had done was terrible in many eyes, and perhaps in his own, too. He had had to justify what he'd done. I thought of the shrug when he had been asked about going to trial. Man's judgment did not worry him as much as God's.

The voice had been there, however, as real in that instant as my voice or any man's. How it must have screamed for attention when Walford's eyes fell upon Arnold Zeleznik alone in the hallway.

Denaro:

"You've got to understand, he's telling me these things, but I know he's still holding back. He had been rambling, the past few days, about John the Baptist and Christ. At one point he said to me, 'Who are you and why should I tell you?' and then he asked, 'And what is your authority?' The words stayed with me. I thought: He wants to kill for God.

"And so I tried to put myself in his position. As a schizophrenic. 'Are ye he who has been sent from above...?' You see, I put his mental existence on the line; remember, this is an intelligent man. Oh, he knew he was insane. He had fought and fought mentally to escape himself. But he had been unable to. And now he had to justify what he had done to God.

"So I told him I was sent from above. I told him that we needed the information to see if what he had done was justified in the eyes of God. And I told him I was an angel. He knew, you see, even the Greek derivation. We think of angels as people dressed in white, with wings. But in the Old Testament they are messengers. And that is what I told him I was.

"And so he told me everything. I took him back—not physically, but mentally—to the airport and then to the restaurant and then to the hallway and finally to room two-oh-six.

"He told me everything. But I still felt there was something missing. He wasn't trying to evade me any longer. He just couldn't remember. I went over it again and again with him: What did you do when you woke up? What did you get dressed in? What did you do when you went out? I didn't know what I was searching for, but something. What did you do when you got your breakfast? And then he said it. He said, 'I sat down at the sofa, and I read the newspaper.' And I thought: He read something!

"Remember what he said in the note that the police found in his pocket. When did he have time to write that? Not after the murder. Things were happening too quickly! Before, before, before.

"You have to think like a schizophrenic."

The note in the pocket. The words scrawled erratically across an empty airmail envelope: "The God of Israel, say so. The God Israel say this temple must not be used for any voilence nor any police office child offer has sacrifices."

Denaro:

"He was caught in the midst of a compulsion to do something he knew would destroy himself. It must have been a terrible thing, to be trapped, to destroy a life for this idea he couldn't control. At that point, he would have killed any child he saw."

I thought of Carter's comment. "In a way, I think Arnold saved his brother and mother's lives. . . ."

Denaro:
"Look in the paper. You'll see the article."

I went to the microfilm files of the *Miami Herald*. I checked the morning of the twentieth. Nothing. I checked the nineteenth, the eighteenth, the seventeenth. the sixteenth, the fifteenth. Nothing. I called Jack Denaro back. "It's there. Think of the note. You've got to think like a schizophrenic!" he said.

I looked again.

And there it was.

It was a small column, written by the editor of the *Tallahassee Democrat*, Malcolm Johnson. The column was barely 300 words long. It occupied a small corner on the *Herald*'s Op-Ed page. To most readers, it must have seemed innocuous, just a few more words in the mass of newsprint that the newspaper disgorged every day. Something for the eyes and mind to scan quickly and just as quickly to consider and forget. But not for Vernal Walford. I could instantly envision the impact it must have had. Explosive:

Court and Church Unseparated
A 5-YEAR SENTENCE: CHRISTIANITY

Musing over the news:

A young woman, convicted of manslaughter for cutting her husband's throat, was sentenced by a Miami judge to teach a Sunday School class for five years instead of going to jail.

Now the very best rehabilitation for this 23-year-old woman may result from preparing her Sunday School lesson and reciting it for the next 260 Sundays.

But what right has that judge to impose such a sentence on the Sunday School and those it hopes to attract by sincere study of the Gospel?

Assuming there is a church willing to put this woman in front of a Sunday School class despite her record of killing her husband plus old arrests on charges of prostitution and narcotics law violations, there is a deeper question involved here.

The sentence amounts to compulsory Christianity, and—though it may lead to sincere conversion of a sinner—it isn't in the realm of the American judiciary to compel anyone to engage in even the most wholesome religious activity.

But as long as we choose our judges by popular election, as we do in Florida, we'll have judicial stunt men playing to the galleries with such judgments from the bench. . . .

The column continued with other "musings over the news."

The temple. Police office. Slashing the throat. A woman. I thought of what the attendants at Northampton had overheard: Men were important, women less so and children don't count hardly at all. The God of Israel say so. Right in Vernal Walford's ear.

"It's crazy, you know," Denaro said. "In a way that's the entire point. As his attorney I saw it as the missing piece. We would have the videotape, the doctors, the act itself. And then this incredible mad logic stemming from reading that innocuous article. It would be inconceivable for anyone to make that up. And, taken then as a whole, I thought that when the case came back for trial, that I would be able to persuade the jury not to follow their emotions but to follow their oath and return what I thought was the true verdict in this case."

Denaro stopped his spinning in his desk chair and looked out from his window, up into the empty, pallid blue of the Miami sky. He took a deep breath and sighed.

"It was such a frightening thing.

"I have handled hundreds of murder cases and seen hundreds of crime scene and autopsy photographs. But when I saw the pictures of that little boy—" he hesitated, searching for the words—"it had a singular effect upon me. He was absolutely beautiful, a perfect little child. It was the only time, in any murder case, where the photos touched my heart.

"You see, that's the way I prepare my defense. I research it and come to know the facts so well that it is like a moving picture in my mind. That happened in this case, and it was terrible. I could see it, the faces, the movements, the actions and the dialogue frozen in my mind. I could see Barbarino, the manager, and the mother frantically searching for the lost child. I could see them opening the door, and I could see Barbarino stepping inside and just out of the corner of his eye, catching the sight in the bathroom, just to the right, and turning, trying to prevent her, but she wouldn't be stopped and pushed by, and the father seeing and falling in a faint. I could see all that."

He hesitated again.

"Many people believe, mistakenly, that because you are a criminal defense attorney, you somehow sympathize with criminals. Nothing could be further from the truth. You are charged with a defense, and that is what you do, to the very utmost of your capacities. Do you know who are the harshest sentencers when they get on the bench? Former defense attorneys. I think that if I were a judge, I would scrupulously ascribe to the defendant all of his rights during a trial. But if I believed, after all that testimony, all that evidence, that beyond the shadow or glimmer of a reasonable doubt that that person had committed a murder or any vicious crime, then my punishment would be swift, fearsome and awesome."

He paused again.

"Those people," he said, and I knew instantly he was speaking of the Zelezniks, "experienced true horror, the horror of fate. I think they were immersed in the ugliest nightmare any man or woman could be subjected to." He waited, arranging his thoughts.

"Perhaps except a concentration camp."

Victory, or a Statement of the Obvious

1. Eight More Years

The Massachusetts Senate inquiry committee held eight public hearings in June, July and October 1982. Seven of the hearings were in Boston; one was held at the Northampton State Hospital. The final hearing, on October 4, was to consider information about Walford and the U.S. Immigration and Naturalization Service. The Zelezniks attended almost every minute of the hearings.

There were many individual moments that marked the sessions: Dr. Angelina Supan, who had authorized Walford's release after just two brief sessions with him, tearfully describing how, on the day of Walford's insistence on his release, she had been the only physician responsible for three of the hospital's five units, more than 300 patients; psychologist Robert Sharon's description of Walford's arrogant initial refusal to agree to any follow-up care if released; Jack Bourgeois, Ed Kubasek and Carol Bombard telling the committee of Walford's explosion in the floor meeting, where he'd leaped toward Bombard and had finally been wrestled into seclusion by the two attendants and several patients; Nurse Phyllis Dandineau describing how she had sat listening to Walford the night after his explosion, as he casually, calmly and lucidly informed her that he was in the hospital under an alias, that he had entered the country illegally, that he was involved in passport and marijuana smuggling—all facts which she had dutifully noted in her nurse's progress notes but which had been ignored the following day by those in charge of Walford's release.

All the moments added up to precisely what Carter had been saying for all those years.

The Northampton State Hospital was built in the 1870s. It is a red-brick Georgian-style complex of imposing buildings, set back some twenty-five yards from the street that runs by. It is situated a short way from the center of downtown Northampton, Massachusetts, the home of Smith College. Indeed, the grounds of the exclusive women's college abut the hospital grounds. Although built to house about 500 patients, the hospital has held close to 2,000. When Walford was there for his forty-odd hours, there were about 700 patients in the hospital. It is not a particularly distinguished-appearing place; in a small New England college-oriented city, it could easily be mistaken for just more dormitories, save for the ubiquitous thick wire-mesh screens that cover the windows.

The inquiry committee heard eventually from thirty witnesses. They heard about Walford, his behavior at Milton Bradley, the fight, the layoff and his subsequent psychological decompensation. They tracked his stay at the hospital hour by hour, his release and some of his bizarre behavior afterward. They analyzed the procedures in force at the hospital (barely any) and the legal options available to the doctors at Northampton to have kept Walford in the hospital (several). What they heard was incredible.

In September I received a letter from Carter. I had spoken with him a few days before about the inquiry, and he had seemed excited and optimistic about the outcome. As always, he defined success purely in terms of the truth emerging.

Dear John,

I said I would call you when I learned the date of the preliminary report... naturally, I cannot find your telephone number now when I need it. I have just a few minutes ago learned that there will be another day of hearings on October 4th and a bomb shell may be exploded at that time.

You will recall that my almost immediate reaction following Arnold's death was that it was somehow drug related and that the FBI should be called. No one would listen to me. I made the same suggestion to the state attorney, Mr. Korvick, in 1977 and I was given the "ho-hum" treatment....

Well, Greg Torres called me today to tell me about some information concerning Walford which he has now verified. It turns out that on December 2,

1974, Walford turned himself in to the Immigration authorities at the Springfield office. He told the entire story to the receptionist who duly recorded it. He told how he had been busy smuggling, how he had been at the state hospital, he showed his fake passport and social security card (he was going under the name of Robert Grant). He told this person how he had been out of the country from November 16 to November 19 and had gone to Jamaica for another load of drugs. However, at this time, "God told him to tell the whole story" and that is what he did. She took down all this information and put it into a memo which was forwarded to the Head of Investigation. Where it sat. Because of budgetary reasons, supposedly, it was standard procedure for Springfield cases to be held until there were several and then someone would be sent on a per diem basis from the Boston office.

Walford's passport, apparently, was turned over to the State Department, which took no special precautions. . . . What is extraordinary about this is that he had a record which went back (at least) to 1972 when he was turned away from the border at Niagara Falls. He was arrested in Vermont six weeks later and deported to Jamaica in 1972. In January of 1973, he was arrested in Detroit in possession of phony birth certificates.

Greg's question has been what to do with the information. They plan to bring in the person who wrote the memo (although the woman has no precise recollection of Walford). She can testify that it was her understanding that he could have been arrested that day.

To me, the news is staggering. To you? To others?

Suddenly I see eight more years in front of me.

> With best wishes,
> Carter

When I read Carter's letter, I recalled something Walford had told Dr. Jacobson, back in January 1975, in the Dade County Jail, a few days after the murder. It had seemed just to be rambling in the midst of his aberrant actions and bizarre explanations of the Bible when I first heard it. Now it took on a totally different importance.

"I took the papers to Immigration in Massachusetts and said, 'I believe in God, not man! This is phony. Send me back to Jamaica. Send me back to my country. I got here illegally, and I got these papers. I was brought here illegally, but God teaches me there!'"

I thought, too, of Denaro's argument: He was fleeing. He was trying to escape. He was caught in the throes of a demand far worse than any, the compulsion to kill a child. He was struggling against it, trying to get home. He turned himself in, knowing that he would be deported. But even the authorities wouldn't take charge; they let him go. How surprised he must have been. So he went to the airport himself and got as close to Jamaica as Miami. He just didn't make it the rest of the way.

When I spoke with Carter, he seemed outraged by this additional piece of what he termed irresponsibility. (Greg Torres, agreeing, pointed out to me that the Immigration office where Walford had come in to confess his participation in serious felonies was one flight of stairs beneath the Springfield branch office of the FBI. All someone would have had to do was walk Walford upstairs and have him start repeating his story. A simple national crime information computer check would have turned up his prior arrests.) It seemed beyond comprehension to Carter; how could one sit blissfully listening to a psychotic describe his involvement in crimes and just write a memo, waving as he exited through the door. Frankly, it seemed just about incomprehensible to everyone connected to the inquiry.

There was another emotion in Carter, however, that paralleled his outrage. For the first time I sensed that in part, he was invigorated by the news. I thought back to what he had said over the years, about Walford's being the manifestation of breakdowns in so many systems, how the murder had symbolized so many evils. How could one debate that? I wondered. Every time Carter turned around, it seemed, another group or authority charged with maintaining the public good had failed dismally to exercise any judgment or responsibility. "Suddenly I see eight more years. . . ." Carter had written. And, I thought, there will be eight more after that. And on and on.

2. The Report

I flew to Boston on November 11, the day before the final report of the inquiry committee was to be released. It was overcast but warm for the time of year. It was Veterans Day; flags protruded from the old brick and stone buildings on Beacon Hill; the Common was busy with strollers, joggers, street musicians and young men hanging out with time and probably trouble on their hands. The state government offices were closed and empty, and my footsteps echoed through the vacant corridors. The buildings were dark, lifeless in the late-afternoon quiet.

I met Greg Torres in the inquiry committee staff chambers. "Here it is," he said, handing over a stapled thick sheaf of papers. I looked down at the words: "Phase One. The Release of Vernal Walford from the Northampton State Hospital on November 27, 1974." The report was eighty-eight pages long. "Start reading," Greg said. He left me alone with the copy while he went to talk to a reporter anxious for details and trying to get the jump on the opposition.

I sat at a desk and started in.

The bulk of the report was the delineation of fifty "facts" that related to Walford's admission and release. The remainder of the report summarized the importance of the facts and placed them within the context of the manner in which the hospital had been run in 1974, and then made findings and recommendations. I read first through the narrative summary of the fifty facts.

On November 25, 1974, Vernal Newland Walford was involuntarily committed to the Northampton State Hospital by a psychiatrist from the Bay State Medical Center. Upon admission to Northampton, Walford, who used the alias Robert Miller Grant, was in a psychotic state. He complained of hearing loud voices which made him lose control, he would suddenly scream, he acknowledged that people thought he was "crazy" and were afraid of him, and he exhibited the behavior of a religious fanatic. Walford was medicated and spent the night without incident.

The following morning, during a meeting of all patients on his ward, Walford attempted to assault the head nurse chairing the meeting. When two attendants prevented him from reaching the head nurse, he assaulted them. A ten to fifteen minute violent struggle resulted. The two attendants eventually subdued Walford with the help of several patients. Walford was secluded, his medication doubled, and he spent the next five hours in prayer-like chanting. Both attendants involved in the struggle sustained injuries.

That same afternoon, Walford was released from seclusion in a relatively lucid state. Informed of his right under the law to petition for his release by filing a "three-day notice" of intent to leave the facility, Walford began to inform the staff that he had signed such a notice. (Note: According to the law, the hospital then had a full three days to evaluate Walford. If, after an evaluation, Walford was determined to be a danger to himself or to others by reason of mental illness, the hospital could then petition the district court for an involuntary commitment. The petition alone prevents the patient from leaving the hospital until after the case is heard by the court.)

Meanwhile, the nursing staff, who had witnessed the violent assault by Walford, attempted to convince hospital officials to transfer Walford to (Massachusetts Correctional Institution) Bridgewater. Although such a transfer was clearly permissible under the law, the recommendation of the nursing staff was denied.

Walford's physician, who assumed that a three-day notice had actually been submitted, began to discuss the possibility of release with the patient.

Although the patient spent the rest of the day and night in a fairly lucid state, he was observed the following morning chanting incoherently in the direction of the exit door at one end of the ward.

Several hours later, approximately forty hours after he had been involuntarily committed while in a psychotic state, and only twenty-four hours after violently assaulting several staff members, Vernal Walford was released from the Northampton State Hospital. He was given a prescription for thorazine; he was told to contact the community care center for additional treatment; and he left the hospital in a taxi. His case was never followed by the hospital even after a representative of Walford's employer telephoned the hospital several days later to report bizarre and disruptive behavior on the part of Walford, and sought to return Walford to Northampton.

On December 2, 1974, Walford turned himself in to the Springfield office of the Immigration and Naturalization Service. Walford claimed to be following instructions from God and admitted to being an illegal alien. He handed over an illegal passport and birth certificate in the name of Robert Miller Grant, identified himself as Vernal Walford and confessed his involvement in criminal activity, provided his current address and a summary of his activities over recent months and left the office. His case was never investigated by the Immigration and Naturalization Service.

On December 20, 1974, at the Crossways Motor Inn in Miami, Florida, Vernal Walford murdered Arnold Zeleznik.

An internal investigation into Walford's release initiated by the Department of Mental Health several weeks after the murder found no negligence on the part of the Northampton staff.

FINDINGS

The committee finds that the involuntary commitment of Vernal Walford by Dr. William Linson of the Springfield Hospital, pursuant to (Massachusetts General Laws) Ch. 123, sec. 12, was handled in an appropriate manner. An accurate diagnosis was made, statutorily mandated procedures were followed, and Northampton State Hospital officials were alerted to the patient's condition.

The committee finds that the admission of Vernal Walford to the North- ampton State Hospital reflected unprofessional and sub-standard treatment on the part of the hospital. Hospital admission procedures were vague or nonexistent. Walford's physical and mental status examinations, required by law upon admission to a state hospital, were of a cursory nature. And no attempt was made to collect relevant background information on a patient who arrived at the hospital in a psychotic state and was unable to communicate in a logical, coherent manner.

The committee finds that the "treatment" received by Vernal Walford consisted almost exclusively of shelter, medication and restraint. Virtually no well-prescribed medical or psychiatric treatment was given to the patient. In fact, the only treatment received by Walford which either met or exceeded standard was that provided by the nursing staff.

The committee finds that Vernal Walford was inappropriately released from the Northampton State Hospital approximately forty hours after his admission and approximately twenty-four hours after violently assaulting members of the hospital staff. Walford had not been evaluated by a treatment team, his records had not been reviewed by the discharging physician, his assaultive behavior of the previous day was virtually ignored and a thoroughly inadequate "aftercare" plan was developed.

The committee finds that in 1974 the Northampton State Hospital:

a) functioned under a severe shortage of qualified physicians and psychiatrists.

b) relied almost exclusively on physicians who were graduates of foreign medical schools and practicing in the United States under a limited license.

c) functioned without written policies and operating procedures relative to medical supervision.

d) functioned without the benefit of legal training relative to the new mental health statute enacted three years earlier.

e) failed to provide pre-service or in-service training to the hospital staff.

f) failed to clearly define the role of clinicians assigned to the patients on a rotating basis.

g) functioned under an experimental organizational structure which was poorly implemented and led to organizational chaos.

h) failed to establish policies and procedures governing admission, the taking of patient histories, discharge, record keeping and aftercare.

i) functioned without appropriate procedural direction, support and administrative oversight from the central office, regional office and area offices of the Department of Mental Health.

j) functioned under enormous pressure to lower the census at a pace which placed both patients and staff in jeopardy and reduced the quality of care at the hospital.

The committee finds the internal investigation of Walford's release, conducted by the Department of Mental Health to have been thoroughly deficient and misleading.

I scanned through all the fifty events uncovered by the committee and listed in the report. They were stated, matter-of-factly, in simple, direct prose. It was the mass of details, one after the other, that presented the portrait of incompetence and error. The report mentioned that after his release from the hospital Walford had returned to the Milton Bradley Company, still complaining in loud terms of glass in his eye. He'd said the glass was making him hear strange noises inside his head. The company had tried to get the hospital to take Walford back but had been told only a physician could arrange admission. Despite Walford's terrifying and menacing behavior, the company's personnel director had still taken it upon himself to arrange for an eye exam. Sure enough, a competent physician had discovered a minute sliver of glass in Walford's eyelid.

As much as anything, I suppose, that infuriated me.

After all, even in the midst of his psychosis Walford had been complaining of pain in the eye. And no one at the hospital had taken a close look.

Outside the small office where I read the report, it had turned black with New England nightfall. The sensation of solitude grew, an eerie feeling of isolation. There were only occasional echoes of footsteps from faraway hallways to indicate that I was not alone in the huge State House.

I stood up and paced the room.

A feeling of excitement came over me. Everything I had read was that which I knew and had known for years. It was everything that Carter had said and said and said again. Finally, there in my hands was the summation in print. I turned to the report's section on conclusions and read: "The patient Vernal Walford was discharged from the Northampton State Hospital in a precipitous and inappropriate fashion. The patient should not have been released."

There were other conclusions, of course. The report didn't back away from concluding that operations at the hospital had been grossly negligent and chaotic, that the hospital and the Department of Mental Health had failed to live up to their responsibility of protecting the public, that the internal investigation had been a sham and fraud and on and on. But seeing the words *should not have been released* was what was exciting. The obvious finally stated. But for incompetence and misjudgment, Vernal Walford would not have been in that hallway when Carter left Arnold alone for those few terrible seconds. For eight years Carter, Betty and Bobby had fought to get someone in authority in the state of Massachusetts to admit that simple, heartbreaking fact.

And someone finally had.

The Zelezniks had won.

But they didn't know that yet.

3. A Distribution of Medals

In the morning I met Carter in the chambers of the inquiry committee staff. He was excited, pumped up, whirling with energy. He grasped my hand, shook it vigorously for an instant, introduced me to a *Boston Globe* reporter and then dashed off to check on some detail or another. Betty and Bobby were upstairs in a coffee shop, he said, and when Carter raced back, we went to find them. The family had been up since 4:30 A.M. They had driven from Ambler, north to Newark, New Jersey, to catch an early-morning shuttle to Boston. Despite all the planning and precaution, they had nearly missed the flight and had gotten the final three seats on the People Express plane only in the last minutes before takeoff. Carter and I couldn't find Betty and Bobby, so we went into the large wood-paneled room where the hearings had been held over the summer and where the morning press conference was scheduled to take place. We watched the television crews set up their cameras and microphones, their business adding to the excitement of the moment.

"Have you seen the report?" I asked Carter.

"No. Greg Torres offered to let me come in early and read it, but I declined. I want my reaction to be spontaneous."

"So you don't know what it says?"

"No idea."

Carter looked at me. "You've seen it?" he asked.

"Yes." I didn't volunteer any details.

"Well," he said, "it won't be long now."

I turned and saw Betty and Bobby enter the hearing room. Betty was wearing a trim brown business suit. She smiled and waved. Bobby was a picture in contrast, all teen-ager. He wore corduroys and a short-sleeved shirt, sneakers that seemed to be heading in directions other than the rest of his body, and he had flung a battered gray parka over his shoulder. He grinned and swept over. Within a few seconds we were engaged in a deep discussion of the damaging psychological effects of a fall without football. He kept kidding me about how good the Miami Dolphins had been before the National Football League Players' Association had gone out on strike. "Tough luck," he said, his voice filled with mock pity.

"Bobby," I replied, "how can you be so cruel as to kick a fellow when he's down?"

He laughed and said, "Well, look ahead. Maybe the Yankees will do better this year than fourth place."

"Bobby," I said, "what have I done to deserve this torture?" And within a minute we had changed the subject to computers.

He wanted to know everything about the word-processing program I was using. "I'm writing my own programs now. Nothing real complicated, you know, mostly different art forms, like making the computer draw different star patterns," he said. "I'm just beginning to get the hang of it."

I nodded. "Pretty soon it'll be running your life."

Betty was listening in. "Sometimes he just disappears," she said, smiling, "and all we can hear is this clickity, clickity, click coming from his room. He always tells us he's doing his homework—"

I interrupted, "But you think he's playing Asteroids, or Star Invaders or Massacre on the Moon or whatever those games are?"

Betty nodded, nudging Bobby in the ribs. "Right."

Bobby shook his head, "I'm not!" he said.

"Lie detector test?" I said.

He smiled. "Gee, maybe not." We all laughed together.

Behind us, Carter was seated in the front row of the audience seats, fielding preliminary questions from the various reporters assigned to cover the press conference. The newspaper, radio and television men ambled over, introducing themselves, checking to see if Carter was aware of what was in the report, trying in that indefinable way that reporters have of assessing the mood of an event prior to its taking place. Betty looked up at the clock. "Shouldn't be long now," she said.

The hearing room's doors swung open then, and Greg Torres entered, carrying a stack of the stapled reports, followed by committee chairman Patricia McGovern and fellow senator David Locke, the man whose motion had established the inquiry committee. They strode across the room and took seats behind a long desk on a small dais. "Let's get this under way," said Senator McGovern in a direct, distinct Boston accent. "Is everybody ready?"

Betty sat down next to Carter, and I slumped down beside Bobby. I looked over at his two parents. Betty squeezed Carter's hand. When she let go, I noticed that his was quivering slightly. He leaned forward, to catch every word.

After having read the report the night before, then having read it again to make certain that what I thought was there was indeed there, Greg Torres and I had repaired to a nearby bar. It was supposed to be an interview, I kept telling him, but instead, we simply talked on and on about the Zelezniks, about our own children (both babies, a few months apart) and how deliciously difficult, frightening, fun and infuriating it was to rear a child. I must have congratulated him a dozen times on the report, on its integrity and accuracy.

I told him that I had read many reports issued by governmental bodies but that this was the first time I'd seen one so openly critical, one that refused to soften its opinions. Greg talked about the decisions that had gone into the writing of the report, how various constructions had been tried and discarded, until only the simplest, most direct statement had remained: "...should not have been released." He said that the impact of the Zelezniks' testimony had been felt by everyone on the committee; they hadn't ever compromised, he said, so why should the report? We had looked across the table at each other and laughed together in relief. We ordered another round of drinks and toasted each other's children. "You know," Greg said, "you work on something, you research it, you get so close to it and then you don't know whether you've really accomplished what you set out to do."

"I wonder," I said, "how the Zelezniks will react."

"That's what has me concerned," he said. "In a way, this is Carter's report. He had so much input. They've had so many doors slammed in their faces; you don't want to be another door. You don't want to be another failure."

I thought of Carter's most recent letter. Eight more years.

"I don't know," I said. "I don't know if anything can satisfy them. I don't know how that report could be any different or any harder, if you will. But whether it will satisfy them..." I hesitated. In my mind's eye I pictured the family in room 216 of the Crossways, each second ticking away Arnold's last moments, and the suddenness of the scream that had penetrated their lives. "I don't know. You've done your best. And it's very good. But will it be enough? We'll have to see."

Greg nodded. "I understand," he said.

Betty clasped her hands together tightly, and Carter leaned forward still farther, perching on the edge of the seat, almost as if he were a bird ready to swoop. He had placed both hands on his knees, as if trying to hold his body together, in check.

Senator McGovern was looking across the room directly at the Zelezniks, ignoring the cameras. She was thanking them for their part in the inquiry.

"...Without their tenacity, their diligence, their willingness to give of themselves to keep this case alive for eight years, we wouldn't be here today.

"Early on in this inquiry I asked Dr. Zeleznik what he wanted to come out of it. He replied, 'The truth.' I sincerely hope that we have done this here today."

Occasionally a radio reporter would get up to adjust a microphone. Around us reporters scratched away in note pads.

Senator Locke was speaking. I kept my eyes on Carter and Betty. I heard snatches of sentences: "turmoil and grief" and "pursued relentlessly."

And then the senator unexpectedly added another suggestion. "I think that what might be appropriate would be if the legislature voted funds to establish the Arnold Zeleznik chair at the University of Massachusetts Medical School in the psychiatry or clinical psychology departments. The purpose of the chair would be to monitor public health care. In that way we would demonstrate the perpetual act on the part of government to be certain that this kind of heartbreak is not visited on anyone again."

Betty leaned over and grabbed Carter's leg. She was nodding her head up and down. She turned instantly to Bobby, not saying anything, but continuing to nod vigorously.

Senator McGovern began to go through the report. She looked directly at the Zelezniks and said, "He should not have been released."

Carter sat back. He put his hand on Betty's leg. He closed his eyes for an instant, leaning his head back. He was pale, and I saw him breathe in slowly. Then he leaned over Betty to Bobby, gesturing toward a small rucksack the family had with them. "The medals," he said. "Give them out."

McGovern's raspy voice was describing how the committee would recommend to the legislature that a $50,000 payment be made to the Zelezniks in recognition of their eight-year fight. Then she started to field questions from the press.

"Well," she said, "the possibility of such errors always exists. But what angers me, too, is that we never even bothered to treat him. And we just let him go. A very sick individual."

There was a question about the $50,000. She replied swiftly. "The issue here has not been the amount of money. The issue here has been getting the commonwealth to get up and say they made a mistake. That's what we're doing."

There was a lull in the questioning. "That's it then," said Senator McGovern. She started to gather papers together to depart.

Out of the rucksack at his feet Bobby pulled three small boxes. I recognized them right away. They contained the small silver medals bearing Arnold's likeness and motto. Bobby hesitated just for an instant at the thought of penetrating the bright television lights and walking in front of the assembled people. Then he squared his shoulders and stepped in front of the two senators and Greg Torres. He handed each the small box and then returned to his seat. The cameras swung over to the family, and they accommodated the photographers by standing up and taking seats on the dais.

Questions flew at them.

"I think they did the right thing," Bobby said.

"The issue is accountability," Carter said for perhaps the millionth time.

"I had the facts. It was only a question whether the committee would have the integrity to face this. They did. I'm very pleased."

"Oh, yes, I'm pleased and happy, too," Betty said. "Especially by Senator Locke's suggestion of a chair at the university. That really excites me, I think that's a wonderful, appropriate idea."

Carter told all the reporters that the state ought to make Greg Torres the new head of the Department of Mental Health. Greg blushed. Carter repeated his statement.

There were handshakes all around.

The family stayed, patiently answering every question, but it was always the same question, and yes, they were very pleased and happy with the committee report. I caught Greg Torres's eye, and we both smiled in relief.

There were more handshakes.

The room began to empty, reporters left to write for early editions, television crews to make early telecasts. Carter, Betty and Bobby posed for the cameramen, holding up the medals and the report. Carter repeated his enthusiastic thanks into the microphones of radio reporters, who needed actualities for their broadcasts. Betty turned and said to me again, "That idea of the chair, that's a great idea."

And then it was over.

Still carried by enthusiasm, the family winged down the flight of stairs to the inquiry committee offices. Greg Torres was captured for lunch; Carter went in to thank Senator McGovern, then emerged, grinning broadly, clapping his hands and waving his arms to collect everyone. Greg led us out through the side door, and we went over to a restaurant to eat. "A place all the old pols hang out," he said. Carter was busy pointing out architectural sights to Bobby, who managed to extricate himself after a minute and come talk more baseball. Martha Woodall of the *Philadelphia Inquirer* was along, smiling, caught up in the family's relief and excitement. We ate sandwiches, and Carter insisted on paying, though everyone else was on expense account. He told his story of going to the Middle East on the CIA expedition, and everyone laughed at the thought of Carter the spook. Betty asked if anyone on the committee had known about Senator Locke's suggestion, and Greg said it had taken everyone by surprise. He liked the idea, too. Carter and Greg described their first meeting, with all the documents, alone in the little room. They laughed together over the idea, now so odd, that they would skip lunch, caught in the intensity of that moment. We left the restaurant and walked back to the State House. By the huge portal doors of the entranceway, between great mock Doric pillars, Carter became a tourist. He arranged photographs: "First Bobby and Greg and Betty, that's right, now just Betty and Greg, good, and now Betty and Bobby, got to have one, now Bobby, you come take one of me and Greg and Betty and Martha, you come get into one of these, you too, John. No holding back." There was a final trip into the inquiry committee offices, and a few more handshakes and thanks, and Carter told Greg that he would be more than willing to help in any way as the committee entered the second phase of its inquiry into the mental health delivery system. Carter wandered off with Bobby for one moment, and Betty turned toward Greg Torres and me. She wore a small, beautifully delicate smile, and her voice was soft yet enthused with a strength of release that I had not heard before.

"I read something in the paper recently," she started, "I guess it was the *Inquirer*. And I can't remember who exactly said it, but it was about grief and loss, and it went something like this: that when something bad and terrible happens and you lose someone close to you, it is like a circle that surrounds everything in your whole life so that it is in everything that you do and say and think. But after a while you get older and time passes and life goes on a little bit and that circle stays there, but new circles develop, expanded beyond that grief circle. So new things come into your life that aren't a part of your sadness. That grief circle never really leaves you; it's always there to remember. But now there are other circles to your life, which is good, and that first circle never goes away, but it grows smaller until it's just there in the core, I guess."

She looked at Greg and me, and she smiled that same way again at the two of us. But there was a small tear in the corner of her eye, which she wiped away swiftly.

CHAPTER 16

Circles

Missing him now, I am haunted by my own shortcomings, how often I failed him. I think every parent must have a sense of failure, even of sin, merely in remaining alive after the death of a child. One feels that it is not right to live when one's child has died, that one should somehow have found the way to give one's life to save his life....

I wish that we had loved Johnny more when he was alive. Of course we loved Johnny very much. Johnny knew that. Everybody knew it. Loving Johnny more. What does it mean? What can it mean, now?

Parents all over the earth who have lost sons in the war have felt this kind of question, and sought an answer. To me, it means loving life more, being more aware of life, of one's fellow human beings, of the earth.

It means obliterating, in a curious, but real, way, the ideas of hate and the enemy, and transmuting them, with the alchemy of suffering, into ideas of clarity and charity.

It means caring more and more about other people, at home and abroad, all over the earth. It means caring more about God.

I hope we can love Johnny more and more till we too die, and leave behind us, as he did, the love of love, the love of life.

> —Frances Gunther, in an afterword
> to *Death Be Not Proud* by
> John Gunther

1. *"...As It Comes"*

It was gray, overcast, with temperatures falling as I pulled into the Zelezniks' driveway on December 19, 1982. I stamped my feet as I got out of the car and drew in air tinged with frost. Betty was at the door, waving for me to hurry in. I saw Carter and Bobby directly behind her.

"We turned up the heat," Betty said. "We were afraid that your Florida bones would start to rattle and freeze."

"I'm grateful," I replied, laughing.

Carter pumped my hand with his usual bearish intensity. Bobby and I ribbed each other, as always, about whose teams were winning and whose were losing. I looked around the house and saw that nothing seemed to have changed. In the living room I noticed that they had returned the painting of Arnold and Bobby to the side of the room. The mosaic of the two baseball players was on the table. Arnold's conductor's cap was still on the bookshelf.

"As you can see," Betty said, gesturing, "we made our usual lackluster effort to straighten up for your visit."

We laughed again. Everyone sat in customary seats, and I passed around photographs of my wife and child. Everyone said how good they looked. I complained that the baby had a cold, and Carter said, "Now, John, you know the difference between a cold and a fever. Children get fevers, and for the most part that's okay. Don't give him any aspirin because the fever is what the body is doing to rid itself of the infection—"

Betty interrupted. "Now, Carter, he knows that. And anyway, you can't tell young parents anything because they have to find out for themselves. That's the way we were."

Carter, in mid-lecture, stopped. He looked at his wife and grinned. "You're right. But, John, if you do have any questions, don't hesitate."

"Carter," I replied, "advice is not something in short supply in my house." I pulled the tape recorder from a briefcase and started it running on the coffee table. "So," I said, "tell me what you think of what's happened."

The family had been on a high after leaving the state government complex in Boston. They had stayed that night with friends. They had bought the papers and read the stories; they had watched themselves on the evening newscasts. Some of that excitement carried over, the following day, when they returned to Newark Airport and then drove out to the house in Ambler.

But it was followed by a letdown.

Though the story had received prominent play on the Philadelphia television stations and in the local papers, not many people said anything about it to the Zelezniks. Two boys at Bobby's school mentioned it; one had lost a brother in a swimming pool accident, and Bobby told me how the boy had sought Bobby out and simply said that he had seen the newspaper and that it was a good story. Carter couldn't think of anyone who had spoken with him; Betty, of only one or two people. "If it had been a joyous occasion, perhaps people would have mentioned it, but because it was based on something sad..."

Betty saw the depression that followed the inquiry committee report as the inevitable result of so many feelings coming to an end. So much time, so many thoughts, so many emotions had been encapsulated in the fight against

Massachusetts. Now, those things defused, she thought it was time to decide what to do with the rest of their lives. And that was a depressing realization to come to. Carter, however, denied the depression, or at least held it at arm's length, as he considered what to do now.

Carter shrugged. He looked across the room at me.

"The thing, John, as you know, is not resolved."

I must have looked startled. He plowed on.

"It is resolved as far as the Massachusetts legislature is concerned. Perhaps it will produce changes in the mental health system. We'll have to see about that. I know it has produced a number of changes at Northampton. That's good. But I'm still concerned with the overall picture of government. The Attorney General's Office, for example, has yet to say anything."

There's only one side when you lose your son, I thought.

"You don't see it as a completion?"

"No, because..." He hesitated.

"Larger issues still remain?"

"Yes, the larger issues still exist. I am concerned that this whole thing would not have come about if not for court decisions that gave them unreasonable power. And then there's the Immigration and Naturalization Service."

"Will you shift your emphasis to them?"

"Well, I'm talking to another lawyer. They have no blanket immunity. Shouldn't they be forced to take reasonable steps to protect us? You might say, 'Oh, now you're angry with INS. Go after them.' But that's not the point. The point is, you have a system totally functioning without accountability that calls itself government. That's a contradiction in terms as far as I'm concerned. But it is what we see..."

"Accountability, I think, was the first word you ever said to me."

"You know, John, we may not even finish out this day because some idiot may blow the world all up. We have the capacity to do this. How? Why can we do these things? Because we have this notion of sovereignty which says, 'I am responsible to no one.' You have to force government to be responsible. We have to win, or we won't survive."

"That task remains?"

"That task remains."

"And Walford?"

"Walford is a symptom of a symptom of a symptom. Let's say he's released again. He is going to be released again. There's a very high probability he'll do it again."

"Do you feel a personal threat?"

"No. I have more confidence in the Ambler police than I do in the Department of Mental Health in Massachusetts. But you know, we can predict what will happen. He will go back to Jamaica. Remember, he's been conditioned by his time here. He's never been better treated in his life! He's got good clothes and good food, and they're teaching him occupational skills. He can watch television. It's a nice warm climate. No work. So he goes back to Jamaica, and it's not going to go well for him. He'll probably be back in the United States with another load of marijuana. He's like a homing pigeon. He'll go back to Florida, to Miami, because that's what he knows. In Miami no one will notice him. In Northampton," he added a bitter sarcasm, "no one would notice him."

Betty interjected. "I don't see any reason why he would come here. I mean, we haven't done anything to him."

Carter continued, flip-flopping the subject back to the INS. "It's bigger. More people, more budget. No controls on them. They can do whatever they want. That breeds arrogance. If we have to make a statement there . . ." His voice trailed off, and he appeared to be thinking heavily.

I turned to Betty.

"I feel personally very relieved by the report. It may seem trite, however, but I never thought that winning would make me very happy. Because it was all over the death of Arnold. I have mixed feelings about it. You want something to happen, but you hate the reason for wanting it. Does that make sense?"

She looked at me, and then she smiled. Her eyes were clear, radiant. Suddenly in her voice, there was none of the freight of emotion, only a freed objectivity.

"I don't think I would have the same depth of feelings if there were another lawsuit. My main thought is the thing in Massachusetts connected directly with the death. Now we would be attacking the overall conditions, kind of an offspring from the original points. It's more universal, not so much personal."

She paused. She leaned back on the couch, gesturing with her hands.

"I personally wanted someone to agree with us. It really bothered me that I had to try to convince people that that man shouldn't have been released. I thought it was so obvious, but it was so hard to get someone to agree.

"But now that's been done, and I feel released."

"What about you, Bobby?" I asked.

His reply was direct. "I was glad. I was glad it was over because it was so close to what had happened with Arnold dying. The two cases were so close together. I think especially the chair idea is good because that's something that can be really positive.

"I've learned that when government is wrong, you've got to try to change it. It will be easier, if we sue INS, easier to deal with because it's not as close. It's something a little bit removed. We can attack it in a less emotional state."

"Do you feel an emotional release?"

"Yeah, I think so. The fact that they admitted they were wrong. My mom said it was important for somebody to admit they were wrong. Well, I thought it was important that *they* admit it. I knew myself they were negligent. It was the fact that they could finally say it that was important!

"If they hadn't said it, well, I would have lost faith in the government itself. We had gone through the courts and they hadn't done anything. This was the last chance for the government to prove that it does have some integrity. If they hadn't said it, it would have been a big blow to me.

"We're studying American history now. We've been reading about how the framers of the Constitution gave us these rights. Well, if they hadn't have said it, it would have shown me that the Constitution doesn't have any meaning. It was important for me to see that the government does have integrity."

And Betty interjected then: "I guess now we have to get back on our feet and take life as it comes."

2. Why Arnold Died

There are many reasons why Arnold Zeleznik died, all elusive.

If Carter and Betty hadn't been such strong, loving parents, and Arnold had grown up less independent and less confident, less curious and less self-reliant, he might have preferred to take his father's hand and trotted alongside him back to room 216 to return the key. Seconds later Vernal Walford would have passed by, unaware of who else occupied that hallway. He would have set his chicken dinner down, opened his Bible to the Book of Daniel and started eating, and another little child, somewhere else, probably would have died. I hated that irony: that all the love and fostering of such a carefree, enthusiastic, bright child had made him the type that automatically gained his parents' trust, so that it was nothing out of the ordinary to leave him alone for those few instants. Would they have done anything different, rearing Arnold? No, I doubt it. Carter and Betty reared two sons and provided them both with far more strength than showed on the outside.

If Northampton had exhibited even a few basic concerns for humanity, Walford would not have been available to be in that hallway...

If the hospital had provided even minimal medical care to Walford...

If the nurses who watched him on the ward and noted his behavior had been listened to instead of ignored...

If the hospital had taken the suggested option of transferring Walford to a maximum security facility...

If the hospital authorities had called the police and filed assault charges after his attack on the attendants...

If the releasing physicians had checked Walford's medical record, if they had understood the laws governing release from the facility, if they had contacted the doctor who initially sent Walford to the hospital...

If the hospital had listened to the Milton Bradley Company personnel supervisor who called, pleading to be allowed to bring Walford back to the hospital...

If his brother or girl friend had called the police in Hartford or Springfield when he started to act so bizarrely...

If that secretary at the INS in Springfield had taken him up a flight of stairs to the FBI...

If there had been a direct flight to Jamaica from New York City, December 19, 1974, or if a ticket salesperson at La Guardia had suggested some destination other than Miami, perhaps Atlanta or Fort Lauderdale, or merely suggested waiting until the following day's flight, Walford would not have been at the Crossways at 4:45 P.M. on December 20...

If a policeman had spotted Walford preaching in the airport the morning of the murder...

If Sirgany International hadn't sold hunting knives...

If the chicken dinner had taken a few more moments to cook...

If Carter hadn't taken the key...

If fate were not so capricious...

Why did Vernal Walford kill Arnold Zeleznik?

Because he thought God told him to.

Because Arnold was there at the moment that any residual ability to contest the demands of the voice evaporated, leaving only a pure homicidal essence.

Because in his knotted view, "children did not count at all."

Why? Perhaps the answer to that is within the loss of his own five children. Perhaps because he had seen God take his own children so remarkably easily, so casually, so innocently and insignificantly. Perhaps that voice came from the twists of his own sadness. That is speculation on my part, however. Ultimately Walford and the voice that coaxes him remain enigmatic. Couple that thought, however, with all the other imbalances in his past, those known and those unknown and probably far worse. Added together, they produced a raging, clashing war of chemicals within his brain, and Vernal Walford seized his knife and tore a great beauty from the earth.

And what should be done with him?

I believe that the system of criminal justice cheated the Zelezniks. They suffered a great loss, and they deserved the opportunity to rise and express that loss in a court of law. That would apply to both the criminal proceedings in Miami and the efforts to sue Massachusetts. The argument against it in the first arena, the criminal court, is that their emotions, their personal loss were in actuality irrelevant to the proceedings. In the idealized view of the court system, we want our criminals to be prosecuted merely on fact and law, in a vacuum devoid of feelings. Of course, the reality is that a criminal trial often swings on extralegal events, emotions, prejudices and strength of personality. That, in its imperfect way, is what maintains the essential fairness of our court system.

From the very beginning of the criminal case the defense lawyers assigned to defend Walford understood that he was very important in a symbolic sense, that the crime was more than shocking, emblematic, one that would test the system. There was no similar recognition by the prosecuting attorneys, which is the reason they were consistently outmaneuvered, outprepared and outargued.

Walford's defense was able to manipulate the proceedings at virtually every stage. Consider this irony: At his first competency hearing, Jack Denaro and Roy Black eloquently and persuasively argued that Walford's bizarre, uncontrollable behavior made him too great a risk to bring to court, and it would be unfair to try a man in that condition; two years later Michael Von Zamft and Michael Tarkoff eloquently and persuasively argued that it would be unfair to try Walford because he was then a quivering, misshapen, drug-laced near-zombie, and a potential jury should have the right to see what Walford was actually like when the crime was committed.

They all are honorable individuals.

Denaro, Black, Von Zamft, Tarkoff and Weinstein for the defense; Glick, Yedlin, Korvick and Kaye for the state; Judges Williams, Wetherington, Ferguson and Jorgenson; Doctors Mutter, Corwin, Jacobson, Jaslow, Weiss and Stillman. Many other men and women also had input into the situations that evolved. All are respected within the community. All have reputations for honesty. Knowing how the Zelezniks felt about him, Michael Korvick never hesitated to answer any question I had and indeed took pains to see that I had a complete record of the case. It was he who showed me the correspondence, replete with Carter's anger. He did not hide anything he did.

Similarly the defense lawyers, Von Zamft, Denaro, Black, Tarkoff and Weinstein, never refused an answer, despite knowing that their actions in the Walford case would be seen by many people as evil and manipulative. They, too, were never ashamed.

No one ever really seemed to doubt that Vernal Walford was legally insane when he killed Arnold Zeleznik.

That is not an answer to a question, however. That statement should pose questions. Much of the effort put in by the defense lawyers was to avoid putting the facts of Walford's madness to a jury for fear that a jury would react emotionally. They chose a much safer and successful course. However, with the outcome of the case, I believe the community was cheated. If the evidence of Walford's madness was so overwhelming, then it should have been put to the jury. A crime, in particular a despicable, heinous murder such as the killing of Arnold Zeleznik, diminishes everyone in the community in which it happens; in an infinitesimal way, it reduces that community's soul. The community never had the opportunity to redress that wrong. If the community, represented by a jury, believed that Walford was so mad that he had to be pardoned for that murder, then so be it. It should have been the task of the defense to put its arguments and its expert evidence to the community, as opposed to the clubby forum of a criminal court hearing.

I think that what angered me so much about the case was the way in which Arnold Zeleznik was forgotten. The psychiatrists who examined Walford sought only to understand the motivation for the crime within the limited context of mental competency and the M'Naghten rule. Even with that minimal scope, the doctors assumed great importance. Their impressions were what dictated the decisions by the four judges who had the case. The community was ignored.

Jack Denaro once said to me that Walford was "the classic irresistible impulse." Of course, he acknowledged that irresistible impulse, the Durham rule, was not the law in Florida. The strictures of M'Naghten applied to Walford only in a square-peg, round-hole fashion. Both Denaro and Roy Black told me that they had thought that when it went to trial, Walford's case would pave new highways in the law. He was so mad, they said, yet the crime was so terrible. How would the law deal with this intersection of absolutes?

The reality was, it didn't.

That seemed true in Massachusetts, too.

The legal position espoused by the Attorney General's Office was one designed to head off the exposure of the state to a decision by a jury whose emotions might award the Zelezniks a great sum of money. The stratagem used by the state—invoking the discredited doctrine of sovereign immunity—

was good legal advice. One school of thought would say it was perfect legal advice: It won. If it had lost that cause and been forced to go to trial, the state would have relied on the contention that there was no way the physicians at Northampton could have predicted Walford's behavior. Modern psychiatry professes not to be in the business of predicting behavior, but it is often called upon to do precisely that. The worth of the state's contention is questionable, but it is equally questionable whether the Zelezniks' attorneys could have provided the direct causality necessary to prove their case. They could have proved that he shouldn't have been released, but there had still been more than a three-week period of time between the release and the homicide. When I put that question to many lawyers, there was great disagreement.

The problem is, of course, that they didn't get the chance.

In matters of the law, I am naïve. I am not a lawyer or any real legal scholar. I am a journalist who has spent much of his career watching lawyers and laws work and not work. I have seen cases won which did not deserve to be victories, cases lost which were tragic defeats. Of the hundreds, perhaps thousands that I have covered, I have come away with one lasting impression, one that is ridiculously trite and simple: A trial is a furnace, wherein fact, emotion, judgment, the law, personality and prejudices all are baked. The finished result is generally imperfect, but at least all the factors are contained in the product. There are often injustices: In one case prejudice is too great a strain; in another, emotion; in yet another, insufficient facts or less competent attorneys. It is ultimately a system that reflects the people who enter through the courtroom doors, and that is something not to be afraid of.

The Zelezniks were not afraid to put their case forward, in either a criminal or a civil forum. They were denied that chance, and that is what, to my journalist's overly simplistic mind, seems unfair. That they were able to persist and discover a different forum in which to air their loss is a testament to the power of that loss and to the inherent reservoirs of strength that they were forced to draw upon. It is a testament, too, to the power of television and, in specific, "60 Minutes." The show only arranged the obvious for the viewers, however; it was the fiber of the family that dominated the airwaves.

They were fortunate to gain the opportunity before the inquiry committee. They were lucky to have people anxious to see the truth emerge in the committee. So many unlucky events befell the Zelezniks they could have been swallowed up and ruined by the repetitive frustrations. They could have entered a state of mind and being beyond bitterness, a realm of acidity, crippled by the accumulated powers of so many small disappointments blending with so many great angers.

They did not.

And that is truly remarkable.

* * *

All the ifs and whys go around and around, back and forth, forward and backward. I wanted all of it to be direct, linear, a mathematical equation of emotions with a simple, unenigmatic answer. I wanted Carter and Betty and Bobby to be freed, somehow, from their grief and loss. But then I realized that was not only impossible but unrealistic.

The Zelezniks need their grief. They need their guilt. They need their anger. There was nothing they could have done to prevent the slaying. They did nothing wrong. But the feelings remain. If they had not allowed them to be expressed, they would have been absorbed by the murder, murdered themselves.

I think Carter will never forget that he left Arnold in that hallway and will continue to pursue whatever institution remains available for him to examine, find wanting and attack. Perhaps, in this way, he deflects the hurt and disappointment and rage he feels within himself. He is an extraordinary man, with a voracious hunger for honesty and knowledge. He is not a man ever to acquiesce to what he perceives as evil or to cower away from a fight. The more he learns, the more wrongs he sees to correct. That his energy stems from the depth of his loss is a hard reality, but it is one that he bears with humor, grace and wit. And if he chooses to tilt with the windmills driven by guilt and grief, well, that is not a terrible thing. The Massachusetts mental health system, the Northampton State Hospital, the Immigration and Naturalization Service, big government, whatever—all are things that need reform. If this drive, regardless of what emotion created it, brings Carter to force attention on those institutions and beget some change, whether small or large, then perhaps some other man or woman or child's sadness will be avoided. There are far meaner legacies to leave in this world.

I think Betty has reached a different emotional location. She was more satisfied with the immediate results of their fight. The admissions by the inquiry committee in Boston cut more of the bonds that looped her heart. In a direct way it closed something that was open, ulcerous and that hurt her constantly. I think she, too, is anxious to fight on against those other institutions, but she sees it more as a choice, whereas the initial fight—the forcing of Massachusetts to admit wrongdoing—came directly from her heart. For so many years she had lived with the idea that Arnold's death had resulted from a specific negligence; when someone had finally agreed, it had been a huge burden lifted from her life, a release from a sentence of anguish. I think that success (what an inappropriate word) has allowed her to place Arnold and that loss within a different context. I doubt there are many minutes in the day when she is not reminded of her sadness, when it doesn't form a core of tears within her, but it does not freeze her in a pit of depression. She is free to remember the many moments that Arnold gave her; she can delight in those too-few years and recall the happiness within them without feeling an unruly, uncontrollable frustration with the murder and the aftermath.

When she mourns, it is unencumbered.

3. Bobby's Room

The conversation turned again to the law and lawyers. Carter cited the two rules of ethical behavior that his friend the late philosopher Warren McCulloch had formulated:

1. You want to play. You want to win.
2. You want to play more than you want to win.

"They're not bad," he said. "More people should learn them. More lawyers especially." He hesitated; then he laughed, as if the concept of teaching ethical behavior rules to attorneys, with their strict—but oft-violated—codes of ethics, was somehow ludicrous.

Carter looked over to where Bobby was sitting. Bobby had picked up a math text and was flipping through it. "You know," he said, "I truly hope that Bobby doesn't want to go on to become a lawyer." He shook his head in distaste at the idea. "Or if he does, he's the type of lawyer that works to bring about good and not merely win cases."

I scratched down Carter's words. I didn't say anything, but I remembered what Carter had said at the end of our first conversation, more than four years earlier, about what he hoped Bobby would become.

Betty said that she and Carter had joined two groups: the Parents of Murdered Children and the Compassionate Friends. These groups dealt with losses incurred by the death of loved ones, but she shook her head and said that there had been so much bitterness expressed at a meeting of the first group, so many people complaining and wanting vengeance, that she had been overwhelmed. She said she thought that she and Carter and Bobby felt very differently. She did not begrudge people their emotions, she said, but she hated to see all that energy wasted on anger.

There was a small silence then.

I closed the notebook and leaned over the coffee table to shut off my unreliable tape recorder.

"Will you stay for lunch?" Betty asked.

I shook my head. "Holidays. Presents. I've got seemingly endless numbers of cousins and in-laws that all require some Christmas showing. My battered bank account has further shocks to undergo."

Betty put back her head and laughed. "How about a sandwich for the road? Or an apple? Anything?"

"I'll survive okay," I said.

"Let me show you the computer first," Bobby said. I nodded, and we all trooped upstairs to Bobby's room. He clicked on a light against the gray pallor of the sky that slid through the windows. "Here we go," he said.

In a second Bobby was clamped down at his desk, typing in instructions on the computer. Various mathematical and computer terms fled across the small television screen in front of him. I saw the words *Program by Robert Carter Zeleznik* flash by; then the computer started drawing star-shaped designs, in brilliant color, one after the other, each line flowing together with other lines, forming points, then rushing off in new directions, only to join with another line in a constant ballet of connection. "Not bad, huh?"

"Not bad at all," I said.

"I'm just a beginner," Bobby said.

"Do you get credit at school?"

"We're working on that."

"He does much of his homework on the machine now," Carter said. Bobby shuffled a bit. "Show him what you can do," Carter urged, always the proud parent. Bobby began to demonstrate other programs and other functions on the machine.

I looked about the room. There was a bed in the corner, almost an afterthought amid stacks of books, baseball equipment, photographs, posters, swimming trophies, medals and other awards. A cello leaned up against one wall, losing out, I suspected, to the computer. I pointed at the autographed poster on the wall of Manny Trillo, the Phillies second baseman. He had just been traded away. Bobby made a joke about its being bad luck to get one's picture on his wall. He got up from the computer and showed me his boxed collection of autographed baseballs, which I admired.

I noticed, then, hanging above the baseball collection, a withered brown palm frond about three feet long. It was stuck in the joint between the wall and the collection box. "That looks like something from Florida," I said.

"Yeah," Bobby said. "It is."

"When we were all out by the pool, when Arnold and Bobby were playing in the water, the boys found it," Betty said. "Arnold especially was playing with it, pushing it through the water, you know how little boys are." I nodded.

"After the murder, I don't know when," she continued, "Bobby went out and got it. When was that, Bobby?"

"I just went out and got it and brought it back," he said. He smiled at his mother.

"And it's been on the wall since?" I asked.

"That's right," he said.

Carter, Betty and Bobby walked me out to the car. The temperature was still falling, and Carter's breath clouded his face with vapors as we all shook hands. They weren't wearing coats, but Carter seemed oblivious to the gathering cold. "I've got a joke," he said. "Listen, you'll really like this one." It was a terrible joke, but Carter roared as he told it.

Bobby looked at me and adopted a fake pained expression, as if the greatest burden of any teen-ager were compensating for the ridiculous behavior of his parents. He dug his hands deep into the pockets of his jeans and shook his head. When Carter finished the joke, Bobby burst out laughing. "Dad! That's not funny! That's a terrible joke!"

"It is not!" Carter replied in mock anger. He threw his arms around Bobby and tried to put him into a headlock. "Egad!" he shouted. "The boy's getting too big!" Betty grabbed each of their arms, so that the three were linked together for a moment, sharing their warmth.

"Come on," she said, smiling toward me, gently rebuking the horseplay. "John has to go, and we've got a lot to do ourselves before Christmas."

I got behind the wheel of the car and started to pull back in the driveway. It seemed the gray sky was framed by the empty black branches of the trees in the yard. Before pulling back, I looked once more toward the family. They were heading inside, but still joined arm in arm. They turned, and then they waved.

That night, the nineteenth, it snowed hard, the darkness broken by a soft, wet coating of deep white. By midmorning the sun had burned away the remaining gray clouds and shone freely, lighting up a great expanse of brilliant blue sky. It had been a day much like that, eight years less three days earlier, on which Arnold had been buried. His body, dressed in his beloved miniature Philadelphia Phillies uniform, had been cremated. His ashes had been placed in a small urn and taken to the burial plot in northeastern Philadelphia where Betty's mother and father were interred. There is a small headstone on his grave. It says:

Arnold Frank Zeleznik

April 7, 1965—December 20, 1974

"With God We Can"

Bobby at Sixteen

> . . . It might have been an hour, or thereabouts, after my quitting the smack, when, having descended to a vast distance beneath me, it made three or four wild gyrations in rapid succession, and, bearing my loved brother with it, plunged headlong, at once and forever, into the chaos of foam below. The barrel to which I was attached sunk very little farther than half the distance between the bottom of the gulf and the spot at which I leaped overboard, before a great change took place in the character of the whirlpool. The slope of the sides of the vast funnel became momently less and less steep. The gyrations of the whirl grew, gradually, less and less violent. By degrees, the froth and the rainbow disappeared, and the bottom of the gulf seemed slowly to uprise. The sky was clear, the winds had gone down, and the full moon was setting radiantly in the West when I found myself on the surface of the ocean. . . .
>
> —Edgar Allan Poe,
> *A Descent into the Maelstrom*

1. Chess Games

Before Arnold's death Carter taught both boys how to play chess. Bobby, in particular, was suited to the game; his quietness, introspection and ability to concentrate silently on a problem all adapted him to the special rigors that chess demanded. By the age of five he was already adept at the wars of the board.

Carter had a rule, though. He would never play at less than his own ability. He made certain, before playing the game with the boys, that they understood that their father wasn't going to compensate for their ages. He would patiently explain to them that he was older, more experienced, a better player and that their likelihood of winning was very slight. He said he refused to condescend to them. Arnold accepted that situation more easily than Bobby; he played, lost and thought little of it, swiftly moving on to another game. Bobby felt these losses all the harder, though; he would concentrate more on the game and envision his moves all the more carefully. When he lost, as he invariably did, he sometimes cried in frustration. Carter would take Bobby aside at those moments and explain to him that there was no shame in losing to someone better; the only shame came from not trying one's best. It hurt Carter sometimes to keep beating the boy when he was obviously trying so hard. Bobby kept returning with the chessboard in hand, however, wanting to play. Carter realized, too, that, his rule established, Bobby would recognize it instantly if Carter tried to throw the game to him.

One day, when Bobby was perhaps six, he brought the chessboard to Carter, and they played. Betty was in the kitchen; Arnold was wandering about the house, playing randomly. She remembers suddenly hearing a shout of mingled joy and surprise from the living room; then there was a roar of laughter she knew was Carter's. Seconds later she heard the roll of sneakered feet running toward the kitchen. Bobby, aglow, threw himself across the room into his mother's arms, shouting, "I won! I won! All by myself!" Carter was behind him, beaming. She looked at her husband, eyes locking for an instant, searching. He knew her question.

"No fix," he said. "Bobby just outplayed me."

Bobby turned to his father. "I won, didn't I?"

"That's right," Carter said. "Fair and square. On the up and up, no holds barred, no punches pulled." He hugged his son. "You won," he said. "You sure did."

In late March 1983 I drove west across the great watery expanse of the Everglades and Big Cypress Swamp toward the Gulf Coast of Florida. Bobby was in Clearwater, several hundred miles from Miami, where he and the other members of the Penn Charter School baseball team were engaged in their yearly spring practice trip. The nineteen squad members had flown south from the still snowy, blustery Northeast, to work out before the season started. For ten days they stayed at a motel near the baseball complex designed for the Philadelphia Phillies team and their minor-league affiliates. The Penn Charter boys worked out on an adjacent field and in the afternoons scrimmaged against some of the younger professionals.

It was the first time Bobby had been on the trip; it was the first time he'd taken a lengthy, more than overnight trip away from his parents.

I checked into the motel and called Bobby. He was expecting me and met me in my room. "Been on the beach a bit?" I asked.

He laughed and half-self-consciously rubbed a red, peeling nose. "Well, not as much as I'd like. They've got us working pretty hard."

"Still stiff?"

He laughed again. "Getting better. But the running . . ." He shook his head.

We piled into my car and drove over to a nearby steakhouse. One of the Phillies minor-league teams was eating there also. Bobby and I discussed the subtle differences between someone who will stay in the minors versus those who can make the majors: a fastball that moves a little extra, a little quicker; a little more foot speed; a stronger arm or quicker release. "Sometimes it's just the stomach," Bobby said. "You know, nerves. Being able to hang in against a ninety-mile-per-hour fastball."

"How have you been doing?"

"Well, hitting . . . not so hot. But the pitching has been good. Especially relief pitching. I really like that."

"That takes nerves."

"Yeah, but I like it. The pressure is greater. You know what you've got to do. There's nothing else to think about, just getting it done. I really like it. I like the responsibility. I've always liked being a little alone. To myself. That's what relief pitching's all about."

He smiled. "A little crazy, I guess."

We ordered thick steaks, shrimp cocktails, salads, baked potatoes, the works. Bobby inhaled his. Enough food to make me sluggish for a week barely registered on his lithe, muscled body. I asked him questions between bites.

"Bobby, would you change anything you've done?"

"No. I mean, I'd rather have Arnold be here, but no, I wouldn't do anything different. You've got to fight. That was always so important. I think what we said is true. Arnold would have been something. I know it. He would have done something in the world. I think it's true that it was up to us to make a mark for him. I'm glad we've done that."

"Do you think about him much?"

He was quiet.

"Yeah. A lot."

"Do you think you have a responsibility, I don't know, to live for two, I guess?"

He thought deeply before answering.

"It's not exactly that. You see, in a way, I feel like he's still there. He's with me. So it's not like I do things for him. It's more like he does things along with me. I still miss him. I guess I always will. Like when I walk out onto the baseball field. He loved baseball so much. I think how much fun he would be having, how much fun the two of us would be having. So in a way, he's still there. It's as if I experience it for the two of us."

"But he's given you something?"

Bobby smiled. "Oh, yes, a lot." He considered for a second. "In a way, I feel a little older, a little more experienced than some of the other guys. It's as if because Arnold died, I've seen a little bit more of life. I know that life's a little more..." He searched for the word.

"Tenuous?"

"That's right. I guess I feel a little more vulnerable. And that means more responsibility. Maybe a little more mature."

Bobby told me that he still thought about death, that it still frightened him. I suspect that he will have this fear for a long time. After all, he has come closer to it than most do, looking down on death at its worst and ugliest. No one who is close to his brother would ever deny that the brother's death seizes a sliver of his own soul and carries it into the grave.

If Bobby walks through each day with this burden, however, at least it is borne on straight, strong shoulders and met with glance unaverted.

I changed the subject while we were waiting for dessert. Bobby had ordered an immense fudge ice cream cake that would have intimidated most people, perhaps even armies. I had forgotten about the teen-age boy's ability to devour more food at one sitting than some entire nations. I asked Bobby about school and if he had started to think about college. He had, he said, but only tentatively. As far as his schoolwork was concerned, well, he was having difficulties finding challenges. The As were too easily obtained. He ribbed me about this. He was spending most of his spare time with the computer or reading. I told him to read more. He said that was predictable. I asked if he had any thoughts about what he wanted to become. Too many thoughts, he said. He really wasn't specific yet. He was fascinated by computers, yet he wanted to master chemistry. At the same time he loved reading and writing. He thought about journalism sometimes; that, of course, I encouraged. Law school remained a possibility, he said. But he was uncertain. He was not particularly worried about his indecision. Plenty of time to figure out the future, he said.

"What was the hardest moment?"

"I think going back to school, alone, just after he died. He was always there, and suddenly he wasn't. But there were a lot of hard moments."

"Did you have nightmares?"

"Yes." He didn't elaborate.

"What about Walford? Does he scare you now?"

"No, not really. I sometimes think it could have been me. I could have been ready first. Or maybe Dad wouldn't have taken the key and I could have been in the hallway. That frightens me."

It is always unfair to be the survivor.

Chance forever rubs the memory raw. There's no real relief from that.

But when we walked outside into the darkness of the Florida night, Bobby said, "You can't be scared to go on."

And of course, he was absolutely right.

Later we talked more baseball and about his decision to run cross-country in the fall. I told him to be sure to get good running shoes, and he ruefully started telling me how he'd begun practicing in tennis sneakers, and the two of us threw back our heads and laughed at the picture his feet must have presented after a few turns around the course.

2. An Anachronism

In tenth grade Bobby wrote a paper titled "The Insanity of the Insanity Defense."

He wrote:

...The M'Naghten rule states that the defendant must have been laboring under such a defective reason, from disease of the mind, as not to know the nature and quality of the act he was doing, or if he did not know it, that he did not know that what he was doing was wrong.

The rule, as stated, involves many undefined terms and implicit assumptions which are, at the least, ambiguous. For example, it is tacitly assumed that knowledge of sanctions strengthens the powers of self-control. Moreover, many words need to be operationally defined, as, for example, the word "know." Is knowledge limited to detached intellectual awareness or is it meant to include an emotional appreciation of an act's impact upon the offender and the victim? Does "wrong" allude to moral or legal implications?

He continued:

...A major reason that the insanity defense should be abolished within our judicial system is that there are no longer the frequent legal executions as previously was the case when the rule was set forth. Its original justification may then no longer be meaningful. Consequently, the insanity defense has tended to degenerate to the point of being no more than a method of plea-bargaining. Many lawyers acknowledge using psychiatrists who regularly testify to the "insanity" of virtually anybody.... Even prosecutors are reported to use the defense in the absence of adequate evidence concerning the actual guilt of the defendant.

Another important reason for the abolition of the insanity defense is that psychiatrists aren't capable of effectively determining who is insane by legal standards. It was concluded in *Washington* v. *United States* that "psychologists ... cannot provide sufficient data relevant to a determination of a criminal responsibility no matter what our rules of evidence are." This inability of psychologists to produce any criteria which can be empirically validated makes an insanity defense meaningless. Even if psychiatrists were able to make such determinations, the rule does not acknowledge different gradations of insanity and its application becomes "all" or "none." It is likely that there are few individuals who are completely insane and with no ability to differentiate right from wrong or to appreciate the nature of their actions. . . .

Bobby continued, analyzing some of the different systems proposed for dealing with mentally ill offenders. He concluded the paper with these words: ". . . The insanity defense, whatever its merits, when originally set forth, is at this time an anachronism which we would do well to do away with."

The paper received a straight A.

Vernal Newland Walford, as of this writing, remains in the maximum security section of the Florida State Hospital at Chattahoochee, outside Tallahassee.

He still hears the voice.

The only real restraints keeping him behind the wire mesh and bars of the hospital are the vagaries of his own mental illness. Under the provisions of his not guilty by reason of insanity verdict, the controlling jurisdiction over his case remains with the Dade circuit judge into whose division the case falls. Before Walford could be released, that judge would have to make a judicial finding that Walford no longer posed a threat to himself or to others. This qualification could keep him behind the mental hospital walls indefinitely, but inevitably, the day when he will be released will arrive. Whether it is a month or a decade away is uncertain. But the day will come. This will undoubtedly happen after the hospital has stabilized him on psychotropic drugs and shipped him back to Miami. There, in the Dade County Jail, just as he has been so many times, Walford will once again be examined by a procession of psychiatrists. The same treadmill of madness. As before, their reports will determine his future, but Carter's supposed scenario is probably as good as any. Walford ties up hospital space, at great cost, in a time when space is at a premium. When nothing more can be done for him, it is likely that authorities will opt to deport him and let his native land take care of him—if it chooses to do so.

What will become of him then?

Anyone's guess.

Will the voice return?

Yes.

And what then will it tell him?

3. A Ride on a Bike

Sometimes, when he has some free time, Bobby will get on his bicycle and
ride up to the old house in Fort Washington where he and Arnold were children
together. If no one is around, he will park his bike by the street and walk
slowly through the yard, remembering the moments the two of them shared
there.

He told me this simply, directly.

He knew it was not something to be embarrassed about.

In the morning I had to leave, to get back to Miami. Bobby was up at
6:00 A.M. to wolf down breakfast with the other members of the team, their
youth and enthusiasm swallowing the too-few hours of sleep they'd put in.
After breakfast the team changed quickly and en masse ran the mile or so to
the practice field. As the sun climbed into the postcard-perfect Florida day
the boys assembled in groups and went through those particularly American
rites of spring: They practiced pick-off moves to first and getting the jump
on the pitcher; how to cut second base close, so as to go from first to third
on a single; how to hit the cutoff man and how to hold the runner close; how
to sacrifice the runner into scoring position; how to tag and score on the
medium fly ball. All those things, and so many more, that make up the small
moments of baseball. It is a young man's ballet, played amid the unmistakably
familiar sounds of bat on ball, ball into glove, voices raised in singsong
accompaniment.

Bobby was in the midst, keeping up the same chatter, the same constancy
of noise. When he did something right—the reliever's quick move to first
which caught the runner by the small half step that is the essence of the
game—there was the usual smattering of applause and "attaboy." Those
mingled with the day's flow, nothing out of the ordinary, small sounds, lost
amid many.

But when I thought about those few enthusiastic handclaps, I wished that
they had grown. The sound should have multiplied rapidly and gathered
momentum, becoming rhythmic. The noise should have gained great strength
and power and filled the air like the sounds from a stadium at that exquisite
moment of victory, when the thunder of applause rises and swells and sweeps
up the currents of air toward the skies, shaking the clouds and riveting the
clear blue ceiling, racing upward to beat on the heavens, before washing back
in great tidal waves of hurrahs over Robert Carter Zeleznik, a young man at
play with other young men, in his element, indomitable.